C000137126

"I've had the pleasure of knowing Sh[...]   im
change the lives of over 1,000 UK [...]
powerful roadmap based upon those   g
closely with some of the UK's most for[...] [...] accounting firms. The ten
parts of this book are the key ingredients that have been proven to build some
of the best accounting firms; ingredients you will need if you want to build a
more successful, profitable and rewarding accounting firm."

Mark Wickersham – Professional speaker, Amazon #1 bestselling author of
'Effective Pricing for Accountants' and the creator of Price Consulting: Changing
clients' lives the fast way by helping them price more profitably

---

"A stunningly useful and practical book that every single
accountant in the world should read."

Steve Pipe – Former UK Entrepreneur of the Year, multiple author
and Advisory to the profession

"By implementing the steps described in Shane's book I've transformed
my Practice, it's profitable and enjoyable, I'm making a difference
to my clients and have a great lifestyle myself."

Val Wishart – Chartered Accountant, Beyond The Numbers, Edinburgh

---

"A great, timely read. Accountants that are serious about
building their own practice need to get themselves a copy.
I particularly enjoyed the mix of personal anecdotes and practical advice."

Mark Rowland – editor, AT magazine (AAT)

"I cannot put into words what Shane and his team have done for our business.
Using the concepts in this book, we have been able to smash through barriers
we previously thought impassable. Accountants need to read this book,
because those who do and apply its principles to their own business
will soar to new heights. It really is that simple."

Phil Tarbun FCA CTA – Managing Director of Blend Accountants,
a business dedicated to making anything possible

Shane Lukas

PUTTING EXCELLENCE INTO PRACTICE

A Proven Roadmap
To A Profitable, Sustainable
And Value Driven
Accountancy Business

Putting Excellence Into Practice A Proven Roadmap To A Profitable, Sustainable And Value Driven Accountancy Business

Copyright ©2019 Added Value Solutions, Shane Lukas

First published 2019 by Added Value Solutions,
7 Midland Way, Derbyshire, S43 4XA

This edition published 2019

A catalogue for this book is available in the British Library

Edited by Harriet Powney

Designed by Charles Bradshaw

Illustrations by Michael Groves

Printed and bound in the UK

Paperback ISBN: 978-0-9957562-2-9
Kindle ISBN: 978-0-9957562-3-6

About The Author

Shane Lukas is a keynote speaker, inspiring accountants to become even more inspiring to their clients. He has spoken for many of the governing accountancy bodies, including ICAEW and AAT and is the author of six books, including International Best-selling book, *'Better Business, Better Life, Better World'* and UK Amazon Best Seller *'What's Next For Accountants'*.

With his business, AVN, Shane has worked with over 2800 accountants since the late 1990s, helping them achieve their aspirations for their accountancy practices. Over this time Shane has built up experience of what works and what doesn't.

AVN is a UK based coaching and training organisation for accountants in practice. AVN delivers powerful hands-on workshops, 'Practice Improvement Training Programmes' and ongoing support for accountants in the form of membership. AVN helps accountants specifically focus on improving their accountancy practice in seven key areas, which naturally results in stronger practices delivering greater value and improving the businesses they work with.

Shane is passionate about enabling better choice for people at all levels. His beliefs are that…
* Success isn't really success if it comes at the expense of family, friends and health
* Most business owners need the help and support of an external business adviser
* Accountancy is a noble profession, one that can make a profound difference
* By helping accountants improve their practice and teaching them the skills to help their clients better, we're affecting countless businesses, boosting the economy and creating jobs
* Businesses can be developed for good.

Dedication

I dedicate this book to my children, Kaden and Chiana, who kindly gave me zero peace and quiet in which to write it! And also to my beautiful wife Jenny, who lovingly kicked me out of bed at 5am every morning – since that's my most productive time – to ensure I finished it.

I will love them always.

In addition to being my wife, Jenny is also a key member of the AVN team. Both she and a colleague, Emma Slack, have formed a core part (indeed, the DNA) of AVN since they joined – respectively in 1999 and 2000. My gratitude for, and appreciation of, their shared passion for our common purpose, their steadfast loyalty and unwavering hard work and dedication, is deeper than words can express.

Contents

Contents

Introduction

I decided to write this book because all too often I see, as an accountant grows their practice, that there's a direct correlation between their success and the number of hours they have to work. As working ridiculously long hours invariably leads to increased stress and anxiety, and also places a strain on their relationships with family and friends, it somewhat defeats the object of this growth. **Remember: your business should always work for you rather than the other way around.**

When most accountants start to build their accountancy practice, they have a defined capacity to which they can work. As they take on more clients, however, this capacity is consumed and then exceeded as they take on ever more clients just to pay the bills. Eventually, of course, maximum capacity is reached, by which point they're working far too many hours, for far too little income, and leaving themselves far too little time to spend with their family, their friends and – worryingly – their own health.

An approach to marketing which simply involves offering cheaper services than their competitors amplifies this situation, and a vicious downward spiral ensues that leads to ever more stress and ever less time. All in all, it's not a pleasant way to work or live.

To make sure you don't fall into the trap I've outlined above, I'd like to share my proven, seven-step methodology with you. The first three steps will enable you to achieve a more efficient capacity level. In other words, you'll be able to work less hours whilst earning more income and gaining a greater sense of fulfilment in all that you do. The next three steps will focus on creating scalability so that your practice can grow without overburdening either you or any of your employees. The final step – the icing on the cake, as it were – will be learning how to become truly purposeful, thereby making a profound difference to businesses (and to the loved ones of those businesses) throughout the world.

The seven-step process has grown from over 20 years' experience helping thousands of accountancy practice owners. These practices have come in all shapes and sizes, but the results have always been staggering. Clients have ranged from a single accountant working from his garden shed who – in just a handful of years – went from earning £50,000 in annual recurring income, to being the owner of a £1,000,000+ practice who now only works three or four days per week and receives 30% profits on top of his salary, to a practice that was already earning £800,000 per partner, but wanted to take this to greater heights. This was convincingly accomplished when they recently exceeded £5,000,000 in revenue.

Throughout the book, I'll be supporting my seven-step process with case studies, providing real-life examples of how various practices implemented the concepts and the great results they achieved. A Practice Performance Assessment (available online at: www.takethetest.today) will also allow you to ascertain exactly how strong your practice is at each of the stages, and offer you further strategies and step-by-step actions to improve your practice.

In fact, why not start by taking the assessment? That way, if you do it again once you've implemented all the ideas this book contains, you'll be able to ascertain exactly how much of an impact they've had.

So go ahead! Grab a coffee, make yourself comfortable, and invest in seven minutes to complete your Practice Performance Assessment…
www.takethetest.today

Before you read any further…

If you enjoy reading this book and find the content as valuable as I hope you will, I'd love you to write a review and rate it on Amazon.

If you do, and are able to email me a screenshot, I'll send you a free copy of either 'What's Next for Accountants' (which, despite my writing it first, is a natural extension to this book) or, if you prefer, Jonathan Holroyd's book, 'Accountancy, It's your Business', offers another natural complement.

With Special Thanks...

The following accountants have kindly contributed their real-life examples to support the concepts I refer to within this book:

- Brian Thompson of CPT, Darlington
- Cathal Cusack of Cusack Garvey, Dublin
- Fiona Jones of Grant-Jones Accountancy, Camberley
- Georgi Rollings and Emma Lawrence of Starfish Accounting, Berkshire
- Jacqueline Hooper of JDH Group, Abercynon
- Jonathan Vowles of Vowles Chartered Accountants, Bedfordshire
- Marie Donaldson of Fresh Clarity, Gloucester
- Michael Hemme of MDH, Croydon
- Peter Disney and Brendon Howlett of Wood and Disney, Colchester
- Rennie Evans of Prospero Accounting, Manchester
- Rob Walsh of ClearVision Consultancy, Bath
- Simon Chaplin of GreenStones, Peterborough
- Steven Carey of Numbers UK Ltd, Plymouth
- Val Wishart of Beyond The Numbers, Edinburgh

1

Inefficient Capacity

Inadvertently, far too many accountants run their practices inefficiently. They dislike change and procrastinate over taking important action.

Does any of this sound familiar?

Whether you've created your own accountancy practice from scratch, or taken over an established one, at some point you'll have thought about how much time you'd like to allocate to your business. In an ideal world, of course, this would also leave enough for you to enjoy spending quality time with your family, your friends and on your health. (By health, I mean keeping active and fit, pursuing interests, and keeping your mind on things outside work).

Your practice and your life balance...

 vs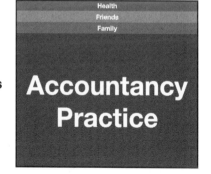

Sadly, the reality for many is that work is all-consuming. You take on ever more clients – many of whom have driven your fees so low that they're barely profitable – who expect you to be at their beck and call but, however hard you work, show little if any appreciation.

Inefficient Capacity

Each morning, you arrive in your office with a plan: to cross just 10 items off your to-do list by the end of the day. But, each evening, you're lucky if you've ticked off six. The phone hasn't stopped ringing, clients have bent your ear, your email inbox has been crazy, and a few prospective customers have made enquiries. (While it's great that new people are eager to work with you, they can also prevent you doing the work you need to do to keep your current customers happy).

Then there are the employees you need to micromanage, those who bring more problems than they solve and whose work you always have to double-check because it's simply not to the standard you'd like.

Day after day you leave work only to sit at home with your laptop in a vain attempt to keep on top of your to-do list and to keep your clients happy. Meanwhile, your email inbox just keeps on pinging.

And that's before you even begin to think about how much the legislation keeps changing, and how you just don't have time to stay up-to-date (unless you make it your bedtime reading). Then there are the endless new technologies to get to grips with. For many people, it's simply overwhelming.

All in all, the money isn't great either – especially when you consider how much time you put in. Worse, you're often challenged on fees. There are so many accountants out there and most potential clients are savvy enough to play you off against each other until you crash the price in the hopes of winning their custom cheaply this time, and generating further work in the future to compensate. However, invariably they go on to dispute the cost of every piece of additional work you do for them as they "assumed it was part of the package!" Finally, you end up writing it off or agreeing to accept a fraction of the price you should be charging in an attempt to achieve a win-win situation. In reality, of course, no one wins. Bit by bit, such clients grind you down.

Most importantly, the result of all this is that what should be an exciting, enjoyable and emotionally rewarding experience – having your own business – isn't. You're working a ridiculous amount of hours for very little financial reward and getting little to no appreciation for any of it.

One of the saddest parts of my work is hearing just how many of the accountants I speak to deeply regret missing out on important times – sports days, nativity plays or parents' evenings – in their children's lives, or simply having the time (and energy) to take them swimming or to play with them.

Their pain, as they acknowledge that they'll never get those opportunities again, never gets any easier to bear.

Similarly, I've seen too many divorces due to the owner of a practice feeling they have no choice but to keep working ridiculously long hours in order to keep their clients happy and to pay the bills – even at the expense of their relationship.

In all the scenarios I've outlined above, the accountants have exceeded their working capacity by far – and yet it's an inefficient capacity.

That's why, in Parts 3–5, we'll cover the first three stages of a proven methodology which has helped my clients who are AVN members achieve an efficient capacity; one that will enable you to work a fraction of the hours you currently do, whilst earning significantly more. Not only that, but you'll be working with fantastic clients who both respect and appreciate you; clients who know they're getting a great service and are happy to pay a premium for it.

But don't skip to that part of the book just yet! To get the most out of it, there's more you need to be aware of first.

Now, what about those for whom none of the above has resonated so far, because you're working a manageable amount of hours and taking home a reasonable income? No doubt you're asking yourself, "Why change?"

After all, as I suggested at the beginning of this chapter, most accountants hate change.

The answer is: Because the world around you is changing.

I've already mentioned the number of cheap accountants who are driving your clients away or forcing you to negotiate your own prices down. Their numbers are only going to increase, and negotiating on price will get even more difficult – especially if you fail to differentiate yourself. Clients will simply think you're delivering the same services, yet charging a higher fee for the sake of it.

Then there are the advancements in technology. I've been talking onstage about the threat of AI (Artificial Intelligence) for many years, but it's only recently – because they're now experiencing it for themselves – that accountants have started to sit up and take notice.

In a process that's only going to accelerate, software is automating more bookkeeping and accounts production than ever before. Many business owners, for example, already think you simply click a button and – voilà! – finalised accounts appear. That may not be the case just yet, but in reality how long will it be before it is?

Even if, as an accountant expert in the art of producing compliance accounts, understanding the intricacies and the need for judgement calls, the thought of a computer being able to take so much into consideration seems a long way off, I suggest we take a step back from the field of accountancy for a few paragraphs.

What is Artificial Intelligence?

Many interpret AI as being the point at which a computer can 'think' like a human. But – although it's inevitable they'll reach that stage eventually – such a point could still be decades away.

Human intelligence can be broken down into many different types. Some of us are stronger at maths, others at literature, art or strategy. Computers are already able to reproduce, and even exceed, human ability in some of these. Not by thinking like us, but by processing permutations so much faster and thereby coming up with an often better solution.

Take chess, for example. Prior to every move, and almost instantaneously, a computer is able to work out all the possible counter moves to each of the choices available to it before making its final decision. By contrast, most of us can perhaps think a couple of moves ahead at best, and our overall strategies have to be reconsidered each time our opponent makes a move.

In addition, computing power and the speed of processing have been increasing exponentially, since even before Gordon Moore, one of the co-founders of Intel, made his famous prediction in 1965 that – because the size of transistors would halve each year owing to advancements in production, (meaning that twice as many could be placed in each square inch of circuitry) – processing speed would double year on year. (A prediction that so far, on average, has been realised. At the time of writing, for example, the latest microchip contains over 50,000,000,000 yes, 50 billion transistors in a square inch.) Processing speed exceeded that of humans many, many years ago, and as they become more intelligent they will form conclusions thousands of times faster than we can.

A new type of computer, the quantum computer, is also being created. To put its potential power into perspective, this computer's first iteration will be over 1000 times more powerful than the fastest processors around today. Imagine that! And it's predicted that quantum computers will be up and running by 2023 at the latest. The applications for such technology are endless.

Already, applications such as Babylon Health, able to diagnose ailments and prescribe treatments, are being used by doctors and patients alike. How many more patients could GPs see each week if the more trivial and easy-to-diagnose ailments could be dealt with by a computer?

Such thinking also applies to accountants. Whereas compliance accounts were once highly valued, few business owners today care about having their accounts produced. It may be a legal requirement – just as it's a legal requirement to take your car for an MoT every year – but most of us simply want to fulfil our obligations in the cheapest, least painful way possible.

Many traditional accountants, however, haven't yet woken up to this. They've been happily producing accounts for many years, talking to clients as little as possible, sending out the draft accounts by post, and they don't want to change.

In fact, they're often working through so many sets of accounts that they simply don't have a chance to analyse them to find out where each business' strengths and weaknesses lie. And, because they have so little meaningful contact with clients, they don't get the chance to understand what each of them really wants to achieve for – and from – their business. As a result, they don't get the opportunity to work with them to help them achieve those things, either.

Charles Handy, author of many great books including 'The Age of Paradox,' uses the mathematical concept of the sigmoid curve to illustrate the typical lifespan of a product, service or business and the demand for it during that lifespan. Typically, a product, service or business is created to overcome a specific problem. If that problem then goes away, the demand for it to be solved – and the need for them – does, too.

A mistake that many businesses make is not to evolve their product or service until demand for it has already begun to wane. In other words, they don't even think about change until they realise that no one wants their product anymore. Unfortunately, by this time it's often too late and their clients have moved on.

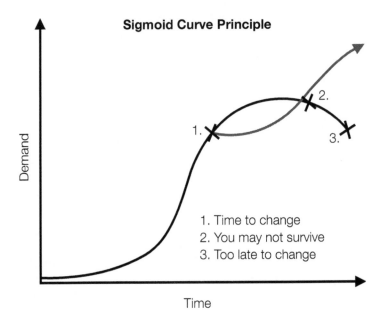

Sigmoid Curve Principle

1. Time to change
2. You may not survive
3. Too late to change

The best time to improve is whilst demand is still increasing

The best time for a business to evolve – or even, sometimes, to revolutionise – is whilst demand for their product or service is still on the increase. Consider, for example, how Apple releases a new version of each of their products every single year. Although the previous one is still great, they need to keep ahead of the curve if their customers aren't to think they've stopped innovating and move elsewhere.

Your accountancy practice is no exception to this and the core services you offer have a lifespan, too. The practice of the future then is one that will be happy for computers to crunch the numbers (and to produce the accounts and the analytical reports that complement them), while the role of the accountant will be directly client facing. In other words, your role will be to sit with clients and to go through the real-time data with them: identifying strengths and weaknesses, producing trends and forecasts, and carrying out 'what if' exercises to examine the ways in which their businesses could be improved.

In this book I don't intend to go into too much detail on the business advisory side, since I've already written a book on that very subject called *'What's Next for Accountants'* (If you haven't read it yet, I strongly recommend you do so after finishing this one).

Indeed, in many ways – since many of you may need to put some crucial foundations in place if you're to deliver the kinds of services I describe in *'What's Next for Accountants'* if your clients are to be receptive to them and (most importantly of all, perhaps) be willing to pay for them – this book is intended to act as a prequel.

To do so, it will take you on a journey that will enable you to overcome the challenges I've described so far. The changes you'll need to make, however, won't be a walk in the park. Many of you may need to step far outside your comfort zone. But, by replicating the environment that AVN create for the accountants we work with, I'll make taking that action as easy as I possibly can.

To give just one example, many of us – even some of the most successful – admit to being procrastinators. To overcome this, we need to put mechanisms in place to ensure we take the action needed to make significant advances in our businesses and our lives. I'll be sharing some of these mechanisms with you later in this book, so that you, too, can implement some of the actions from your to-do list. (But don't worry, I'll address this early on so you can take action straightaway rather than simply adding to your to-do list!)

The book contains ten parts. Here's a brief insight as to what you can expect from each:

- **Part 1** Why it's so important to change the way you run your accountancy practice – not just to improve your own life, but so you can provide significantly more help to the businesses you work with.
- **Part 2** Based on my learning from working with accountants across the length and breadth of the UK, I'll focus on the typical inhibitors they face in making fundamental changes and share mechanisms to overcome these.
- **Part 3-5** How you can attain a new, efficient capacity – one that (if you choose) will enable you to work less hours, for more income, while delivering greater value to your clients.
- **Part 6-7** By helping you change your mindset from building an accountancy practice to building an accountancy business, I'll take you on a journey of creating scalability by developing a team of people as committed to growing your business as you are. As a result, you'll create a team with a purpose-driven culture who understand the value of using systems to ensure consistently high standards.

- **Part 8** Once that's in place, you'll be ready to attract even more of the right kinds of clients in a way that requires little effort, yet keeps a steady flow of new business coming in. I'll also share how you can make sure the clients you'd most like to work with seek you out.
- **Part 9** Throughout your journey, your sense of fulfilment will have been increasing. Now, I'll touch on the impact this could have on the lives of your family, on the lives of your clients' families, and even on the lives of others around the world. (Most accountants I know have a genuine desire to make a difference. If you're one of them, this section is for you).
- **Part 10** What does excellence look like in an accountancy practice? I'll explain exactly what it means.

2

A Noble Profession

"Accountancy is a noble profession that can make a profound difference to its clients." Steve Pipe – Founder of AVN.

Although I strongly agree with the above quotation, disappointingly, and for the reasons I've described, too few accountants are able to set aside the required time to make such a profound difference.

However, before I share how to move to the more efficient capacity that's crucial to your being able to achieve this, I'd like to share the opportunity that you have waiting for you right now.

Research shows that there has been a significant increase in the number of new businesses being created in the UK. In fact, setting up a business is easier than it's ever been. Website designers, virtual administrators, content writers, and anyone else you can think of, are all only an online click or two away. Technology, and the ease of outsourcing, means that anyone can set up a business in their spare room and build a website that includes e-commerce to sell their products or services in a matter of days. Next, they simply need to create ads on social media or – using only their smartphones – create a sales video to drive people to their websites.

Or at least that's the way it seems, which is why there are so many new businesses. The reality, however, is a little different. Very few of these businesses survive more than five years and, of those that do, very few do more than survive. In fact, just like those I described earlier, most are barely ticking over, with their owners gaining no enjoyment from it whatsoever.

The good news is that as an accountant you're in a wonderful position to help, which is why, in *'What's Next for Accountants'* I'll teach you everything I know about coaching business owners to run better businesses. But first there are a few hurdles you need to overcome.

Chief amongst these, perhaps, is that your clients see you as 'just' an accountant. Worse, if you respond to emails, texts or phone calls in the evenings and at weekends, then they'll see you as being just as busy as they are.

If this describes your position, to suddenly offer them advice wouldn't only come as a surprise, they'd also probably question what – if anything – a similarly overworked 'mere' accountant could teach them.

That's why I intend to help you reach a position where not only are you practicing what you preach, but where you can demonstrate to clients and prospects that you've created a successful accountancy business that enables you to work fewer hours for a better income.

Accountants often tell me they hide their income and success. I've even known some who despite having two cars, make a point of visiting clients in the older one so that they can't be accused of overcharging! As an anecdote, it's mildly amusing. As a strategy, however, it's completely mistaken. Whether it's working less hours, having a nicer house or taking more holidays, always let clients see your success.

If, as a result, they accuse you of overcharging, politely point out that they're being short-sighted. If they'd like, you can help them to achieve the same!

After all, would you rather be coached by someone who looks like a failure, or someone who's living the dream? I know which I'd choose, and I'd pay good money for the privilege, too.

3

The Forward-Thinking Accountant

Of the many accountants I've met, some are best described as 'traditional' and others as 'forward-thinking.'

To illustrate the difference, and to find out which you are, here's a great method used by many AVN members.

The old-fashioned Nokia phone on the left, which allows you to make phone calls and texts but little else, represents a traditional accountant providing the basic services you'd expect.

The modern Nokia smartphone on the right, however, not only provides these basic services but much more, too. Just like the forward-thinking accountant!

Of the two accountants, which would you choose? Which of the phones is on the desk in front of you right now?

Of course, some accountants claim to be forward-thinking because it sounds good, but when challenged on the definition, are unable to provide a meaningful explanation of what it actually means, let alone be one. Others (far too many) fall into the traditional camp – whether they want to or not – simply because they haven't consciously decided to adapt to our changing times.

Although it's true some business owners still require a traditional accountant, they represent a minority that will continue to shrink, which means that if too many accountants remain traditional their practice will die.

So let's take a closer look at the differences between a traditional and a forward-thinking accountant.

Traditional = Functional, Forward-Thinking = Vital

Whereas traditional accountants simply deliver a commodity by performing a legally required function for a business, forward-thinking accountants are deeply involved with the business as a whole. By seeking to understand their clients' goals, they're able to spot and to present opportunities to make sure they achieve them. The forward-thinking accountant is a vital component of the business they work with.

Traditional = Performing a Job, Forward-Thinking = Making a Difference

Traditional accountants focus on delivering the core service of compliance work and are either deeply involved in doing this themselves or in double-checking the work their employees do.

In contrast, forward-thinking accountants help clients to grow their business and as a consequence change lives. That's why they're able to spring out of bed every morning knowing they'll be making a profound difference.

Traditional = Replaceable, Forward-Thinking = Sought After

Someone who simply performs a function that anyone (or at least any accountant) can do is easy to replace. Business owners will always seek the cheapest alternative.

The forward-thinking accountant, however, is sought after. By raising both their online and offline profile they've become known, liked and trusted – including by business owners they haven't yet met in person. Their reputation for making a difference means that business owners will do whatever they can to remain one of their clients.

Traditional = Overworked, Forward-Thinking = Choose Their Role

The default position for traditional accountants is to take on any client, however large or small, and allow themselves to be negotiated down to rock-bottom fees. They then have to work with a high volume of clients in order to achieve an acceptable income. In short: they're overworked.

Forward-thinking accountants have a different mindset. Their clients aren't interested in which of a forward-thinking accountant's team physically produces the work; they're interested in having the meaningful conversations that result from it. That's why forward-thinking accountants are always happy to delegate work – it frees them up to deliver business advisory solutions to clients.

Traditional = All Things to All People, Forward-Thinking = Rigid on Ideal Client Profile

By taking on any client, traditional accountants are forced to accommodate so many different wants and needs that they run themselves ragged – and all for very little appreciation or respect.

Forward-thinking accountants take time to work out who they most like to work with, the type of business or circumstances their skills are best suited to and – most importantly – the type of personality they prefer to work with. Once they've done this, they can choose to work only with those who fit the bill and to refer on any others.

Traditional = Resist Change, Forward-Thinking = Keep Evolving

New legislation is forcing many traditional accountants to get to grips with technologies that forward-thinking accountants embraced long ago. 'Making Tax Digital,' for example, was something that forward-thinking accountants readied their clients for early on. Traditional accountants are – often reluctantly – catching up, but they'll always be several steps behind. (And not only with technology. They also lag behind with the types of services and support they offer).

Traditional = Fear the Future, Forward-Thinking = Embrace the Future

The future looks bleak for traditional accountants. The rate at which technology, legislation and the environment in general is changing is rapidly increasing. The new strains of entrepreneur want – and need – a lot more from accountants.

Forward-thinking accountants are excited about what this future holds – for both themselves and their clients. They're tapping into the likes of AVN because they know it will help them develop an accountancy practice which is able to thrive in the years to come.

So which camp do you currently fall into? But, more importantly, which do you want to be in going forward?

4

All The Right Notes, Now In The Right Order

Before I share the model that has helped so many accountants transform their business with such success, it might be useful to explain how and why it was developed in the first place. It was created through a process of learning that included not only careful research and long experience, but also from making more than one mistake and the wisdom that ensued. A crucial first step was to recognise the inhibitors to implementation and progression that so many business owners experience, as only then could we develop the mechanisms to help them overcome these.

Since the late 1990s AVN has been helping accountants in practice by providing training on leadership, team building, marketing, value pricing, customer service, systemising, opportunity spotting, delivering added-value services and business consultancy. Our ever-evolving software tools help shortcut the implementation of many of these areas and we also provide access to intellectual property that includes a full suite of ready-to-tweak practice systems and growth strategies. In addition, we provide coaches to challenge, advise and provide accountability.

Despite this comprehensive support, not every practice we work with achieves the level of success they – or we – would like. I'm sure you've heard the expression: *"You can lead a horse to water, but you can't make it drink?"* Well, disappointingly, there was more than one instance where the partner of a practice admitted that although they were inspired by the possibilities, they were too afraid to take the necessary action. They simply felt that it was too big a risk.

This, of course, is understandable. It often takes years to build and establish an accountancy practice and, even if the owner(s) don't have complete choice about their hours, role, income and the difference they're able to make, it does put food on their table. After all, fear of rocking the boat is common to us all.

Then there were others who did take action but whose journey took much longer. Why? They had the same training, the same access to the same tools and strategies, the same coaches, and yet they hit more challenges.

To find out why, in 2015 I went on a mission. I travelled the length and breadth of the UK visiting as many of our AVN members and former members as I could. Over the course of a few hours, I sought to understand their circumstances when they first joined us, the approach they'd taken so far, the results they'd had, and the challenges they'd faced.

My results revealed that some had simply been overwhelmed by the amount of 'stuff' available to them as part of their membership. In fact, there was so much they could use to make their practice stronger, they weren't sure where to start.

Others had chosen one thing, put this in place, and then moved on to the next. But this 'next' might depend on their own intuition, on a conversation with a member of the team at AVN, or simply on the fires they were fighting at the time.

And that's how I established that there was a clear pattern to the approach of the most successful firms in implementing our concepts. It wasn't purely about taking action, it was about taking action in the most appropriate order.

To give just one example, many practices had jumped straight in to offer business advisory services in the form of coaching and consulting programmes. However, the reasons some had struggled to promote these services to their clients quickly became obvious.

The firms that failed were overwhelmingly still seen as 'just an accountant' – because that's all they'd ever been in the eyes of their clients and prospects. In other words, the offer of business advice represented such an extreme upshift in services it was as though your window cleaner suddenly offered to rewire your house. It's a big leap.

Also, to be clear, by 'just an accountant,' I mean a traditional, compliance-only accountant. As I've already emphasised, I firmly believe that accountancy is a noble profession that can make a profound difference both to individuals and to the world. Sadly, however, a common stereotype persists. In a survey carried out a few years ago, business owners were asked to give three words that described their accountant. The four most commonly used were 'introverted,' 'systematic,' 'antisocial' and 'boring.'

We may know that the reality is very different, but it's the perception that matters, and until that changes (or is changed by us), clients and prospective clients will remain less receptive to accepting business advisory-type work from their accountant (and even less receptive to agreeing to pay for it).

That's why I decided to develop a brand-new approach to helping accountants improve their practice. (Albeit still with the aim of delivering business advisory and added-value services as the core of their practice – rather than compliance being their core service with business advisory and added-value service added on).

This new approach fell into two stages:
- **First** I identified seven key principles that would lead to a far more profitable, enjoyable, scalable and purposeful practice. These, and the methodology around them, form a structured process that I call the AVN roadmap since, effectively, it's a journey. The aim is not for each accountant to create a clone practice, but through a series of strategies and actions, to develop the practice to which they aspire.
- **Next** I identified a better way of helping the accountants we work with to take action to implement the necessary changes more effectively.

Although the bulk of this book will focus on those seven principles, it's logical to address the second stage first by looking more closely at what can typically get in the way of you taking fundamental action.

5

The Keys To Taking Fundamental Action

At the beginning of this book I mentioned how the most successful people put mechanisms in place to overcome any tendency they may have to procrastinate.

While I'm not suggesting for a minute that the accountants I work with don't work hard (indeed, most of them work too hard!), often they'll describe themselves as procrastinators. By this, they're referring to their failure to take specific action that will fundamentally change the way they run their business.

And please note, I deliberately use the term *fundamental* action to differentiate it from the type of action we're all taking, all the time. After all, we're busy people. It's just that sometimes we don't take the *right type* of action. In other words, the *fundamental* action that could prevent us from being so busy in the first place.

There are a number of factors that can prevent you from taking this fundamental action and I'll start by giving you a brief understanding of each. Chances are, only some will resonate. It's useful, however, to be aware of all of them as the content in this book can equally apply to the businesses that you work with.

Factor 1: Overwhelm

In today's fast-paced world it's all too easy to be overwhelmed by the constant emails, telephone calls, meetings – whether with clients, team members or suppliers – the necessary (and ongoing) CPD and the daily ad hoc questions from colleagues. And that's before we even factor in actually doing the work we're paid to produce.

In fact, by the time you've got to the end of each day, all you want to do is relax. Not that you ever really can. Your feet may be up, but I bet your mind is still churning away: running through your day, thinking about the unfinished jobs, worrying if clients will be chasing you, worrying about how you're going to get the information you need from the clients who keep promising to drop it off, but don't. And this is just the ongoing operational work in your business. In these circumstances, how can you ever be expected to find time to work on your business? The result of all this is a build-up in stress which can lead to anxiety, depression and – in the worst-case but all too frequent scenario – a breakdown or heart attack.

Factor 2: Confusion

Let's say you do manage to find time to work on your business. What should you focus on first? What might offer the quick win which will remove your financial worries and free up more of your time so you can focus even more on improving your business?

When so many things don't feel right, it's difficult to know where to start.

Factor 3: Perfectionism

Accountants are by nature perfectionists. It's understandable – and sometimes even necessary. But not always, and therein lies the problem.

I've seen too many instances when a project hasn't got off the ground because it was never quite good enough. That's why at AVN we offer a piece of software called 'Time's Up!' We created its first iteration in 1998 to help accountants price without using time-based billing – hence the name. In fact, it was the world's first value-pricing tool for accountants as not only does it help you to produce a fixed price, but a value-based one. Its development included pricing principles and psychology from many years of research.

It's a great tool, which is why it's continued to serve accountants so successfully since then. Those who've used the software more or less 'as is' have seen immediate and incredible benefits, including both increased fees and conversion rates, as we have simple ways of customising it for each practice. Those, however, who wanted to tweak every single aspect, whether the pricing, the wording or the way in which we advised them to go through it with clients, either failed to see any results – since they never quite finished this tweaking – or failed to see the results their peers who used it 'out of the box' did.

While I'm not suggesting you should blindly use our products without gaining a good understanding first, trying to drill down into too much detail in the field of pricing psychology rather defeats the object of us using decades of experience to create a shortcut for you!

Factor 4: Fear

Sometimes fear can drive us to succeed. At other times it can prevent us from even starting.

It also comes in many forms. A few common ones, to give you a flavour, are:

- **Fear of failure** What if it goes wrong or I mess up? I'll look bad and then how will I live with myself? Will others see me as a failure?
- **Fear of rejection** What if I offer a new service to a customer and they say no? Will they think I've been too 'salesy?'
- **Fear of conflict** What if they get annoyed with me? Or complain, or ask a question I don't know how to answer?
- **Fear of insecurity** What if things go wrong? Will my business fall apart? If so, how will I pay the bills and support myself and/or my family?

Fear is an incredibly powerful driving force and our reactions to it – fight or flight – are instinctive.

Factor 5: The Bright and Shiny

The 'bright and shiny' has distracted people for millennia. I imagine at some point we've all been guilty of taking our eyes off our main goal because of something that looks as if it'll make our lives easier. Right now, amongst accountants it's generally a new piece of software or the consultant who tells us that *"with just a little tweak to our websites"* we'll have more enquiries than we can handle.

'Bright and shiny' can come in many forms, but in many cases it can distract us from achieving a better business.

Factor 6: Comfort Zones

Sometimes, in order to see the results we want, we need to do things we're uncomfortable with. To stand on a stage and present to an audience, for example, or to part company with an employee who's not performing or lowering morale within a team.

Putting off taking action simply means the problem persists and the results are deferred.

Factor 7: Not Enough Pain, Not Enough Gain

At a basic level, most of us are motivated to take action that will take us away from pain and/or toward gain. In chapter 1, I described how the capacity of most accountants has become over-consumed and the effects of this on their time, their income, their status and their home life. Did reading that open your eyes to this being the perfect description of your life? Or did you read it and think that it was simply a normal description of what running an accountancy practice is all about? If so, I'm here to tell you that it isn't. It's only become the norm because it's happened so gradually.

The boiling frog fable offers a perfect analogy here. If you don't know it, the fable explains how if you place a frog in hot water, it will immediately jump out to escape such a hostile environment. If, however, you place the frog in tepid water which you then gradually heat to boiling, the frog will fail to detect the change and either be boiled alive or only try to escape when it's too late.

You're probably facing plenty of pain: you're working too many hours – but you've become used to it; you're not earning a fair or even a respectable income – but you've become used to it; your family relationships are at breaking point – but you've become used to it.

Once you're in this position, it can be difficult to see what else you can do other than keep going and hope that one day you'll have enough of a recurring fee from your client base to be able to sell your practice and retire. Sadly, old age can often arrive before the value of your business is enough to offer you this option.

I'm sure, like me, you've seen a picture of Dory, the fish from *'Finding Nemo'*, on social media with the quote: *"Just keep swimming!"* Although it's meant to inspire you to keep going if you want to get results, there's another expression that I think is far more appropriate: *"If you always do what you've always done, you'll always get what you've always got."* Even that expression isn't accurate by today's standards, the world is changing too rapidly to expect to get what you've always got from doing the same thing.

From my personal research and experience, although other factors exist (after all, our brains are great at rationalising irrational thoughts, feelings and decisions) those I've just discussed are the seven most common inhibitors to progress.

So now let's visit each of them in turn. That way I can share the mechanisms I've used to overcome them myself (or that I've found through research), which have been proved to work.

But, before we start, remember there's no magic wand. You'll need determination to succeed – just as you would with overcoming any obstacle, either physical or emotional.

Overcoming Factor 1: Overwhelm

There's a huge difference between *feeling* overwhelmed and *being* overwhelmed. We all have lots to do, but it's how we manage our workloads and, even more importantly, how we manage the distractions, that makes the difference. Below are some suggestions to help get you started.

Reduce the Distractions: When we set up a business, we first buy or rent our premises, then equip them with what seems a never-ending list of telephones, desks, chairs, computers, stationery and Internet access, right down to a kettle and tea and coffee. Ironically, while our intention was to create the most productive environment ever, in reality we've done the exact opposite!

That's because, although we might believe that the moment we sit down to focus on a project – whether this is to produce a set of accounts or to create a business plan – our brains are fully engaged, in reality it isn't true. In fact, our brains are more like a car that needs to accelerate through the gears if it's to reach top speed. Research suggests that it takes an average of 11 minutes for our brains to achieve their equivalent of a top speed, which is quite a long time – particularly when you consider that an interruption of just 2.5 seconds is all it takes to have to start again. To return to my car analogy, think of it like hitting a set of traffic lights on red. Each time you have to go back to first gear and start again – until you hit the next set of lights, that is…

Just think about how many times you – or the members of your team – are interrupted each hour. The impact this has on the overall productivity of your practice is often what leads to the feeling of being overwhelmed.

Let's see if you can relate to this hypothetical scenario, for example. You have a major task to complete, so have shut yourself in your office to allow yourself to focus. As you start work, your brain gradually begins to move through the gears toward maximum concentration and speed – and remember, this process typically takes around 11 minutes.

Five minutes later, however, there's a knock on your door and a colleague pops their head in to ask if you'd like a cuppa. Boom! Even as you reply,

"Oh, that would be lovely! Thank you. Tea with two sugars, please," your brain has gone right back to the beginning. Then, five minutes later, just as you've got back down to work, there's another knock: *"Here's your tea."*

You're now ten minutes in, but I bet you won't have appreciated the effect of those two interruptions. As far as you're concerned, each has just been a few seconds and then you've cracked straight back on.

Another five minutes, and the phone rings. Not the phone in your office, the one outside but, probably without even being aware, you listen to hear if it's for you or not. Nope, it isn't. Great! You can carry on.

Ding! I bet you recognise the horrible noise your computer makes every time an email arrives? Sometimes (depending on your settings, and to really rub it in), it even shows a little preview in the corner of your screen. You see that little preview, notice it's an email from an important customer and think, *"I'll just see what they want."* Phew, it's okay, it's not anything you need to deal with now. You can carry on with what you were doing.

Brrr Brrr, Brrr, Brrr! This time it is your phone as your receptionist has a customer on the line who wants to speak to you. You ask her to say you're in a meeting and will call them back in an hour. *"Yes, no problem."* Then it's back to work again.

Another knock on the door, from a different colleague: *"Sorry to disturb you, have you got a minute?" "Yes, of course, but could we talk in about an hour or so?" "Yes, no problem. See you then."*

A few minutes later, ding! Another email; junk this time. Then, just as you've settled down again, there's another knock at the door: *"Have you done with your cuppa? I know you're busy, so I'll wash it for you."*

I've just taken you through a 45-minute period, during which you've had no less than eight interruptions. And if you think I'm exaggerating, then I challenge you to create a record of your own. Research shows that on average we're interrupted 36 times per hour by email, 14 times per hour by people (in an office with four members of staff) and 21 times per hour by people (in an office with eight members of staff).

Not only that, but most of us try to respond to emails as quickly as possible for fear of complaint if we don't and, when the phone rings, we feel we have to drop everything to talk to clients.

Is it any wonder then that our to-do lists get longer instead of shorter?

So what's the solution? My recommendation is to set aside some quiet time each day – or at the very least each week – and make sure your team does the same. This quiet time will not only enable your brains to reach maximum productivity and allow you to nail the actions you need to take, it will also reduce your feeling of being overwhelmed.

I'd also advise you to:
• Stop email notifications making a noise or displaying a preview
• Batch-process emails and phone calls
• Allocate one or two slots per day to read and respond to emails and only open your email programme at these times. In between, set up an auto-response to inform senders when they can expect a reply. That way they won't worry their email has been lost or that you're ignoring them. (In fact, if you explain your reasons, it may even inspire them to take similar action – after all, I'm sure they face exactly the same challenge!)
• Similarly, set aside one or two time slots each day to return phone calls – and get people used to the idea that you won't take phone calls outside those times.

Although, as I wrote that last point, I could already hear some of you shrieking, *"WHAT?"* If you're someone who believes that taking a call from a client or prospect is of the utmost importance, let me put it to you this way. If you were in the middle of a meeting with one client, would you accept a call and then have an in-depth conversation with another in front of them? I'd like to think you wouldn't! Instead, you'd ask the caller to be informed you're in a meeting, but will call them back at a certain time.

Although most people AVN work with find the above relatively easy to implement, the difficulty comes when they're working on a business-related project of their own. That's when it's important for them to remind themselves (or be reminded) that actually their own business is their number-1 client. So what does this mean in practice?

If you have a receptionist, and a call comes through while you're working on a project to develop your own business, ask them – *just as you would if you were with a 'real' client* – to say you're currently unavailable and to schedule a time for you to call back. (If you don't have a receptionist, then I highly recommend tapping in to a virtual one. By taking messages and arranging calls at times that suit you, they'll enhance your professionalism. But, as part of your due diligence, do ensure they meet the level of professionalism you expect).

I promise you'll be amazed at how much more you can achieve by following the above. And, if you have a team of people, imagine how much more productive your whole practice could become!

A Trusted System for Actions

Another reason we might feel overwhelmed is because we're failing to transfer everything from our heads into a trusted system. This can be a major obstacle to getting a good night's sleep because stuff like *"Must remember to do this"* or *"Oops, I forgot to do that"* keeps popping into our heads.

Sadly, if we say we'll do something, but don't write it down, our minds don't work like a computer. They don't remind us at 6.15pm to call for groceries on the way home, they remind us when we're already there and are just opening the cupboard door to make tea. Likewise, when we're in the office they don't remind us about that one last (but vital) item on our to-do list, they remind us as we're about to fall asleep that night.

The only way to be certain that we won't forget something is to have a trusted system in place. The exact form this takes is up to you, but to get you started I can share my system which – even if you choose not to replicate it exactly – will give you some useful pointers to help you create your own.

Remember, while keeping a to-do list is good, if it's only accessible from one place then it starts to fall down. That's why I use Trello™. (It's such a great online tool that I still can't quite fathom why it's free!) I record all of my tasks on it and each of my days is allocated to a certain type of activity. Monday is 'Leadership,' Tuesday is 'On (rather than in) My Business.' Wednesday is 'Prospect Conversations,' Thursday is 'Customer Retention,' and Friday is 'Marketing.'

As each of my to-do items will fall under one of these headings, it's relatively simply to assign them. I also guesstimate how long each is likely to take and label it accordingly. I spend my mornings on larger projects but – and this is key – in the afternoon I stop so that they don't consume my entire day and (within reason) only resume the next time my day is allocated to that project type. I then work on medium-sized projects from lunch until about 3.30pm, before finishing up with the smallest projects.

As the day progresses this means I'm able to tick off more and more items, while also making sure I work on the large important projects that can get neglected if you allow the small stuff to consume your day.

But what if I'm driving home and suddenly remember something I need to do? No problem! I simply say: *"Hey, Siri! Remind me tomorrow at 9am to call X."* (Assuming that was my thought, that is!) I know Siri will remember to remind me at 9am the next day and I can add it to Trello™ then. Or if I'm out running or cycling - or even swimming - I can do exactly the same using my Apple watch.

To summarise, I can make a note, or request a reminder, that ensures I'm able to add stuff to my Trello™ *at any time*. Admittedly, saying *"Hey, Siri!"* in the middle of the night might not be popular with my wife, but, at the same time, it's important to get the thought out of my mind if I want to get to sleep! That's when a good old-fashioned pen and notepad comes into its own – particularly as taking my phone out would activate parts of my brain that prevent good quality sleep anyway.

It's important then to design your trusted system so that it offers multiple ways of capturing the thoughts from your head – and in such a way that they all end up in the right place where they can't be forgotten.

But what if you keep forgetting to look at this right place?

To guard against this, my Trello™ has two additional boards labelled 'DOING' and 'COMPLETED'. In the spirit of Kanban (A Japanese manufacturing system that uses visual cards to organise projects and determine progress), each morning I identify the actions I need to carry out that day and drag them to the DOING board. Then, as I complete each one, I drag it to the COMPLETED board. If I don't complete an item, I state its progress in the comments section before dragging it back to where it came from.

At the end of each day and week, being able to see everything I've completed gives me a great sense of achievement. And then I'll archive those items.

We all have lots to do but - and this is my key point - if we manage our to-do list properly, we won't feel overwhelmed.

In the interests of avoiding overwhelm, why not take a break and grab a cuppa! I know this has been a fairly sizeable section. Although, if I'm honest, I've barely touched the surface of the importance of improving productivity. It's a subject I'm passionate about because I firmly believe that 21st century technology – technology that is meant to improve our ability to be more productive – is in many instances having the reverse effect. In fact, look out soon for the book on productivity I've been procrastinating over writing!

Overcoming Factor 2: Confusion

In the previous section I explained the importance of assigning your actions/tasks/projects to a trusted system. I also explained the process I use to ensure that I'm working on similar items on any given day since this enables me to better switch from one project to another.

Although such a system undoubtedly helps, confusion can still arise if (or when) you have so many tasks in your system that it's difficult to determine the order in which to focus on them. There's also a huge difference between actions and projects on your to-do list.

There are two main areas involved here.

1: Prioritisation

The best way to prioritise is by using the four quadrants that Stephen Covey developed in his book *'The 7 Habits of Highly Effective People'*:

1. Important *and* urgent	**2.** Important *not* urgent
3. *Not* important *but* urgent	**4.** *Not* urgent *or* important

Quadrant 1 – important *and* urgent – is otherwise known as firefighting.
Quadrant 2 – important *not* urgent – contains the tasks you keep meaning to do (because they'll help you to grow your business) but which you never get around to because of the firefighting in Quadrant 1.
Quadrant 3 – *not* important *but* urgent – are the tasks you respond to because of pressure from someone to do so. Taking just a few minutes to ascertain the importance of your to-do items will help you realise when something falls into this category. That way, you can then decide whether or not you need to do it or whether you can delegate. (I would always suggest that if it's not important, delegate).

Anything that falls within **Quadrant 4** – *not* urgent *or* important – bin! (The fact that this can sometimes be difficult to work out, particularly when you're feeling swamped, shows the importance of this exercise in helping you realise what, in the grand scheme of things, doesn't really need doing).

I find it helps if I label all my Trello™ items with one of these quadrants. Otherwise it's easy to spend all your time on firefighting when actually taking a day, a half-day, or even just an hour each week to focus on Quadrant 2 stuff will soon begin to eliminate the causes of those fires.

2: Actions vs Projects
Sometimes we look at an item on our to-do list and simply don't know what to do. Typically, that's because it's a project rather than an action. In other words, you need to start by breaking it down into its constituent actions.

To clarify, an action is something simple such as *'call restaurant to book a meal for 10 people for 7pm.'* There's no ambiguity; it's straightforward.

However, an item on your to-do list that says *'organise a meal for the entire family'* leads to more questions than actions. Questions regarding when, where, who, cost, formal or informal… you get the idea!

Next time you look at your to-do list, decide whether an item is a project or an action. If it's a project, then you need to break it down into actions so that you can carry these out one at a time and check them off. Only then will you be able to ascertain the progress of the overall project.

This will help overcome the confusion that you may experience when you look at a to-do item and are not sure where to start.

Overcoming Factor 3: Perfectionism

It's natural – particularly for accountants – to want to get things right. We want to feel comfortable, even proud, of our work.

But at what point is something good enough?

There's a simple way to find out that will also help you overcome perfectionism: Set a tight deadline that you can't get out of!

To prove it, below is a perfect example of its success.

A while ago Mike, an accountant based on the south coast, made the decision to join AVN and, by becoming a member, gain access to our training, coaching and tools. That's why, the next time he had a prospective client meeting, he decided he would use our 'Time's Up!' software.

During that meeting, Mike followed our process to the letter: asking the right questions, setting the correct parameters to match his prospective client's business, going through the service levels starting with the top (level one) and then selecting this to display the fee. At this point, Mike told me he was shocked to see the price that came up. He'd been expecting something a lot less. Never in a million years would he have quoted at that level.

Of course, this fee wasn't based purely on producing compliance accounts. The top-level service offers a packaged solution that we've created which includes many of the products and services you probably often do, but don't charge for. This time, by using 'Time's Up!' and following our process, Mike had talked the prospect through all of these before displaying the fee on the screen.

By now, Mike was dying inside. All he could focus on was the price.

But, when he finally plucked up the courage to look at his prospect, they simply nodded and began to enquire about some of the optional extras also presented on the screen.

The prospective client had been blown away by Mike's professionalism and by his run-through of everything the client could expect within the package he was being offered. This so far exceeded the explanation given by most accountants that when he saw the price, he felt it was right.

Mike came away with a new client and at a fee level significantly more profitable than that of any of his existing clients. A profit level that truly reflects his worth.

Now, to return to perfectionism: Imagine if Mike hadn't set himself a tight deadline to use our software – in his case the following morning. If he'd had more time, he might well have spent longer going through it, or decided that the pricing either simply wouldn't work in his area, or for the types of clients he sees. He might have gone through everything making judgements about how receptive prospective clients would be to the packaged solutions. As a result, he might have reduced the fees, or changed the language we use, thereby transforming a value-pricing tool that helps accountants offer high-level packaged solutions, into a piece of software that gives a 'competitive' (i.e. low) price for a mediocre set of services. In other words, into something that simply wouldn't have the same appeal for prospective clients.

There are other reasons why it's important to commit yourself to a tight deadline. Whenever I need to create a new presentation, for example, I know I can be too much of a perfectionist. As I don't like to use bullet points, I need to create slides that visually complement my points. This means it could easily take me days just to create a slide deck. However, if I don't start work on a presentation until two days before I need it, I know I'll work flat out, but only make it as good as it can be within that timescale. In my experience, it's always been more than good enough, whereas if I had three or even four days, I'd easily use them up by continuing to tweak my slides right up to the very last moment – for little or no benefit in the grand scheme of things.

To give another example, in the 1990s, when Microsoft were in their heyday, you probably remember how they would release new versions of Windows even though they still contained bugs. That's because Microsoft knew that it was better to get their software out than to wait until it was perfect, as by that time their customers might have moved to the latest release from a competitor. They'd also have been seen as less innovative and, as a result, lose market share and consumers' confidence.

Overcoming Factor 4: Fear

Did you notice that every bullet point in the section on fear began 'What if?' That's because fear comes from our brain's ability to run through every worst outcome possible before we act. I don't know who originally created the acronym for F.E.A.R., but 'False Evidence Appearing Real' is spot on.

To be fair, our brains coming up with all the potential pitfalls ahead of doing something rash has, I'm sure, often proved a good survival mechanism. But we should never allow ourselves to become so afraid that we fail to act at all. Instead, we should log every possible negative outcome and focus on how we'll prevent it happening or what we'll do if it does.

A few years ago, for example, I made a solo parachute jump for my 40th birthday which involved two days of training. This was a lot of training, particularly as before the jump the trainers would help us on with our gear and ensure it was safe, functional and working.

So why did we need all that training? Why didn't they simply let us turn up, don the gear and jump out of the plane?

The answer is: What if...?

Of the two days, around ten minutes was spent on learning how to land correctly, and perhaps a further 20 on how to sit on the edge of the plane cabin and push yourself out. The rest was all about the *'what ifs'*.

What if the chute didn't open? What if it got tangled? What if the pull cord kept you attached to the plane?

We spent those two days carrying out role-play after role-play. Inside the training room, hanging from special frames, we were shown picture after picture of different scenarios and practiced what to do again and again.

When the day of my jump finally came, I sat in the plane as it ascended high into the sky and the instructor signalled for me to sit on the edge of the open doorway (tethered, of course, to both the pull cord and to an additional one to prevent me falling out of the plane prematurely!).

As we reached the correct height and I had the nod from my instructor, I threw myself off, counted "1000, 2000, 3000, 4000," as I'd been taught, and looked up at my chute to ensure it had opened correctly. It hadn't!

But seeing that it was twisted didn't fill me with dread. Instead, I simply reacted in the way I'd practiced over and over again. I pulled the twisted cords apart, kicked my legs to spin my body around to untwist them and, voilà! The chute opened and I enjoyed a gentle descent before landing flawlessly – even if I do say so myself!

Remember: We can either use fear to help us prepare for situations so we're able to face them head on, or we can allow it to prevent us from taking action at all (action that might take us on to experience amazing things).

Even the trembling you might feel prior to giving a presentation is simply adrenaline pumping through your veins, preparing you to be at your best. Rather than see it as trembling with fear, try seeing it as trembling with enthusiasm.

So stick your chin up, take a deep breath, and crack on!

Overcoming Factor 5: The Bright and Shiny

In most cases, people are drawn to the bright and shiny because they're looking for a quick fix to a problem, or to avoid facing one. A clear strategy, however, will keep you on the straight and narrow.

The seven principles I'll be sharing in this book will help you to form that strategy. Only by focusing on enhancing these seven principles, in the order I share them, and then maintaining and refining them, will you be able to build the practice of your dreams.

No matter what the marketers of innumerable bright and shiny objects would have you believe, there's no magic shortcut.

Overcoming Factor 6: Comfort Zones

Stepping out of your comfort zone is closely linked to coping with fear. Sometimes though, no amount of role-play can help. Some things – parting company with an employee, for example – are never pleasant, but they have to be done. The support of others who understand your situation can help, of course. They can share coping mechanisms and approaches. Sometimes though – and I speak from personal experience here – you just have to disconnect yourself and make it happen.

Overcoming Factor 7: Not Enough Pain, Not Enough Gain

As I've said, I strongly believe accountancy is a noble profession that can make a profound difference. If you agree, who do you want to make that difference to?

A good place to start might be with yourself. After all, you've trained incredibly hard and have spent years building up your experience. Surely you now deserve some choice over the number of hours you work, your role, your income, and the difference you're able to make?

If, at this point, you're thinking, *"But I do have a choice in all of those"*, my question would be: *"If you were to halve the amount of hours you work right now, would your practice continue to earn you the same income and function in the same way?"*

If you suddenly had to go into hospital, would your practice continue to support you and your family or would it deteriorate?

In fact, this is probably a good moment for you to make a cup of tea and spend a few minutes taking stock of your situation. In terms of profitability and enjoyment, for example, is your practice where you hoped (or expected) it would be by this point?

How many hours per week do you work? (Even if you're a workaholic, there's a difference between *wanting* to and *having* to work). Similarly, how many holidays can you take each year? And, of those, how often are you able to fully relax, with no phone calls, emails or texts that you need to respond to while you're away? Then there's the impact of all this on your family and friends. When you spend time with them is your mind still on work? (That handful of questions should help you consider where you are right now. If you'd like a more in-depth analysis, you can go to: www.takethetest.today).

If your answers to the above have helped you to realise you don't actually have the level of choice you'd like, that's great. But what about the opposite end of the spectrum, the gain? How *could* things be?

Often it's difficult to imagine a better practice, or we fall into the trap of plotting the future based on our past. If, for example, over the past six years your turnover has undergone a steady increase of 5%, you may forecast that it will continue to increase by this same amount. You may even set targets to ensure that it does.

But what if you were to decide you want to triple your turnover in the next 36 months, with a 30% profit margin after your salary has been taken out? And what if, on top of that, you decide you want to work half – or even a quarter – of your current hours?

How differently would you have to plan? How would achieving it make you feel? Imagine the holidays you and your family could take if you could leave your business for longer, but it continued to thrive in your absence! And imagine the impact it could have on others, such as helping your team in their career development, or your clients to grow better businesses.

Whether any of the above resonates with you or not, finding what drives you is incredibly important. Discovering my own purpose was like switching from pulling upstream on the oars of a rowing boat to driving a speedboat. What had previously seemed an effort became effortless.

If you don't yet know what motivates you, I suggest you grab a sheet of paper (or your digital device of choice!) and note down what you're not happy with in your practice, and in your life, too, for that matter. Next, describe your ideal scenario and decide when you want to achieve it by. Don't worry about being realistic, in fact be as ambitious as you like! If you could wave a magic wand, for example, what would your dream accountancy business look, feel and even sound like? How would your clients describe it to others? That should help to focus your mind.

6

REACHing For The Stars

The previous chapter shared a few of the common reasons why some accountants don't take the fundamental action they need to, as well as some proven mechanisms to overcome these.

In order to improve AVN's ability to help more accountants achieve the success they aspire to and deserve, I also took that learning and applied it to our support framework.

I'd now like to share this with so that you, as an accountant in practice, can replicate the attributes that will help you accelerate your journey towards achieving your ideal practice.

This support methodology can be described by the acronym REACH:
- **R**oadmap
- **E**nvironment
- **A**ccountability
- **C**ommunity
- **H**uman to Human and handholding.

Roadmap
Once I'd identified the seven principles, my team and I were ready to create a roadmap methodology. Of course, although every practice we work with starts from a very different place, with very different problems and aspirations, the overall blueprint to success remains the same. That's why I'll be sharing those seven principles with you later in this book.

Environment
What's the best environment in which to focus on your business? It's probably not your office as you're too likely to be distracted, plus – as the environment you're used to working in operationally – it's difficult to think strategically.

Perhaps, then, you should aim for total isolation in a different setting? The trouble is, that way you miss out on being able to bounce ideas off others, which is a great way to accelerate the development of ideas.

How about a mastermind (a peer-to-peer mentoring) group then? Again, it depends. If you're surrounded by people who face similar challenges (and with the mindsets that created those challenges in the first place) it can simply end up as a venue for chewing the fat. Any ideas that do arise are often more akin to a sticking plaster than to a fundamentally different way of running your business. (Another challenge with mastermind groups is that different people progress at different rates. The faster-paced then get frustrated with those who want to proceed more steadily– and vice versa).

In my experience, the best environment is one that places you in a room with non-competing peers, where you can bounce ideas off each other but an expert is on hand to lead the discussion, challenge the status quo, and share their expertise.

If you're not convinced, let me give you a personal story to illustrate this.

Many years ago, some friends were encouraging me to join them on a skiing holiday. I hadn't been on one before, but frankly, it didn't appeal as I expected cold, miserable conditions. Despite this, I eventually agreed and was, of course, proven utterly wrong: the weather was glorious and the scenery was stunning. The only problem was I couldn't ski.

I'd had a few lessons on a dry slope before I left and - somewhat optimistically as it turned out - thought I'd be able to figure out the rest when I got there. I spent the first morning on the nursery slope, practicing the snowplough, but I couldn't nail it and I had no one to discuss what I was doing wrong with.

In the afternoon, when many of my friends joined me, each of them had a different suggestion. One told me to lean forward, another tried to explain where my weight should be and, all in all, it became thoroughly confusing. At this point, they suggested I just follow them and it would simply 'come.' It didn't.

By the third day I'd had enough and decided to plump for lessons. After a brief assessment I was placed in a group which consisted of others at exactly the same level as me, led by an expert – the instructor. The instructor started by asking us all to focus on just one thing and to support each other to make sure we got that right first. I remember thinking I'd got it right at one point, but the person next to me was able to see that actually I was still leaning in the wrong way. Likewise, I was able to help others. Once the instructor was happy, we moved on to the next thing.

For me, something clicked, which meant that I was able to progress more quickly than others in my group. Luckily, my instructor recognised this and, by moving me to another group that was a little more advanced, allowed me to continue to progress at my own pace.

The environment I've just described is exactly the one we aim to replicate within AVN: expert-led, with each person able to focus on very specific things, but also to bounce ideas off one another. That way, once they're back in their office, they'll know exactly what they need to focus on because they'll already have done much of the foundation work. And, just as importantly, they'll have had the opportunity to practice through role-play, which is particularly useful when it comes to areas such as pricing and pitching.

Accountability
Even if it's impossible for you to attend the ideal environment I've just described, you can still make progress. However, to do so you'll need to work with an external individual who can hold you accountable.

Most of us have a tendency to respond to whoever's shouting loudest at any given moment and, frequently, that's a customer. The challenge is that many customers make demands even when it isn't actually that important to them whether you drop everything to deal with them instantly or not.

And who suffers as a result of this? Your practice. (Yes, that same practice which, as I explained earlier, is your real number-one client; the one that needs to be in great shape if you're to serve your other clients well). That's when an external person, able to act as a louder version of that little voice inside your head asking *"What about my practice?"* is so important. By holding you accountable for at least one period each month, they keep your momentum going.

You'll also find them a great sounding board. You're free to air your dirty laundry in confidence, whether it's related to your team or to your partner, and even talk through any personal barriers that are getting in your way.

A word of warning though, working with the wrong type of person can be costly. There are many, many people out there who call themselves a coach, a mentor or a consultant but not all of them merit the title. I'd also encourage you to work with someone from outside your practice.

In fact, here - in an extract from one of my other books, *'What's Next for Accountants'* - are some of the criteria I use to identify suitable practice growth experts for our AVN members.

First things first: A coach, a mentor or a consultant?
I'm sure you've heard all three terms used, but here's my take on the differences between them.

Consulting
A business consultant is academically qualified. Perhaps they have a high-level degree and/or significant experience in a particular field. Examples might include a fire and safety or a marketing consultant.

Consultation tends to be reactive. You have a problem and so you consult an expert in that area. A consultant will listen to the particular challenge you face, assess the situation and provide a set of recommendations – a prescription, if you like – that you can follow to overcome that challenge.

In other words, a consultant tells you what you need to do.

Mentoring
A mentor has been there, done that and got the T-shirt. They've gone through a particular journey, experienced the pain, overcome the challenges, and gained a wealth of experience.

Because of this they're able to relate to your situation and suggest ways you can improve. They can teach you to think like they do and share the processes that worked for them.

In other words, a mentor relates, suggests and teaches.

Coaching

In my view, coaching is about getting you to think for yourself and helping you to improve your thinking.

A coach isn't afraid to ask obvious questions; to ask you to explain why you're doing what you're doing and how things could improve. They won't give or suggest answers. Their role is to ask thought-provoking questions – not to get a predetermined answer, but to keep drilling down until you develop a solution yourself.

Even if the coach is able to provide a solution, they won't (or at least they shouldn't). Helping you to discover the answers for yourself is a key part of your development and, in addition, often helps you to uncover something unique.

In other words, a coach questions in ignorance.

Personally, I want to keep developing my skills and strategic thinking and I feel it's best done through a coach. Moreover, times are changing so rapidly that, from a mentor's perspective, what worked five years ago may not be the best approach now. However, we're all different, which is why we make sure that the practice growth experts that we work with at AVN possess the skills to adapt to each individual case, starting with the coaching approach and modifying this as they go.

Whether you decide to work with a coach, a mentor or a consultant, before you commit make sure you gauge the types of questions they ask. Do they tend to jump in with solutions before you've even finished talking, or do they listen and probe first? Are their questions open and exploratory?

As a few further pointers, at AVN I ascertain that all potential practice growth experts have been a success in business themselves and have great business acumen. I want to know that they have a variety of industry knowledge and that it's current. Of course, I also want to know that they help their clients get the results and success they expect. Then, and only then, are they invited to become part of AVN and trained to become a practice growth expert.

I recommend you follow a similar process in terms of the business credibility of anyone you're considering working with.

Community

It can be lonely running an accountancy practice. In our personal lives we have family and friends we can share things with, or to air our feelings and vent our frustrations with. Sadly, our business lives don't always offer us the same opportunity. Even if we have a team of people or co-partners or directors, it's not always easy to be completely open or to get fresh insights about the challenges we face.

As humans we love to surround ourselves with others who share our values. It's why so many of us join clubs or become members of organisations whose beliefs we share. Being part of a community - or at least the right community - is composed of three key elements:

1. Common purpose This is being part of something that can achieve more than is possible for a single individual on their own. Aligning ourselves with others who feel the same way, and being part of a facilitating organisation driving that common purpose forward, enables each of us to feel that we're contributing.

2. Camaraderie Being able to connect with like-minded individuals gives access to a greater level of support from non-competing peers who genuinely want you to succeed. Through sharing your personal experiences, these people become friends and part of your social network. Progression and improvement take place because concerns, obstacles and insights can be openly voiced.

3. Brand Being a member of an organisation that represents everything you're passionate about enables you to proudly share that fact in your marketing. Doing so will not only inspire others, it will demonstrate to customers that you're serious about your purpose.

In addition, being part of an organisation that offers continuous development grants you access to research, training, learning and a structured approach.

Human to Human and Handholding

Business-to-Business sounds so inhuman, doesn't it? Behind every business though are people, each with their own individual concerns and aspirations. That's why it's so important from our point of view to really understand what you want to get out of your practice if we're to help you build a practice that's going to give you this. If you're already working with a coach, a mentor or a consultant, make sure they're not telling you what your practice should be like.

As *your* practice it should reflect *your* personality; have the reputation that *you* want it to; and develop at a pace that *you're* comfortable with.

7

The Seven Key Principles

Below is a brief introduction to the seven key principles. I'll be expanding on them in the following chapters, at which point you can begin to implement them and turn your accountancy *practice* into an accountancy *business*.

1. Clarity
- Developing a clear vision for your practice
- Reverse engineering that vision to form a strategy that's clear on how to achieve your vision in the timeline you want
- Defining a marketing strategy (to attract your ideal clients) and a pricing strategy that reflects your true worth and rewards you for the value you bring.

2. Positioning
- Overcoming the perceptions of both existing and prospective clients that you're 'just' an accountant
- Differentiating yourself from your competition so that price is never the deciding factor
- Getting your positioning right so that clients are more receptive to added-value services.

3. Value
- Improving the value you offer across the entire customer journey, leading to enthusiastic and grateful clients who refer you on
- Delivering valuable business-growth solutions for which clients are happy to pay a premium.

4. Gearing
- Engaging a fantastic team and developing a great team culture
- Nurturing top client managers to look after your clients
- Outsourcing effectively and improving general productivity so you (and your co-partners or directors, if applicable) can better leverage your time

and transform your owner-centred accountancy practice into an accountancy business that doesn't rely on its owner(s) for day-to-day running.

5. Automation
- Ensuring high standards and consistency
- Enhancing systems and embracing technologies that automate and shortcut processes.

6. Profile
- Building on positioning by raising the online and offline profile of your practice, its owner(s) and its team, leading to your practice becoming highly sought after by your ideal clients.

7. Purposeful
- Taking the concept of making a difference and changing lives to a much deeper level.

As I go on to describe each principle in more detail, I'll break it down into its constituent parts and share the common threads that, from my research, each of the most successful firms were following. I'll also introduce excerpts from case studies and interviews with accountants who are already reaping the emotional and financial rewards of focusing on these principles.

The first three focus specifically on moving you away from working at an inefficient capacity. However, in order to achieve efficient capacity a number of things need to happen first. It won't be easy but they're important.

Oh, and before we start, one final thing. Please forgive the regular references to AVN, but the stories and examples I share are based on the experiences of our members and their successes. Every single one of whom – prior to becoming a member – was experiencing similar challenges to those I imagine you're facing now…

Are you ready to share the success they do and improve your lifestyle as a result?

8

Identify Your Aspirations

I vividly remember visiting Robert, one of our AVN members, who was struggling to come up with a pricing solution for his practice. When I offered my assistance, it soon became clear that he was trying to accommodate such a wide variety of clients that every scenario he considered contradicted a previous one.

I quickly stopped the discussion on pricing as there was obviously a far more fundamental question that needed to be answered first. What did Robert really want from his practice? What was his vision?

As initially this wasn't something he had clarity on, after exploring a little we started to focus specifically on his *'why'*. In other words, on what he saw as his true purpose. (Our 'why' comes from our hearts and – once we've achieved a necessary level of financial security – is what gives us our sense of drive). What was Robert really passionate about?

This is often a tough question to answer. Many of us might not feel that we have a purpose. Many a strapline on a practice website, for example, is chosen not because it comes from the owner's heart, but because they think it sounds attractive to potential clients. But our true purpose is never simply a set of words that sound good. It's something we all have, without necessarily realising it. And it's something we should discover not invent.

In my own case, for many years I simply did what I did. Work was fulfilling, but I couldn't articulate exactly what my purpose was – apart from the fact that I enjoyed making a difference. However, once I discovered my purpose I was able to connect it to everything I loved and, as a result, I'd never felt so motivated.

If you haven't discovered your purpose yet, the story of how I found mine might help.

Many years ago, whilst in a pub with some friends one evening between Christmas and New Year, one of them mentioned that someone he knew had completed an Ironman triathlon. As none of us had heard of one before, he explained how - during a period of 17 hours - participants first have to swim 2.4 miles in open water, then cycle 112 miles, and finally run a full 26.2-mile marathon. Each discipline has a time limit which, if you fail to meet it, means you'll be disqualified and prevented from continuing.

It sounded pretty gruelling but, fuelled by several pints of Guinness, the friend telling the story and I committed there and then to competing in one, setting ourselves a target of 18 months to get fit enough. (As neither of us did any exercise at all at that point and were both starting to develop quite an impressive spare tyre, we felt that it would also convince us to do more exercise and eat more healthily).

In fact, we were so enthusiastic that we booked and paid for it online that very night, even opting in to the organiser's chosen charity. The next morning, I remember hazily thinking about what we'd committed to and saying to myself, *"Best start training tomorrow!"*

Tomorrow, however, never came. Every now and again I'd think about it, but I hated running, always had. Even at school I'd try every way possible to get out of cross-country runs. I did cycle occasionally, but I ended up having to get lessons to sort my swimming technique out, since I couldn't even manage a length without being exhausted no matter how often I went.

Six months later I'd still barely started training or cut back on food. In fact, when some training plans arrived from the organisers, I even laughed at the intensity of training they suggested I should be at by that point. Once again I decided that 'tomorrow' I'd start doing more. More successfully, however, they also reminded me that I needed to start asking people to sponsor me. All proceeds would go to Cancer Research and family, friends and colleagues happily signed up to £5 and £10 donations which was great. Now I just needed to make sure I did enough training to be able to complete it.

Exactly one year later, we all met in the same pub again. My friend asked how my training was going and I confessed to having done barely any –

as did he. With only six months to go, we agreed we'd best start 'tomorrow.'

Isn't it funny how tomorrow never comes? By February, I still hadn't gone on a single run, cycle or swim. At this point, I clicked that things were getting serious. I needed to get fit otherwise I'd fail, so I decided to go on a big run to try to catch up with where I should have been according to the training schedule. I went hell for leather, but before I'd finished, suddenly felt excruciating pain in both legs. I limped home and put ice packs on them. After a couple of weeks the pain still hadn't gone and it hurt to walk, let alone run. I decided to go to the doctor who told me I had shin splints and that if I continued to run I could cause permanent damage to the muscles that attach to the bone in the shin. The pain was because these had begun to tear owing to the stress I'd put them through. The prescription was rest for at least six - if not eight - weeks.

This worried me as the deadline was getting closer. In fact, I was more or less resigning myself to the fact that I wouldn't be ready. During those weeks though, I went on holiday with my family, and, when I'm on holiday, I enjoy alternating between reading a new murder mystery and a business book. This time Paul Dunn, a good friend of mine, had recommended 'Start with Why' in which the author, Simon Sinek, shares how the most successful businesses differ from the rest, His conclusion? Because they've recognised that people don't buy what you do, but why you do it. As he gave example after example, I was forced into some self-discovery. What was my 'why'? I didn't know. Even as I read his book, nothing was flowing. Nothing I read struck a chord.

Later, however, during this same holiday, my wife, Jenny, mentioned her cousin Sam, which did strike a chord. Every time we see Sam it bothers me deeply. When Sam was just four years old, he was on a zebra crossing with his big sister when they were hit by a car. The driver was speeding and simply hadn't been paying attention. Sam took the brunt of the collision, hitting his head so badly that it severely damaged his brain. He was in a coma for months and when he recovered was so severely mentally handicapped that he needs constant 24-hour care. Now, although I don't have a close relationship with Sam from a family point of view, his situation bothers me. It makes me realise how fragile and easily damaged the brain is. Why aren't we able to fix it?

Thinking about how much Sam's situation bothered me made me realise that choice is what's most important to me. Whether – as in Sam's case – it's the brain's ability to be able to choose at all or – in the case of many people in the developing world – it's choices around food, education and medical care that most of us take for granted. I also realised that, somewhere amongst these, is the business owner who feels they have no choice but to keep working endless hours in order to pay the bills.

I'd discovered my purpose: To enable people to have a better choice.

Once I realised this, Jenny and I also talked about me raising money for Headway, the charity that had helped Sam after his brain injury and, when we returned from holiday, I suddenly found I'd developed an overwhelming urge to get out and train. No matter what the weather was like, or how steep the hill, I'd think of Sam and it drove me on. I had connected my purpose to the Ironman event.

I went out with a new sponsor form and this time I shared why I was raising money for this particular cause. I found I was no longer receiving £5 and £10 donations, but £50, £100 and even £150.

I completed my first Ironman in 14 hours, 55 minutes and raised almost £3000. And I've continued to participate in the event every year since.

Discovering my purpose and connecting it to what I was doing had given me the drive and motivation I needed. It no longer felt like hard work. It became effortless. And connecting that same purpose to my business – enabling better choice to people in business who often feel they have no choice but to keep on working an endless amount of hours in order to generate the income they need - had exactly the same impact.

The lesson to be learnt is that discovering your purpose has to start with 'WHY?'

In Robert's case, after quite some time digging ever deeper, we ascertained that he's most passionate about helping people to be the best they can. Next, we looked at his personal goals. For Robert, working with his local children's football club is important. He produces their accounts – for no charge – and also helps to coach the children. His personal goal was therefore to ensure he had enough time to continue do this while also spending quality time with his own children. Although he'd managed to do this very successfully so far, he was starting to struggle. For example, he wanted to be able to attend his children's sports days and other events without worrying about his business demands.

So what's important to you? How much time would you like to be able to spend with your family or friends? How does that compare to your current reality? How many holidays would you like to take and where to? Are you hoping to exit your business soon and want to sell it for a premium to fund your retirement, or would you prefer to build a business that you can continue to own in your retirement but don't need to work in?

You need to be clear on your personal goals, because only then will you be able to develop your business in such a way that those things can happen. Otherwise, you'll have no choice but to continue fitting your personal life around your business.

Next, Robert and I looked at his business vision. In my view, a vision is exactly that. It's how you 'see' your business in a few years' time and what it'll be doing both for you and for your clients. This vision is less about numbers and more about what those numbers represent. The numbers come from your goals.

In Robert's case, he wanted a practice that would be helping his clients to grow their businesses *and* give them their lives back. He realised that behind each business were people who he wanted his practice to create a better life for. He recognised that the accounts and financial reports he produced were the means to an end – in this case, of starting conversations – rather than the end in themselves. He also wanted his practice to be a great place to work, where all his team enjoyed coming in and received a huge sense of fulfillment from what they did.

To help make sure he'd be able to achieve this, we went on to discuss some specific goals for his business. And, at this point, I'd like to remind you what I said about a common mistake being to look at your progress over the last few years and project this forward. It's easily done, but it limits your thinking.

If, for example, you've been gradually increasing turnover by a steady 20% each year, you might think it made sense to project that same level of growth going forward. But what if you made your goal 100%? Or even 1000%?

You might think that those seem ridiculous figures. But what if you really committed to them? What different ideas might you begin to have? What help could you get to achieve them? Perhaps you could take a shortcut through acquisitions, or come up with a new, innovative way to grow.

I'm not suggesting that you aim for something so extreme that it's impossible to buy into, but do make sure you pick the middle ground that's leading towards being very ambitious. I promise you'll be amazed by how much it changes your thinking and approach!

A few years ago, an accountant called Phil took a leap of faith and joined AVN. At the time, he was operating from his garden shed with a steady turnover of £50,000 per annum, but an employee ate up some of that and he was struggling to pay the bills for the home he, his pregnant wife and child were living in. Within four years of joining us, Phil had grown his practice by over £1,000,000. (If you don't believe me, you can find an interview with him on our website **www.avn.co.uk** within Testimonials and Case Studies. In fact I suggest you do, it's completely inspiring). My point is that if he'd simply projected his historic growth forward and focused on continuing to meet that, he wouldn't have seen the growth he did. The conclusion is: Always think big!

Robert set some very audacious goals during my visit, including ensuring that absolutely nothing in his practice would rely on him being there. Every part of the service-delivery, including advisory, would be delivered by his team. In fact, as per his original plan, he intended to run his practice as a business. He also assigned target dates by which to meet them, which played a key part in making any goal seem real. Action needs to be taken.

By this point in our meeting, Robert had achieved clarity on his purpose, as well as on his personal and business vision and objectives, so I asked what proportion of his existing client base he was already delivering this ideal service to. The answer was *"none."* In response, I asked him to describe the type of client who would be receptive to this kind of work, in other words, to describe his ideal client.

Next, I asked how many of his current clients fitted this description, i.e. how many might be receptive to working with him for a higher fee in return for this higher level of service? He identified about 10. To reiterate: out of 180 clients, only 10 might be open to receiving the types of service that he really wanted to offer. The rest were either compliance-only accounts or – at best – management accounts offered as an additional service.

As we explored this fact further, it became clear to Robert that not only were his compliance-only clients the hardest work, they were also the least profitable. Their books and records were frequently in such a mess that they needed a lot of extra work, plus they often needed pestering before they handed over the necessary information.

I asked Robert, if he were to start his practice again from scratch, which clients would he choose to work with and what would he choose to deliver? As he described his ideal scenario, it became clear that this would include getting the accounts produced externally and then using the information he gleaned from these to help his clients analyse their businesses and look for opportunities to improve them. He could benchmark the accounts to identify the strengths and weaknesses of each business and then – using the AVN Performance Measurement and Improvement methodology – take each client through a journey of improvement. As Robert described the impact this could have on his clients, he came alive and his energy became infectious. Imagine the impact that could have on a team of people!

At the start of our meeting, because he'd been considering all his different types of client, Robert had been struggling to come up with an effective pricing solution. Now, however, we were easily able to create a package of services that we then broke down to three levels, developing a pricing formula for each by building them in to our value-pricing tool 'Time's Up!'

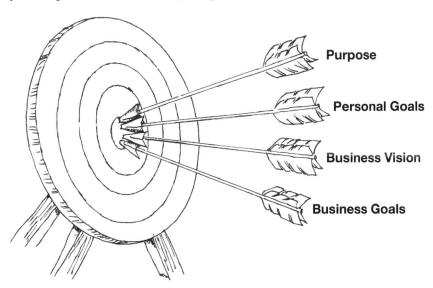

9

Reverse-Engineering Your Vision

Having a strategy means that you have a well thought out plan in place to help you reach your desired destination. To strategise is the process of developing this strategy. Although having a strategy in place is important, it's fair to say that in our present times you'll need to continually modify this as technology improves, legislation changes and competition threatens to undermine you. To succeed, you'll need to be in a continuous state of strategising.

Satellite navigation systems are a great example of how a strategy can get you from where you are now to where you want to go. You simply key in your destination and from amongst hundreds, if not thousands, of possible routes it presents you with two or three options. Through being connected to traffic-monitoring systems, modern Sat Navs are even sophisticated enough to take queues and roadworks into consideration, as well as strategising whilst on your journey as new obstacles arise.

Once, during a tour around the Pyrenees with a group of friends, I'd been using my motorbike's built-in Sat Nav as a guide. Although strictly speaking I was breaking the group's rules of no tech, just old-school map and compass, I felt more comfortable if I had a rough idea of our arrival time and knew we were headed in the right direction!

One day, however, when I tried to set my Sat Nav up it wouldn't work. The connection to the satellite receiver had broken. It was then that I realised that no matter how good your chosen strategist is, it's impossible for them to plan a route to where you want to be if they don't know exactly where you are right now.

Although we usually have the option of several routes whenever we travel to a destination, essentially our journey is linear. We travel in one direction and, if it's not right, adjust our course. Business is a little different. There are multiple factors and many different parts of each business to focus on. Which needs our attention first – marketing? Sales? Operational? Or financial?

If you decide to focus on improving your sales strategy, can you deliver on it? Are you pricing profitably or will more sales simply mean you have to work more hours – perhaps over and above what you really want to? Or, if you'll struggle to cope with the additional workload, do you risk making mistakes or reducing turnaround times, which could damage the reputation of your practice? On the other hand, focusing on increasing your ability to take on more work without generating extra sales could also be costly.

In business, it's important to strategise parallel streams if every aspect is to grow and develop together, which is why the seven principles I've developed are so important. They'll help you to do so in a simple, straightforward and logical way. (But don't worry, although AVN will take on the role of strategist for you, our overarching aim is to help you achieve the practice that you want).

The first of these seven principles is clarity, which involves knowing exactly where you want to get to, and where from. One of the key areas that we focus on first is to help accountants reverse-engineer their vision so that it becomes a step-by-step strategy. As a complement to this, we also help them to create a pricing and a marketing strategy to ensure they're able to attract the types of clients they'd most like to work with and charge appropriately for their services by better communicating their value. (Of course, this also means they deter the ones that don't fall in to this category, which is no bad thing).

But how do you begin to strategise if you can't see the wood for the trees? If your cashflow is up and down, if your clients are continually on the phone, if members of your team are constantly coming to you with new challenges or – worse – you don't have a team and have to do everything yourself, how can you even begin to work methodically through a strategy?

The short answer is, by taking stock and finding out where you are now. It's the only way to discover what you need to focus on first. And don't forget I've created a free online tool that will help you do just that. In fact I highly recommend you spend a few minutes going through the questions right now by heading to: www.takethetest.today. The Practice Performance Assessment takes about seven minutes and will give you an instant visual report on exactly where you are now and how strong you are in each of the seven principles.

As you read this book further, I'm sure you'll come up with lots of ideas about different actions you need to take, but this report is an incredibly useful guide as to how to prioritise them. Remember: If it ain't broke, don't fix it. And if it ain't *too* broke, it can always wait a while.

10

Remove The Restraints

Sometimes, you know where you want to go, but something – or some things – are holding you back. At this point you need to decide whether or not you're going to let them.

Some of the common restraints I've witnessed accountants having to remove before they can progress are:

- Franchises
- Partners – either in their accountancy practice or their life
- Clients and/or team members (of the wrong sort)
- Self-limiting beliefs.

Franchises

After joining AVN, an accountant was delighted to be able to achieve clarity on exactly how she wanted her practice to look, feel and act only to find that the franchise she was part of wouldn't permit her to develop it in that way. It then took her two years of trying before she was able to get out of it. Although the franchise had been useful in helping her to get established, it was now preventing her from making the choices she wanted.

Sadly, this is all too common, and very few of us are brave enough to escape and pursue our own aspirations. As a consequence, we carry on working more hours than we'd like, not delivering what we'd love to, and not enjoying what we do.

Partners (business)

Over the years I've seen many accountants held back by the other partners in their business. Many have given up. Others, by dragging their partner - often kicking and screaming! - to an AVN masterclass, have finally persuaded them to see what they want to achieve and to get on board. (Although, to reiterate, we never try to brainwash anyone. We simply show people how they *could* run their practice but, at the end of the day, this has to fit with their own values and aspirations. If it does, then they'll be inspired to embrace our philosophy. If not, they'll simply go home feeling they've wasted their time).

Sometimes a partner just doesn't get it and sometimes they don't want to. Some people are happy to churn out accounts production-line style, as many as they can, as fast as they can in a stack 'em high, sell 'em cheap approach, while others would prefer to use these accounts to have meaningful conversations and to make a profound difference. If a multi-partner practice is made up of partners on different sides of that divide, it will hold back the partner who wants to do more.

Despite this, I've seen very few partnerships split, but when I have, both partners have come away happier because they're now doing what they enjoy – without the constant disagreements.

Partners (life)

Although initially I wasn't sure whether to include this section, I believe it's important. The people we spend the most time with have a huge impact on us, on our mindset, on our confidence and on our self-worth. Often, of course, it's our life partner, but friends and relatives are also important. Do they have a positive or a negative impact on your self-esteem and on whether or not you believe you can (and should) do what you most believe in? Are they supportive or are they holding you back? If it's the latter, you need to have that conversation and stop the negativity.

Clients

I hope you remember Robert? Robert may not have had other partners to deal with, but he wasn't able to deliver the services he really wanted to because too much of his time was taken up in meeting obligations to current clients. (Yes, those same clients who were neither his ideal nor interested in the services he really wanted to deliver).

For some years, he'd been taking on clients at the compliance-only level in the hope that one day they'd embrace his higher-level services, even though he knew in his heart that most of them wouldn't. They wanted their year-end accounts doing to meet what they saw as an annoying legal requirement and that was it.

Together, Robert and I explored his options. He could either choose a gradual shift toward the type of practice he really wanted, or a radical one. The former involved talking to one existing client at a time, either trying to persuade them to upgrade or pricing them out so they'd go elsewhere. Another, more radical strategy, was to free up his time instantly by selling the clients that weren't right for him to another accountant as a block of fees.

Robert decided to be radical. Ridding himself, in one go, of the majority of his clients who were preventing him from spending time with the minority he felt he could really help meant a huge drop in revenue and profits, but a huge increase in time. Crucially, however, he could use this time not only to better serve his preferred clients, but to market to and acquire more of them, too.

Additionally, Robert didn't feel that his team was quite right as some of them were focused on compliance-only with no desire to develop their skills. As the move offered him a fresh start, one option he chose to explore was to help these team members set themselves up to deliver compliance services to those clients he wanted to say goodbye to.

Although Robert told me that part of him felt he'd failed when he took this decision – failed to develop the team and the culture he wanted, failed to acquire the right type of client – I strongly believe it would have been a bigger failure to continue in a direction that was taking him ever further from his aspirations, simply to soothe his ego.

My session with Robert was a purely coaching role. I didn't encourage or lead him in a particular direction. A decision such as the one he made, could – and should – only come from him. In sharing his story, I'm certainly not recommending that you sack most of your clients, although neither am I opposed to the idea! Robert's decision to take such a radical step came only after he'd gained absolute clarity around what was really important to him.

And Robert's story isn't an isolated example. Helping AVN members identify the clients they should stop working with – based on both personal fulfillment and profitability – is something we do regularly. For example, if you were to list all your clients on a spreadsheet and rank them in order of profitability – not fee – you'd likely discover that 80% of your profits come from only 20% of your clients. If, as a result, you decided to say goodbye to the bottom 20%, you'd save a lot of time whilst facing a negligible loss of income. The 80/20 principle is only a starting point, but it does offer a very quick win in terms of freeing up your time. (Just remember to say goodbye to those low- to no-profit clients in a way that doesn't hurt your reputation and leaves them happy!)

Team
As alluded to in Robert's story, another restraint is working with the wrong people. Not only can this demoralise you personally, but also the other members of your team. I'll explore this more in the fourth principle: Gearing.

Self-Limiting Beliefs
These often reveal themselves in the form of excuses: *"My clients wouldn't be receptive to me delivering higher-value services such as business advisory or coaching."* Or, *"This area's a little run down and the local businesses aren't interested in growth."* I've heard them all but, frankly, they're all simply rationalisations for self-limiting beliefs. The real reason is that, at heart, the practice owner doesn't believe that they can deliver on their aspirations. Of course this then becomes a self-fulfilling prophesy.

Having worked with more than 2800 accountants over the course of 20 years, I'm here to tell you that you can. So say out loud: *"I am a tiger!'"* and make it happen.

11

Commit Yourself

You've created your vision and your masterplan. You've identified the restraints that are holding you back but, the problem is, you're comfortable.

You've become used to things the way they are. Despite not earning the fee income you want and need, despite working more hours than you'd like, despite your practice not delivering what you really want it to, you're comfortable. As the saying goes: "Same shit, different day."

In one presentation I run, I encourage the audience to produce a bucket list of things they'd love to do and then commit the next 10 years to making them happen. On one such occasion a few years before I wrote this book, Marie Donaldson from 'Fresh Clarity,' an accountancy practice based in Shropshire, told me she'd spotted how my own bucket list (I show it on screen with the items I've ticked off so far and those I've yet to tick off) included a family trip to Lapland under the ticked category.

When she told me how that was something she'd always wanted to do, I had a conversation with her along the lines of 'JFDI' (just flipping do it!) and, a few months later, I was tagged in one of her LinkedIn posts. I'm not ashamed to say, that when reading it, I welled up with joy for her that she'd done it. With her permission, I've reproduced it below.

 Marie Donaldson • 1st
Sustainable Business Success | Profit Improvement accountant
3mo

For the last few years I've had a personal goal. I hadn't shared it with anyone, it had just been in my head amongst everything else. Needless to say nothing happened. About 18 months ago I shared it, out loud with Shane Lukas at an event, and his advice... just book it. If I booked it I'd find a way to do it. Sounds simple really, doesn't it. So home I went with this new possibility.

Running my own business meant I needed to believe in my business & myself enough to make it happen. I needed my business to deliver. Now I'd be lying if I said it I didn't have the odd wobble along the way, but it appears I'm quite stubborn when I've set my mind on something. I don't give in easily. Apparently wasn't a surprise to my husband.

So on the 15/12/18 we flew to Finland. When we landed and saw all the snow I felt quite emotional that I'd achieved it. We've had 4 fab days visiting Father Christmas, sledging, snowballs fights...

The point of this story is not in what we did or where we went, it's about the importance of sharing your goal/s with someone out loud.

If you've got a goal and you're struggling to make youth business deliver what you need, come and talk to me in the new year, we'll work out the numbers together.

#smallbusiness #christmas #goals

My advice to you is the same: whatever your dream, commit yourself to it in a way that'll give you the impetus and drive to make it happen. Whether it's a family trip to Lapland, a new home or something else, book it 18 months in advance, pay the deposit and then commit to making the improvements in your practice that will allow it to happen.

12

Commit Time

One thing shared by the most successful firms I visit is that they've all committed serious time to chipping away at their strategy and to the actions they know will help them improve their practice.

Always remember: Your practice is your number one client. As such, it needs time allocating to it. Not after a hard day's work when you can barely think straight, but your best, most alert time.

The dilemma is, how much? Unless they're doing chargeable work, many accountants feel they're wasting time or are letting their clients down. By putting the needs of their own practice last, is it any wonder they don't see the results they once hoped for?

The amount of time the most successful practices dedicate to their strategy is almost directly related to the pace at which they see improvements in their time, cashflow, profits and enjoyment.

For example Michael, an accountant based in Croydon, set himself the target of achieving AVNExcellence in 12 months. (I'll expand on this later, but in a nutshell AVNExcellence is a set of standards we've collated based on the UK's best accountancy practices). To do this, he knew he'd need to sacrifice client time, but with the help of Natalie, a team member, he set aside every Wednesday for them to work on the practice. Implementing one of the standards we set out at a time, often working late into the evening to make those standards an everyday part of their business, they completely transformed the practice.

Then there's Brian, an accountant from Darlington, who assembled a team called the AVN Steering Group. I'll feature his story in more detail later, but for now I'll just share how Brian reported that involving others in moving the practice forward on a strategic level led to much faster progress as team members felt empowered. In fact, the steering group was chaired by the least experienced member of his team as they were the least likely to have been influenced by how the profession had always been run and Brian specifically wanted someone who would ask questions and make suggestions that challenged the norm. (I'm delighted to report that this model is working so well that Brian won AVN's Firm of the Year award).

The key lesson to be learnt is: Assigning time to your practice is paramount to its successful development.

13

Progress

The firms that make the most – and the fastest – progress toward the owner's aspirations are those in which this progress is regularly tracked and, depending on the results, specific actions assigned.

To return to my Sat Nav analogy, there are many key measures we need to be aware of throughout our journey to our destination. Our Sat Nav will record the remaining mileage and our ETA, while the main dashboard will tell us, amongst other things, how much fuel we have left, our speed and the engine revs.

Some of these measurements allow us to make decisions that will affect our overall journey. For example, if we're going faster than the speed limit, an instant correction is preferable to the delay involved in getting a speeding ticket or even a driving ban.

It's exactly the same in business. Just as with a Sat Nav, we need to measure our overall progress toward our aspirations as well as to measure our current position. Sometimes it's easy to measure these in real-time, others less so. With a business, it's also useful to track trends over a few months rather than viewing a data 'snapshot.'

If practice size is important, some measurables of your overall journey might include turnover and profits. However, these are a consequence of your actions and as such are your lag indicators. Other measurables – your lead indicators – will indicate whether action can be taken to better influence the former.

To give another example, if you've set goals around reducing your hours, the number of hours you work each week will be an important measure – and that's where the importance of measuring trends comes in. One week you might work 35 hours, the next 37, the next 36, and the next 38. Compared to a starting point of, say, 60 hours per week these figures may look good in isolation but, when viewed as a trend it's clear that they're volatile and, on average, heading back in the wrong direction.

Another current measurement that will warn you when tweaks are needed is customer happiness. If this drops, it's far better to do something sooner rather than later, i.e before clients move to another accountant. Similarly, if your team's happiness drops, it can affect productivity and accuracy (which will then impact on customer happiness), which is why it's crucial to maintain a happy team. (Of course it can also reduce the risk of an unhappy team member moving on and the concomitant costs).

The numbers that matter most to you and your practice will be largely down to the type of practice you want to create but, whatever they are, you need to identify them quickly so you can tell whether you're on track or not.

I often ask people what their true measure of success is – although their first answer isn't usually their final one. When they really think about it, their true measure of success invariably comes from something much deeper. Perhaps, for you, it's capturing case studies that demonstrate you've changed lives.

Whatever your answer, I strongly recommend you don't keep this measurement to yourself. Involve your team as much as possible: *The more you share, the more they'll care*.

Georgi and Emma, for example, have a practice based in Berkshire. One of the most important factors in the progress they've made is that they now measure the numbers that matter to them and then involve their team by sharing these in various meetings and discussing how they can improve them.

One of these meetings is their weekly 'Trello™ Monday,' when they sit with their team and review workflow and priorities, then shuffle these to ensure that no one feels overwhelmed. They also have a monthly 'First Thursday' meeting when, as a team, they focus on the strategic numbers to ensure they're on track, as well as our AVN OnePagePlan™ which they use to measure their key numbers. They've also benchmarked themselves using the AVN BenchMark software, which shows how they're performing compared to thousands of other accountants around the UK using many pre-determined, accountancy-specific key performance indicators. Last, but by no means least, they have regular meetings with their AVN Practice Growth Expert who helps them monitor their progress and plan the actions they need to take.

Having meetings for the sake of it is, of course, a waste of time.

Although they're crucial for communication and planning, unless meetings are structured and timed, they can dissolve into digression, with many items rushed (or not even addressed) and little action being agreed. For meetings to be effective, you need to set an agenda that not only contains the overall purpose of the meeting, but specific outcomes for each item. I'd also recommend allocating a specific amount of time to each item and making sure you keep to this by setting a countdown timer. Strict adherence will ensure that the topic is adhered to and the outcomes are met. If you allocate an hour, it will take an hour. If you allocate ten minutes, it will take ten minutes! This is because our brains don't fully engage until a deadline approaches.

14

Bite-Sized Chunks

Not that long ago, I remember visiting Andrew, an accountant based in Birmingham, who at the time had a team of eight people. Andrew told me how, shortly after joining AVN, he'd approached his clients with excitement and enthusiasm to offer the additional services he'd discovered through us. Most of his clients were happy to accept as well as to pay a premium fee for them spread across monthly payments.

Andrew's challenge was that he then began to struggle to deliver on those services. Although he was sure he had the right team in place, they were struggling to keep up and to integrate the additional services into their workload. Embarrassingly, Andrew had over-promised and was under-delivering. In his case, this wasn't down to resistance from his team but simply because he hadn't appreciated the impact the level of take-up would have on their workload.

Although over the years I have witnessed countless examples of practice owners (or one partner of a multi-partner firm) striving to make changes that will have a positive overall influence on the practice only to be met with resistance from their team and / or the other partners, the flipside of this is that I've also visited practices where it's the members of the team who feel they're being held back. The owner – despite being excited about the concepts he or she has learned, and despite sharing these with their team – when it comes to actually making the necessary changes, resists. Why? The obvious answer is fear, and the *'What ifs'* I referred to earlier in this book.

Ironically, some of the firms I've seen grow the most have been those in which the owners started from a point of absolute despair. They felt under so much pressure – both at work and in their private lives – that they decided it was all or nothing. No one and no individual thing would be allowed to get in the way of them implementing the changes they wanted.

To illustrate this, here are two great examples.

You may remember that earlier I told you about Phil, from just outside Leeds. Phil had been trying to build a practice and, to keep his costs down, had bought a large – admittedly fancy – shed for the bottom of his garden. His thinking was that it would also mean he was closer to his wife (then pregnant with their second child) and son.

However, because Phil was making the same mistakes as so many others, his practice wasn't profitable. He was working 70 hours per week, trying to churn out as much work as possible in order to support his family, but he was struggling even to do that. In fact, he was scared that the bailiffs would be around any day to collect the furniture.

Things had reached such a low point that, despite being at the end of the garden, he was having less and less contact with his wife and their marriage was on the rocks. In fact, if he was in a room of people, his son would come to him last and that really hurt.

Phil knew something had to change. He'd heard of AVN and decided to come along to one of our events. His thinking at the time was not to join AVN, but simply to take some ideas away to implement in his practice. But, when he discovered that membership is on a month-by-month basis which can be stopped at any time, he felt he had nothing to lose. He decided to try it for a month and to soak up as much help as he could. After all, if he didn't see any benefits we'd even promised to give him his money back!

Phil went on to grow his practice by over £1,000,000 in just four years. How? By not holding back. He didn't let fear of risking everything stop him from taking action because, in reality, at that time he felt he had nothing to lose.

Another example of this 'nothing to lose' mindset is offered by Paul, who has an accountancy practice in Nuneaton. When Paul was a junior partner in his six-partner firm, he and a couple of other partners attended an AVN event and signed up for membership, although disappointingly they were met with too much resistance from the senior partners who were approaching retirement and refused to implement the changes they suggested. Although Paul had seen the potential impact the practice could have on their clients, he finally had to terminate his membership. Over the next few years, his fellow partners gradually retired, selling their equity to the remaining partners each time until, eventually, only Paul was left.

At the same time, Paul's workload had increased with each partner's retirement. Now, as the only partner left, each client wanted his time. There were still enough clients for a six- partner firm, and a team of 30 people, and yet the turnover of circa £800,000 didn't support that number of employees. Being at the beck and call of every client, Paul was barely generating any income and at one point could barely pay the bills. He'd had enough.

He came back to AVN and together we looked at how he could restructure his practice to make it more profitable and reduce the burden on his time. Commonly, a quick win is to price services better and it's true that in Paul's case cashflow and profits were in a terrible position. His mental state, however, was worse. To ease the burden, we suggested that he implement a strategy whereby clients would deal directly with team members who he would rename client managers.

This is often a difficult action for practice owners to take. First, because they feel that clients have bought into them as the partner; second, because they don't want to lose control; and third, because they're worried their team might run off with a pool of their clients and set up in competition. We'll address all three of these fears under 'Gearing' later in this book, but the point I'm making here is that Paul, by having a 'nothing to lose' mindset, implemented actions that enabled him to build a practice that's grown at an exponential rate. (The last time I checked turnover had exceeded £5m, just 18 months prior to that it had been £3.2m). He's gone from working 60-70 hours per week to one day per week – primarily to go over the KPIs from our AVN OnePagePlan in team meetings.

Phil and Paul's stories prove that one of the biggest obstacles people face is whether they're prepared to take action. And, at AVN, we understand this. It's frightening to think that something you've spent so long building up may simply fall apart if you rock the boat. But not everyone has to take action at the incredible rate Phil and Paul did.

Take Andrew, who I mentioned earlier, who had over-promised but under-delivered. He realised that, although he was surrounded by a great team, his rate of change needed to be slower. Since then he's made steadier, more incremental changes at a rate his team are comfortable with.

To reiterate: There's no right and wrong speed as long as progress is being made.

We all move at different speeds. Many of us don't like changes and so put off making any to 'another day,' which means we – and our practices – fail to progress. On the other hand, you may be someone who has an idea and wants to make it happen. If you're a one-person band, then that's fine, but what if you have a team of people and/or other partners? It's important to understand how they'll cope if you make changes too fast.

If your team are struggling to embrace change as quickly as you, then a decision must be made. Is it better to move at a pace they can all cope with or do you need to take the tough decision to let some of them go? It may be the right thing to do if the survival of your practice – or achieving the practice you want – depends on it.

But remember: The only pace that's intrinsically bad is stationary.

15

Pricing

Once, sitting in on the Board meeting of a five-partner firm we were working with, I was challenged on pricing. *"We're offering a far better service and charging on average 10-15% more than our competitors and yet prospective clients still choose those competitors over us,"* one of the partners told me.

"I'm not surprised!" I replied. I went on to explain that building additional value into your services is incredibly important and although they'd done that really well, they weren't charging enough of an additional fee to reflect this. Potential clients simply didn't believe they could deliver that level of value at the prices they'd set, and assumed they were offering the same level of services as their competitors but at a slightly higher price.

Psychology has taught us that most people judge the value of something almost instantly based on its price. If it's cheap, it must be poor quality. If it wasn't, how could they afford to produce it for that price? At some point, too, we've all learnt that buying cheap is a false economy – whatever it is it never lasts very long. And so, subconsciously, we learn to identify price with value.

If you increase your fees so they're at least 50% higher than those of your competitors, your value becomes believable. People will happily pay more as long as you explain the value they'll gain from doing so. Value pricing isn't about ripping off clients by over-charging them and then failing to deliver to a higher standard. It's about enhancing the value proposition, enabling you and/or your team to spend more time analysing the data, identifying and presenting opportunities to clients that will improve both their business and their life.

But how do you know you're charging the right price? If you simply base your fees on those of your competitors, how do you know that they didn't undercut their competitors, who in turn had undercut theirs? Undercutting each other is a vicious downward spiral of reducing profitability in which no one – neither you, nor your clients – wins. You're working more and more hours just to pay the bills but spending less quality time with your clients to help them spot opportunities.

That's why we teach the accountants we work with seven methods to increase their prices in a way that demonstrates to even the most price-sensitive client that they're delivering greater value. These seven methods are:

- Package your services and provide choice
- Add more value
- Explain this value
- Link price to value
- Communicate payment terms
- Make the price seem smaller
- Include power strategies such as guarantees.

By following our processes, AVN accountants tell us again and again that they've doubled, trebled and even quadrupled their fees.

To illustrate my point, I'd like to share a story that Cathal Cusack, of Cusack Garvey in Dublin, Ireland, told me recently about a phone conversation he'd had with a client who was complaining about turnaround times, and their not doing this, not doing that. Despite remaining as patient as possible eventually, out of frustration, Cathal told him: *"To do all of that in the time frame you wanted would have cost €20,000."* The client's reply, however, was a real wake-up call. He simply said: *"I've never refused to pay what you ask. Why didn't you tell me that that's what it would have cost to get what I want?"*

The client's actual bill was €6,500 and Cathal realised that he'd been guilty of making assumptions in his own mind about how much the client would be prepared to pay and quoted based on that. The result was a dissatisfied client. (Although thankfully one who, by complaining directly rather than simply moving on, allowed Cathal to respond by significantly increasing his fee so that in future he was able to deliver exactly what they wanted).

16

Gaining Clarity –
To Start, You First Need To Stop

This chapter has kindly been written by Val Wishart of Beyond The Numbers Chartered Accountants in Edinburgh. I asked Val if she would contribute to this book following a presentation she delivered to AVN members at our annual conference. I was inspired to adopt her suggestions myself and I recommend you take them on board, too.

I'd like to share with you the way I worked to achieve clarity, not only for my business but for my life, and the difference doing so has made to how I approach everything.

The first and most important step in gaining clarity about my life and my business was to find some headspace so that I could regain focus in a very murky and busy mind. I realised that in order to start changing things I needed to stop. To stop doing and thinking all the time and allow myself to just be.

I decided to try meditation, and from there to move on to visualisation of how I wanted the future to be. I have to admit that when I first started to work on mindfulness and meditation, some people were simply sceptical while others looked at me as if I had suffered a knock on the head!

Like them, some of you might think it's all a lot of mumbo jumbo, but if you're struggling to find clarity about the way forward, what have you got to lose? Why not give it a try? And, if you're still not convinced, I suggest you have a read of *'What Got You Here Won't Get You There'* by Marshall Goldsmith, one of the world's most respected coaches. It might make you think about making some small changes in your life which can have a huge impact.

Let's start by doing an exercise to see how mindful (or not) you are in your daily life. Answer yes or no to the following questions:

1. Do you ever arrive at work in the morning with no idea of how you actually got there?
2. Do you ever walk into a room and find you've completely forgotten why you went in there in the first place?
3. Do you forget birthdays/anniversaries/appointments until they pop up on the calendar on your phone and it's too late to do something about them?
4. Do you get to a Friday evening and wonder what you did all week?

If you answered yes to more than one of these questions, the chances are that you're not living mindfully. And, if you're not living mindfully, the chances are that you don't have clarity about your purpose, your goals or your vision.

I'm sure you're all familiar with these famous phrases around planning in business:
- Failing to plan is planning to fail (attributed to Benjamin Franklin)
- Begin with the end in mind (Stephen Covey)
- Start with Why (Simon Sinek).

These are all really useful, positive and inspiring quotes by people who share their beliefs, philosophies and methodologies in order to help us work out a plan and move towards it.

But how do you go about planning and getting clarity if your head is full of whizzing thoughts, feelings, problems, appointments, deadlines, clients, family, money, teams and systems?

Whatever it is that's clogging up your thinking (and it might be all of the above if you're anything like I used to be!), when you sit down to plan it means you'll struggle to see into the future and visualise where you want to be. I've been in this position myself and I know how it feels and how difficult it is to see your way out of it.

When I decided to try meditation, as I'd tried it before and been unsuccessful, I knew that this time I wanted to get some help. After doing some research, I came across an App called Headspace. Although I can recommend Headspace from personal experience – in a moment I'll tell you why I like it so much – there are many other ways to find out about meditation and lots of online tools to help you out. (In fact I've listed some helpful books and websites at the end of this article).

As Headspace is available on desktop or as an app on mobile devices, you can access it wherever you are. It's full of information about meditation and mindfulness, and its calm and careful teaching of the basics of meditation had a profound impact on my life.

I found that by sitting down for 10 minutes each day (yes, that's really all it took) and dedicating myself to following the instructions, I began to see, think and feel more clearly. I started to notice all kinds of things that had previously passed me by as I hurried through the day lost in thought.

This clarity of thinking had a really positive effect on my business, as I was actually able to sit down and visualise where I wanted to take it. Then, with the help of the AVN team and my business coach, I put in place a plan, figured out my *"Why"* and set about finding the best way to communicate my values to my team and to our clients.

If I hadn't allowed myself the space to just be, I know I'd never have started to make the changes I needed - and wanted - to make in my business.

If you need to gain more clarity in your life and/or your business, why not give it a try? If you're interested in finding out more about mindfulness and meditation before you jump in, I strongly recommend Andy Puddicombe's book *'The Headspace Guide to Mindfulness & Meditation'* as a starting point.

There are also many websites dedicated to the subject which include videos, blogs and/or podcasts and YouTube offers an incredible wealth of videos and guided meditations to help you.

Some of the resources I've found most helpful are listed below.
Books
* *'Mindfulness in Plain English'* by Bhante Gunaratana
* *'Meditation for Beginners'* by Jack Kornfield

Websites
* Headspace.com
* Jackkornfield.com
* how-to-meditate.org
* Gaia.com

I dare you to have a go – but watch out, the effects can be life-changing!

My thanks to Val for her contribution in this part of my book, I've personally benefited hugely by practicing mindfulness.

17

Clarity – The Principle

Clarity is the first stage on the AVN roadmap. As I hope has become clear, it's about establishing clarity in what you really want from your practice, where you are now, how you're going to get to where you want to be, who you want and need to take with you on your journey and who you want to work and operate for.

Without clarity, it's easy to miss what's really important to you.

For example, if your personal goals include spending at least two hours of quality time with your family on a weekday evening, you'll become more mindful about your focus during the time you're with them. Being in the same room but thinking about how you'll present a quote to that prospective client in the morning isn't really being with them at all.

Likewise, once you've established your ideal client profile, your language will reflect this whenever you describe who you'd most like to work with. This will help you with marketing and if you speak at networking events your pitch can include it, too. Turning away prospective clients is never easy but the rewards of choosing to work only with your ideal clients are huge.

In psychology, it's known as selective attention. Once we start to focus on something specific we often develop tunnel vision and can see nothing else. (Obviously the results of this can either be good or bad depending what we choose to focus on).

It's why goal-setting in business is so important. Once we start to focus on achieving them, it's almost as if antennae spring out of our heads specifically looking for everything that will help us achieve them and filtering out everything that won't. (A caveat is that although goals are important, they need to reflect your overall vision. If, for example, you focus on turnover as a goal, you may take on any client to try to achieve your target with the consequence that you end up working far too many hours).

Once you've achieved absolute clarity on your vision strategy, your marketing strategy and your pricing strategy – not independently but collectively – you're ready to embark on the journey to achieving your ideal practice.

At AVN we hold an annual conference and awards ceremony at which we recognise improvements and the high standards our members have achieved. Themed around the seven principles, the awards look at how a practice has benefitted from implementing the concepts within each principle and the results that ensued. To reflect this, as I end the discussion of each principle in this book, I'd like to share the award-winning entry for that principle.

With regard to the winner of the Business Clarity Award, I'd also like to point out that when they entered, CPT Chartered Accountants and Business Consultants had only been working with us for four months, and that their entry was written by a team member rather than by the owner, Brian Thompson.

Winning Entry for the AVN Business Clarity Award:
CPT Charted Accountants and Business Consultants
Before embarking on our AVN adventure the practice had become stale. Both workflow and cashflow were poor, and morale throughout the team was at an all-time low. We only had time to deliver compliance services to our clients, and whilst we hadn't started to lose clients, we felt it was only a matter of time before we did. The practice was at breaking point and therefore it was critical we stopped the rot.

There was consensus amongst the team that changes were required to improve the practice, but we didn't know where to start. It was recognised that revolution, rather than evolution, was required but we knew that if we tried to change every aspect of the practice overnight we would fail.

Brian watched an AVN webinar and was captivated by its underlying message. There were numerous lightbulb moments and afterwards we didn't hesitate to accept the invitation to attend an AVN masterclass and made the decision to join AVN as a member.

We needed a driving force in place throughout the team, so two key team members attended a further masterclass and were also enamoured. Within the practice, the AVN Steering Group was formed. This now meets fortnightly after hours, usually in the local pub, but with a strict agenda to drive the practice forward.

These meetings are chaired by the youngest member of the team and together we have set out the bite-size chunks we require to progress, with the structured programme of the AVN roadmap as the tried and tested method of success.

Our first action was the benchmarking of the practice using the AVNBenchmark to understand how we were performing compared to other accountancy practices. There were a lot more red areas than we were comfortable with and it was clear the practice was underperforming.

We discovered that we were significantly undercharging compared to the UK averages, and AVN gave us the courage and reassurance to increase our prices across the board, by 10% minimum, and without exception.

To date not one single objection has been raised. This gave us confidence to hone in on specific business services where we were found to be undercharging. For example, we increased our company secretarial services by 300%, with only 1% of clients opting to do their own.

We also implemented an 'Extra Work Order' system, which was useful for fee-sensitive clients where we anticipated a potential dispute as it allowed us to agree the fee before work commenced.

Achieving our desired level of billing on a regular basis had become a problem so we completely rebuilt our billing procedures. Historically, billing was done by the partner in between his other work commitments, the whole process was cumbersome, and many days could pass before bills were sent out to clients.

We now have a system in place in which each team member is responsible for their own billing. Bills are produced on the morning of the 1st of every month and sent out electronically by the end of the day. The team are encouraged to bill throughout the month where possible to keep the work-in-progress down.

Fees for the three months following implementation were up 55%, 52% and 85% respectively on the previous year and cashflow was noticeably improved. Administration time was reduced, freeing up the team to focus on chargeable work and giving Brian more time to work 'on' the business. This system also empowered team members as each took responsibility for their client portfolio, improving morale and making each team member feel like a valued stakeholder.

Our approach to prospective new clients was also reviewed. At initial meetings, all prospects are now presented with three clearly defined packages, illustrating service levels ranging from three to five stars, and a monthly investment for each. AVN's 'Times Up!' system is a crucial part of defining and value pricing these packages.

This approach has also proved effective when renewing current clients' fees. A recent example is a client for whom we prepared company accounts for a fee of £2.5k. When the fees were up for renewal we offered the three packages and the client chose the five-star version, which included management accounts and bookkeeping. The resulting fees rose to £8.5k and the client kindly offered to pay in advance!

Next, we graded our clients from A to D based on AVN's suggested criteria. Each team member graded their own portfolio and results were discussed at the steering group. It was found that 79% of our fees came from the A and B clients, who often demand less time than the C or D clients. We could therefore afford to be more bullish with our D clients, either bringing their fees in line with the work required, promoting them to C or above, or parting ways.

We discovered we had more A clients than we realised and decided to select 10 of these for our A★ programme with a view to maximising future fees, referrals and the client's personal objectives. This is an evolving process, but we believe in the potential of these clients to transform both our practice and their business.

During the implementation we have improved various other systems including:
- Standard phone-answering script, ensuring all team members answer calls consistently, thus improving the professional image of the firm

- Accounts passed for review should now be processed within 72 hours, and review points cleared within another 24, thereby reducing the bottleneck. The key control here is the Review Clipboard which details and prioritises jobs in progress
- Action planners – these ensure action points from client meetings are officially recorded, allocated and completed in a timely manner so clients aren't let down
- Agendas sent out ahead of all client meetings. This gives the client the opportunity to ask questions ahead of the meeting and for us to approach subjects such as referrals without putting the client on the spot.

We've only been on this journey for four months but our achievements so far are already having a tangible impact on the partner's role in the practice. Most notable is the fact that the partner is now able to dedicate one day a week to working 'on' the practice away from the office.

The systems that we've put in place mean that the practice is becoming more autonomous, requires less of Brian's input on a day-to-day basis, and provides peace of mind for succession.

18

Changing Perceptions

Most often the prospects and clients of an accountancy practice perceive their accountant – in fact accountants in general – as a traditional compliance-only accountant. The result of this is that no matter how good your business-advisory and value-adding services, or how much they'll improve the value of a client's business, unless you first change this perception, clients are unlikely to be receptive to receiving these services from you.

I know this because for many years we taught additional skills to AVN accountants in these areas, and provided ready-to-use coaching methodologies and consulting programmes that they could provide to clients, and yet selling these services proved difficult for a significant proportion until we changed our approach.

It's crucial to get your positioning right first. The most common feedback you're likely to receive if you don't is, *"But you've been my accountant for 20 years. Why are you suddenly trying to offer me this now?"*, followed by, *"Let's just stick with the accounts work, shall we?"*

You may remember that in Chapter 4 I shared the results of a survey that asked business owners for three words that best described their accountant, and how the four most commonly used were: introverted, systematic, antisocial and boring. (Of course, more positive words were also used, but not with the same frequency).

Eight years later, I decided to conduct a similar survey myself. As I have access to many groups of entrepreneurs and business leaders (from the owners of micro-businesses through to those heading up multi-million-pound ones), I posed them exactly the same question and received hundreds of responses. Disappointingly, the most commonly used words this time showed only a very slight improvement: efficient, supportive, distant and uninspiring.

The fact is, most business owners don't respect or see much value in their accountant. There are many reasons for this, but a major one is that accountants have been gradually undercutting each other through a short-sighted stack 'em high, sell 'em cheap model. Another issue is the ever-evolving software, the impact of which many business owners see as a reduction in their need for (or even a replacement of) their accountant. Indeed, many now see their accountant as simply a bookkeeper who tidies up their records.

This is why positioning – from first impressions through to how you deliver your meetings and everything in between – is so important. And why, in the following chapters, I'll be sharing ways in which AVN members are able to differentiate themselves from the competition.

Before a business owner chooses a new accountant, they'll usually talk to three other ones. Unless what you're offering is significantly different, that means the only comparison available to them is price and – if we're simply talking bookkeeping to fulfill their legal requirement to submit accounts – the cheapest will invariably win. (This brings us back to the topic of inefficient capacity. Accountants who fail to differentiate themselves need to work with far more clients than they'd like because they aren't able to charge sensible fees).

As long as you differentiate yourself sufficiently, value rather than price will become the differentiator. The right clients will see that your value outweighs your fee and be happy to pay it, thereby enabling you to deliver great services *and* at a premium price.

By charging better prices for the services you offer, you'll be able to spend more time analysing the data in your clients' accounts. As a result, you'll be able to make recommendations that your clients will be not only be grateful for, but in many instances this will also lead to additional work.

AVN accountants regularly tell us that by applying the suggestions I'll be talking about in this section, they're able to find the right type of clients and to part ways with those who don't fit their ideal client profile. They're able to refine their client base and work with fewer, high-fee income clients who they thoroughly enjoy working with and who in turn respect and appreciate them.

So let's explore some of the things that will help to improve your clients' and prospective clients' perception of you.

19

The Castle

For many of us – particularly those with children – the image of a certain castle will inevitably trigger an association with Disney. And it should do; after all it's their logo and they ensure that you see it every time you have any kind of Disney experience.

In fact, not only does your brain associate the logo with the name 'Disney,' it associates it with everything – great days out with your friends or family, your children enjoying watching their films or playing their computer games – that name means to you, too. And this, in turn, whether you're consciously aware of it or not, reinforces your level of liking for and trust in Disney. Their entire reputation, values and quality are summed up in a single association with their logo.

That's the power of a brand.

However, brand-building isn't something you can simply pay experts to do for you. Your brand is a reflection of you, your reputation and every interaction people have – and have had – with you. That's why it can never be purely about a name, a colour scheme or a logo.

What does your brand say to your clients and prospective clients right now? Does it have an impact on them? If so, is it a positive, a negative or an indifferent one?

Your brand stands for your principles, your reputation, your vision and purpose, as well as the value you offer and who you offer it to. The only way to ensure that your brand has the impact you'd like is to be consistent in the way you act and communicate and to make sure you're different from your competitors. But how do you differentiate yourself from them when essentially you're delivering the same services?

One powerful way is to focus on what makes you unique. When I look at most accountant's websites I see the same tired old phrases over and over again:
- *"We're Accountants and Business Advisors"*
- *"We're different..."*
- *"We're proactive..."*

And then, on the same page: *"We do accounts, bookkeeping, payroll, audits..."* How exactly does that demonstrate that you're different or proactive? I once made this point at an event I was running, before which I'd taken the time to assess each of the delegate's websites. However, after I'd argued that all of them were pretty much the same, one person raised his hand to object and said I must have missed his. I couldn't possibly have seen it because, to ensure it was different, he'd asked one of his clients who designed websites (for nightclubs) to create it.

Of course I apologised and, during the lunch break, spent some time with him going over his site. However, although it certainly had glossy images and impressive onscreen animations it still said exactly the same things: *"We're different"*, *"We're proactive"* and *"Accountants and Business Advisors."* At that point he realised he'd been more focused on his site looking different than on the message it was actually portraying.

In other words, remember to look past the jazziness of your website to what it actually says. Otherwise, every time a prospect compares you with a couple of others on Google, their first impression will be that you're all the same - in which case the only differentiator they'll look for is price.

Earlier, in the Clarity section, we looked at understanding your 'why' and your purpose. Now you've ascertained these, make sure you put them on your website. In the words of Simon Sinek: *"People don't buy what you do, they buy why you do it."* Your purpose will inspire people.

> As part of our members journey with us, the positioning section of AVN roadmaps is kicked off with a workshop at which we help delegates to find their 'why' and their values (amongst many other aspects). At one of these, one delegate, Martin, discovered his 'why' and told me that doing so was a huge lightbulb moment. He told me that when he was a child his parents had owned a hotel and were quite wealthy as a result. They had a huge garden he could play in and he pretty much got everything he wanted. Apart, that is, from what he most wanted: to spend time with them. His parents were so busy running the hotel that they never had time to spend with him. And that's why, he realised, his 'why' was now to help business owners work less hours so they could be there for theirs.
>
> Martin's 'why' – that message and that story – is powerful and that's why it should be on his homepage. It sets him apart and will inspire business owners who have children and want to spend more time with them to want to work with him. (The specific services you provide can be listed in a tab under services, instead). Remember, your website is often a prospective client's first impression of you.

Of course, some business owners might be put off by Martin's 'why.' They might not have children, or already feel they're there more than enough for them. But do these sound like Martin's ideal clients to you? No, they don't to me either. Not only will their values be different, but as clients they're likely to be less receptive to the type of advisory services he can provide.

Remember: Your purpose and the story behind it should always be included in your communications – from a short strapline to the full background – so that people are reminded of them, inspired by them, and continue to associate them with your brand.

20

Your Values And Beliefs

Do you find that – in life, as much as in business – there are some people you instantly connect with, and others you take an almost instant disliking to? Often, this is down to how much our values and beliefs align. To explain the difference, our values are pretty much set by the time we reach the age of seven. They've been influenced by our parents, our relatives, our teachers, the TV we watch and the games we play. Generally speaking, after that – other than through genuinely life-changing experiences – our values don't change.

Our beliefs, however, continue to evolve. In fact, those of the human race as a whole have been challenged time and time again. To give just one example, the belief that the earth was flat was eventually overturned by the evidence.

The good news is that this means that those self-limiting beliefs that prevent so many of us from taking a certain action, can also be changed. Although for this to happen you need to keep an open mind. (Many people, for example, believe that they're doing their absolute best in their business and that it's simply not possible to improve it).

The combination of values and beliefs peculiar to each of us is what makes us who we are. And it's the people whose values and beliefs are a near-perfect match to ours who tend to become our loved ones and best friends.

Next come the people whose values and beliefs are still in tune with ours, only not as closely. We'd still call them friends, but the relationship isn't as strong. It probably includes people you chat to at the gym or in the pub, but your interaction rarely moves beyond this.

Finally, there are the people whose values are the complete opposite to ours. In fact, they see the world so differently that just a few moments of conversation will generally leave us feeling infuriated! (I'm not saying they're bad people, just that they see the world in a different way).

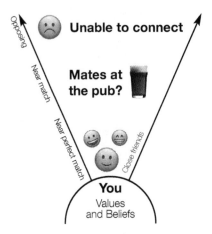

Why am I discussing this in this book? Because the same applies to your business.

Your clients whose values and beliefs are the closest match to yours will invariably be your best advocates. If you make a mistake, they'll be forgiving; if you have a new idea or a new service, they'll be the ones who want to hear about it; if you're looking for new clients, they'll be the ones who are happy to refer you.

Similarly, those clients whose values are a near match to yours will be okay. They won't be perfect, but they won't be the worst either. Perhaps they've driven you down on price, or aren't receptive to added value and advisory work. Or perhaps they never send the information you need and you always have to chase, or don't sing your praises enough to win you any new referrals or, if they do, bring more clients like themselves rather than the type you'd really like to work with.

Then, of course, there are the clients whose values and beliefs are completely opposed to yours. At AVN we call these 'BMWs': Bitchers, Moaners and Whingers. Nothing is ever good enough; nothing is ever fast enough; nothing is ever cheap enough. They complain the most and give you and/or your team the hardest time.

If you have clients like these, you probably spend more time trying to appease them (despite the fact that they're your least profitable clients) than you do on your best ones. In many cases, the better clients then feel neglected and eventually end up moving on, leaving the poor accountant (you, if you recognise this scenario) with the worst clients who seem to relish making their life hell.

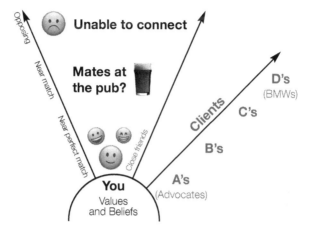

We help AVN accountants to grade their clients using many factors, but their clients' values and beliefs (as far as it's possible to know these) are one of the most important. Life's too short to work with people whose values and beliefs are not aligned with your own. No matter how much you try, you'll never enjoy working with them and they, in turn, are unlikely ever to respect or to appreciate you – or to want to pay you an appropriate (and fair) fee for the work you do.

Remember: Ditch your D's and up your fees!

In addition to your purpose and your 'why,' your values and beliefs also make you unique. By communicating them, you'll attract clients whose values and beliefs align with your own and deter those whose values and beliefs don't – which can only be a good thing.

Once you've ascertained your purpose, values and beliefs, make sure you capture them in all your communications, whether on your website, in your marketing emails, your letters, proposals or agreements. It's crucial to express such an incredibly important aspect of yourself.

I also strongly believe that the values of your practice should be determined by the partner (or partners) only. I've spoken to many business owners who made a point of involving their team in developing their company values to make sure they got buy-in. The problem is, what happens if the values of some people in your team aren't in line with your own? What you then get is a diluted set of values which, in reality, no one buys into and are too generic to inspire anyone.

(You'll often find they include words such as 'honesty,' 'quality' and 'integrity.' In other words, such basic values that, quite frankly, they should be a given).

With multiple partners, it's also important to make sure that your values align as, if not, there'll be too much friction to allow your practice to grow successfully. If you really don't have any common values or business aspirations, the best thing is usually to go your separate ways.

With AVN, I followed exactly my own advice. First, I ascertained the values and beliefs that were important to me, and then I analysed the team to determine who was a good fit with them and who wasn't.

Here are my (and therefore AVN's) values:

And my/our beliefs (which are equally important):
- Most business owners need the help, support and insights of an external expert
- Success isn't success if it's at the expense of family, friends and/or health
- Accountancy is a noble profession, one that can make a profound difference to its clients

- The well-known adage: Give someone a fish and you feed them for a day; teach someone to fish and you feed them for a lifetime
- By helping accountants become more successful first, and then teaching them the skills to help their clients, we're affecting many thousands of businesses and the families behind them
- A business can and ought to be a powerful channel to help its local and wider community through giving and playing a socially responsible role.

Have you defined your values and beliefs?

21

Effective Communication

So just how do you go about differentiating your practice from that of your rivals? Before you start, it's important to understand *how* our brains handle communication. *(Please understand that what follows is based on personal research and experience rather than me expressing any claims to be a psychologist!)*

You've probably heard the often used expression that, for someone to be ready to buy from you, they have to know, like and trust you. (How long it takes is something I'll be expanding on later). As 'know,' 'like' and 'trust' can be broken down and mapped to different parts of our brains, once we understand how these different parts need information we can reduce the amount of time it takes to win each of them over.

In his book *'The Triune Brain in Evolution'*, Paul D MacLean breaks the brain down into three areas that reflect the way it has developed. The earlier part, which he refers to as the reptilian brain, deals with instinct and reflexes in the same way a reptile would.

For example, I'm sure you've walked into a room when, for reasons you can't explain, alarm bells have rung in your head. Something just doesn't feel right. This is the reptilian part of our brain detecting something and the best way it can communicate this to (and warn) our higher-level brain is through this instinctive feeling that something is wrong.

Our reptile brain is the first to interpret information we receive through our eyes and ears. As long as it feels that the environment, object or person we're getting to know is safe and trustworthy, it's happy. If, on the other hand, it isn't sure, any information that filters through to the rest of our brain will be tainted by this instinctive feeling that something isn't right. The reptilian brain is our most powerful influencer.

Paul D MacLean refers to the next part of our brain as the paleomammalian (you may also know it as our 'monkey brain'). This part is pure feelings. It's motivated away from pain and toward gain. It wants an easy life, to have fun and enjoy itself. As such, our monkey brain is emotional and will also influence our decisions. It's incredibly powerful and is often the first to react in situations, for example when we fly off the handle or insist on buying that flashy sports car. In such cases, an emotional decision has outweighed a rational one. (Although later we may try to rationalise our purchase rather than sharing the real reason, which is because it made us feel good!)

The third part of the brain is the neomammalian, which many call the 'rational part' as it's more analytical and logical. However, despite this, it's often the weakest part of our brains when it comes to decision-making as it can be easily overpowered by the monkey and reptile parts. (This is often what lies behind our regrets: it's our rational brain regretting a decision made by our monkey one).

For your communication to be most effective, you need to be mindful of all three. On your website, in your brochures and emails – wherever you communicate with clients, in fact – you need to use language and content that will persuade people's reptilian brain to trust you, their monkey brain to like you, and their rational brain to know and understand you.

Establishing your credibility and trustworthiness quickly is important. You might not know (or even necessarily like) a doctor, but because of their qualification you trust that they're able to do their job. You can and should replicate this method of establishing trust by communicating your qualifications and supporting these with testimonials and case studies where possible.

However, to convince people's monkey brains, you need to communicate the potential emotional impact you can have. This is where your purpose, vision and mission come in. To be most effective, you should also share your values and beliefs, as well as case studies which show how you've affected the lives of business owners you've worked with (as opposed to simply sharing figures, such as how much tax you've saved them). Helping business owners isn't purely about increasing their profits and cashflow. It's about the impact you can have on their lives and what this means for their families. This that will strike an emotional chord, so make sure you include it in your communications.

Finally, the rational part of potential clients' brains will want to know the outcomes you can achieve for them. It wants facts and figures. It wants to know what the short and the long-term benefits will be and it wants to be able to calculate the ROI.

Introduce a combination of all three factors into your website and other communication channels and you'll communicate with your target audience considerably more effectively. (I'll address some of the other things you can do with 'know,' 'like' and 'trust' in the Profile section).

22

Positioning Through Exclusivity

Is it better to be seen as a generalist or a specialist? People will pay far more to see a specialist, they elicit a great deal more respect and are perceived as having far greater authority, and yet many accountants continue to take on clients of any size, from any industry and in any set of circumstances. If this sounds like you, I'm afraid all this does is to position you as a generalist – which is fine if all you're interested in is producing compliance work, but less so if you'd like to offer business-advisory and added-value services. Then positioning yourself as a specialist becomes important.

There are many ways to achieve this, but let's start by looking at the benefits of defining your ideal client profile as specifically as possible.

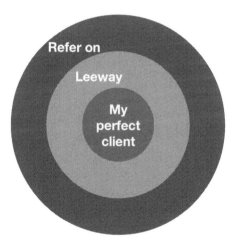

Firstly, although it's a misconception that to niche means you have to work in only one specific sector, it's true that many accountants choose to as it enables them to get a much deeper understanding of the sector and, importantly, the language and terminology used by the people within it. For example, Rob Walsh – from Clear Vision, based in Corsham, near Bath – has been specialising in the dentistry business for many years. As a result he's referred to other dentists by current clients and is recognised as an expert accountant and business growth within the sector. Here's what Rob has to say:

"Some time ago, in one of our practice's Board meetings, one of our non-executives challenged us to have a niche in dentistry. Having a niche means becoming an expert and therefore we created a wheel of opportunities to get to know the sector.

The first thing we did was to work with a client very intensively to understand the language, to put in all the necessary systems, to have monthly Board meetings and to do the management accounts. This was very grounding as it gave us the knowledge that we needed and helped us to understand how the sector works.

We then created the wheel, which was: Who can help us make sure we're known as experts in the industry? Some answers we came up with included:
- Banks
- IFAs
- Solicitors
- Valuers
- Companies offering private patient plans
- Finance companies
- Manufacturers of specialist dental chairs
- Software companies.

We then decided on our package:
- A vision day
- A team day
- A project plan
- All the financials required to run the business from bookkeeping and management accounts through to benchmarking and upside-down forecasting (where we look at the personal goals first and then work out the turnover at the bottom) and packaged these into three different areas. Once we'd built up trust in Board meetings, it was actually very easy to cross-sell into accountancy because clients could see the work we were doing on consultancy, so there was no problem at all in obtaining the above work.

We then set up a marketing strategy to make sure existing clients – using their contacts and talking at events – got our name known by introducers that we'd identified in the wheel. For example, speaking for half an hour at different events on how to run a dental business (rather than a dental practice) was paramount in getting our name known around the country. At the same time we produced a book called 'The Business of Dentistry – How You Run a Successful and Profitable Dental Business Not a Dental Practice' and offered it at the events. This gave us huge credibility and people who had seen us talk would then come and speak to us about their requirements and we would convert them as well. We also took on some of our introducers as clients on the consultancy side so that they understood what we did. They became very good 'gold' introducers because they could see what we did first-hand and relate it to their client base.

We also produced articles in the dental press talking about how our approach was different to make sure dentists knew that. By doing so, we've built up a good network of IFAs, banks, solicitors and valuers who refer work to us. Most of our work, however, now comes from existing clients, because we've done such good work for them that they keep referring. In addition, we always look at clients' lists to see how these match with our ideal profile and to decide whether we should market to them.

40% of our business is now in the dentistry and veterinary sectors. (We went into vets because as the problems in both industries are similar, we were able to transfer our knowledge successfully).

If it wasn't for our niche, we wouldn't be where we are now. I believe it's key to the success of your business, but first you need to make sure you get the language right and gain an in-depth understanding of how the industry works. The benefits of doing so are huge as you'll gain credibility, referrals and good margins, plus it's easier to cross-sell and to convert. We've now published our dental book many times (at 250 each time) and we've also produced a vet-related book which is selling on Amazon on a monthly basis.

In order to be seen as the experts in an industry, you need to get on stage and also write the book."

My thanks to Rob Walsh, Managing Director of Clear Vision Accountancy Ltd for contributing and sharing his insights and experience of identifying an ideal client profile and focusing on attracting that niche.

It's important to note, however, that rather than going all in, Rob limits his sector exclusivity to 40%, as this ensures his practice is still exposed to other industries and allows cross-fertilisation of ideas and concepts. Also, although having a niche within a specific industry works incredibly well for Rob and for many others, your niche could just as easily be to a specific set of circumstances. For example, the ideal client profile of Robert (who I referred to in Chapter 6) was based around a specific set of circumstances and aspirations, in his case business owners with a turnover of £1m-£2m who wanted to grow this to £10m and then sell. By specialising in this way, Robert was able to appreciate the very specific challenges that businesses face at this point in their growth journey and use his specialist knowledge to help them achieve their objectives.

Another example is offered by Georgi and Emma (first mentioned in Chapter 12), who balance running a highly successful accountancy practice with being great mums. As a result, they're perfectly placed to understand the specific challenges that many female business owners face, not only if/when they become mothers, but also in general. (Disappointingly, the chauvinism and prejudice you'd hope would be a thing of the past these days is still hanging on). In fact, their mission statement was born from a supplier's email which they imagine was intended to be internal-only, but he clicked 'reply all' by mistake. Basically, its message was that it wasn't worth dealing with the two women from this particular accountancy practice because they were 'on a mission to help women in business.' They liked the phrase so much they adopted it as their mission statement!

By being specific about the particular industry and/or circumstances of a business you work with, you'll also be able to be specific as to exactly how you can help them, using your credentials as an expert in that area. You'll be better able to relate to these particular business owners, and to explain that similar businesses you've helped tend to experience X, Y and Z problems at this particular point in their growth journey, and that your strengths and experience can help them to overcome these.

If you remember, right at the start of this book I described how running your practice probably feels right now. I described the specific challenges you're probably facing and the impact this is having on your life. However, my description won't have resonated with everyone. For some, it might have resonated completely, for others, mostly, and for a few, not at all. But this book wasn't written for them. They don't need it. My experience lies in helping those it did resonate with. Imagine if I'd made that description too vague, in a misguided attempt to relate to everyone. I'd have ended up not relating to anyone at all. And that's the point of defining your ideal client profile: you understand them, you can relate to them, and you can refine your approach specifically to make sure you help them get the best results. Even if they only represent a small percentage of the total market, this small percentage will happily pay to work with someone who really gets them.

23

Producing Collateral That Differentiates And Helps You To Sell

I've visited a huge number of businesses and accountancy practices and one of the things I've discovered is that many of them don't have any form of professional collateral to help them promote their services.

True, some have created mini-brochures but – like the websites I referred to earlier – these generally simply describe the basic services they deliver and then go in to detail about what these mean. (Often, it has to be said, in language that only another accountant would understand and that fails to connect with potential clients at all).

Although there are many different types of collateral you can create to better position yourself and to promote your services, in this book I'm going to talk about the impact of just one: creating and using a sales brochure. (And please note, I use the term 'sales brochure' rather than simply 'brochure' because a well-structured sales brochure will complement your sales process and make teaching your team members to sell on your behalf far easier and more effective).

A great sales brochure will not only increase your percentage of conversions from enquiries, but also allow you to charge a considerably higher fee because it increases prospects' perception of your quality and professionalism. Since most accountants don't have one, it sets you apart from – and above – the competition.

Before we start, it's important to emphasise that no matter how good your brochure, never send it as a pre-meeting read or use it as a replacement for a sales conversation. Think of it as the slide deck of a keynote speaker. You wouldn't expect to receive one as a substitute for someone actually speaking, nor would they want to send you their slides in advance. Rather they use their slides to complement their presentation. (If they use them in any other way, then they're probably guilty of 'death by PowerPoint').

A sales brochure should be structured to reflect how you would structure the perfect sales conversation. For example, it should contain the typical problems, trials and tribulations your (ideal) clients face. Once you've asked questions of a prospective client and let them air their challenges, then probed as much as you can to make sure you really understand everything they've said, you'll be able to refer to your brochure which lists those same (or very similar) challenges. That way, when you say, "We specialise in dealing with these very challenges," they won't think you're simply saying it. They'll be able to see for themselves that what they've just told you is also written there in front of them.

To ensure your brochure is structured like a good sales conversation, it should:
- Relate to a prospect by stating the typical problems clients faced before they chose to work with you
- Explain how the solution you provide helped these clients overcome their problems and how, in turn, this enabled them to take their business forward
- Contain your 'why' so prospects understand why you do what you do, and why helping them is important to you
- Offer three simple options for them to choose from (rather than trying to promote lots of different products and services), and explain what they'll get in each (I'll explain this further in the next section, Value).
- Include the description of your ideal client (to reinforce your exclusivity and, as it should match them, so they can recognise themselves)
- Contain at least one case study of how you've helped a client through the same process.

Once you've written your content and are sure you've covered the points above, go over it again to reduce the amount of text to the absolute minimum. Remember, your sales brochure serves to complement – rather than replace – the sales conversations of you or your team. Too long and you'll find that you're simply reading out the words verbatim, which is never good, and the brochure will be too wordy. Use bullet points and keep it succinct.

24

A Proactive Accountant, You Say? But Are You Really?

I regularly present to a room full of partners and directors of practices, most of whom refer to themselves on their websites as 'proactive accountants.' However, when I ask what exactly they mean by 'proactive'? I'm generally met by a stunned silence. Eventually a few suggestions are made but, despite so many advertising that that's what they are, no one has a clear answer.

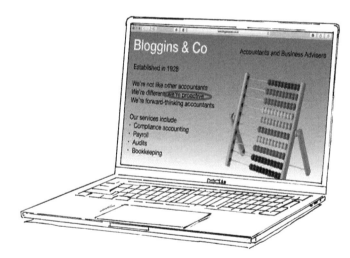

Here's my take on what being proactive really means:
- Making recommendations without being requested to do so. Genuinely proactive accountants pick up the phone to their clients and present opportunities monthly and quarterly.
- Your recommendations are relevant to the client – otherwise, what's the point?
- Your recommendations are valuable, so clients appreciate them and are grateful
- Your recommendations are free – in the first instance.

A Proactive Accountant, You Say? But Are You Really?

What do I mean by that last bullet point? What I mean is, although you should take the time to present a recommendation, there's no need to carry out rigorous investigations immediately. Simply suggest that it might be prudent and timely for your client to have these investigations or work carried out. Tell them what they should do, not what they should buy from you.

For example, let's say a client of yours is about ready to incorporate. Rather than saying, "We recommend you incorporate," or "We recommend that you pay us to work out how much you could save by incorporating," try: "I've taken a preliminary look and I think now might be a good time to incorporate your business. Our initial estimate is that it could save you £2,000 a year, or a total of £50,000 between now and when you retire, so I recommend you take a good look at all the pros and cons."

By doing this you've been proactive, you've spotted and presented an opportunity, and now you're recommending that they incorporate. Your next question can simply be: "Would you like some help with that?" If they say yes, you can present your fee for investigating the pros and cons for them. (To help AVN members be proactive on an ongoing basis, we provide access to many resources and tools that help them spot opportunities quickly, easily and even at a junior level, simply by punching in a few details).

Of course, even if you already deliver to this standard, simply stating that you're proactive isn't enough. You need to back it up with proof from clients, otherwise – having seen the same message on so many other websites – business owners will simply dismiss it as marketing blurb.

25

Be The Professional That You Are

It's natural to want to please clients: to want to deal with their emails as quickly as possible (never mind that it's the evening, the weekend or that you're on holiday); to give them your mobile number; to give away a lot of free advice – advice which doesn't lead to additional income. And yet none of this leads to their respect or even appreciation.

In fact, it seems the more you go out of your way to accommodate them, the less they respect and appreciate you. Instead, they begin to take you for granted, and to see you as less professional and authoritative. That's why setting terms and agreeing exactly what will and won't be covered in the services you provide – in a polite way of course, as part of the sales conversation – is so important. It helps to establish your authority.

To illustrate this, once, many years ago, before I signed up to a course, I was invited to a meeting at which I was asked a series of questions to ascertain my specific needs. Next, these were mapped to the course to check that it would enable me to achieve exactly what I needed it to and, once this had been confirmed, I was told that there were a number of terms I needed to agree to before I could join.

This proved to me that the company wasn't desperate for work, that it only wanted serious people to join its course, and that it wasn't going to be taken for granted. My respect for the company increased and, as a result, I wanted to prove my worth in order to be allowed to work with them.

So be specific about your terms: Are you on 24-hour call or only available 9-5? Are calls outside a specific time charged at a premium rate? Do you set deadlines for information being submitted, or impose penalty fees if these are missed? (These are just a couple of examples that some AVN members use to great effect).

26

Measuring Your Success

A common set of metrics that accountancy practices use include turnover, gross recurring-fee income, profits, and average fee-per-client. But do such metrics resonate with you? Do they move and inspire you? Some of them don't necessarily reflect success and some are simply the consequence of doing the right things.

But what's the right thing for you?

Drive to Strive

While having the right measures in place can unleash a drive to strive that you never thought you had – or had forgotten you had – measuring stuff that's not important to you can leave you feeling unmotivated to change those numbers, especially if they're not too bad.

So what really matters to you in your accountancy practice?

Recently, while I was speaking to a partner from a two-partner firm, it quickly became apparent that his passion was to make a profound difference – both to the lives of his team in their future careers, and to his clients in terms of helping them improve their businesses so that they could spend more time with their families.

For him, success could be measured in the number of prospective clients who approached him on the strength of the reputation of his practice and the number of people who wanted to be part of his team.

Remember: Profits are a consequence of doing the right things for the right people.

So what does success mean for you? And how might you measure it?

Depending on your answer, you could:
- Collect case studies that demonstrate you're making the difference you want to (That's certainly one of mine).
- Record how much tax you've saved clients
- Keep track of how much time you've helped owners save from working in their business, enabling them to spend more time with their families and doing the things they love
- Share the impacts your practice is making in the local or wider community, such as its contributions toward the UN Sustainable Development Goals. (This is another one of AVN's).

What is it in your accountancy practice that you have an emotional connection to?

Same Shit, Different Day

A common mistake is not to measure anything. This often leads to a syndrome that I call 'Same shit, different day.'

To avoid this, think about what really moves you, either positively or negatively. If it's the former, what can you do to replicate that more frequently or on a grander scale? If it's the latter, what can you do to reverse it? Whatever your answer, make that your measure of success.

NB. I'm not suggesting that you don't use any of the metrics that I mentioned at the start of this chapter (after all, it's important to see whether what you're doing is generating the results you need), but remember that these are often consequences and lack the emotional connection that I've been describing.

Listen to your heart. What are the things that tug at your heartstrings? If you're not sure yet, be mindful when it does happen and ask yourself: "When this happens, does it bring me closer to my purpose?" If it does, then start to measure it. Doing so will focus you on making it happen more frequently and increase your sense of achievement.

27

Your Elevator Pitch

Your elevator pitch is your 30-second chance to make a great first impression when you answer the question, "What do you do?" at networking and social events. Yet, despite the impact of getting it right being immense, it's often something that business owners fail to work on. In addition, as so many people have a predetermined opinion of what accountants are like, the answer, "I'm an accountant" can lead to an awkward silence. To avoid this, you need to add more.

So far, we've looked at the importance of knowing your purpose, your values, your aspirations and goals, who your ideal client is, what their problems typically are, and how you measure your success. Now you're clear on these, you need to bring them together in such a punchy, meaningful description of what you do that it leads to the response: "Tell me more."

Of course, it would be impossible to get through all of these elements in 30 seconds. However, done properly, each should lead the person you're speaking to, to ask a question that leads on to the next. For example:
"What do you do?"
> *"I'm an accountant and I use my expertise with numbers to change lives and to make the world a better place."*
"Tell me more!"
> *"I'm passionate about... And, for me, a measure of my success is..."*

28

Positioning Yourself As An Expert

This section will help you build your reputation so that it becomes your brand, and people associate it with everything they come across that's connected to your practice – whether it's your website, your business card, an email, a member of your team or, of course, you. Everything needs to be congruent. It's pointless stating your values if one of your team then plays them down to either a client or another team member.

As I've described, you need to show that you have a deeper purpose (one that people will emotionally buy in to); that you have strong values; and that you'll only work with people whose values align with your own. In addition, you need to show that you only work with a very specific type of client, and that you know and understand the specific business of these clients *as well as* the problems they might face and how to overcome these. If you portray this on your website, in your sales brochure and conversations, and in your elevator pitch, then you'll change how clients perceive you from being 'just' an accountant (in the traditional, undervalued sense of the word) to being an expert in their business affairs.

Obviously, though, you first need to gain this expertise. You need to learn about the common mistakes clients make, the challenges they face, and how you can help them overcome these. (Overcoming these challenges is where Business-Growth Advisory comes in, which I'll address in detail in later chapters). Before you can help, you need to understand exactly what you're trying to fix, so don't be afraid to ask your clients what their dreams and aspirations are for their business, or to ask what's holding them back from achieving these. Often, the mere act of doing so will reignite their passion for their business. Ask them why they think these problems exist – and what they believe they should do about them.

As you do this with more clients, you'll start to discover the commonalities. Remember though, if you have a mixed bag of clients (including some you don't actually want to work with) the challenges and mistakes you collect will also be such a mixed bag that they'll fail to resonate with your ideal clients.

Considering how hard it is to qualify as an accountant, I'm always saddened that the profession doesn't have the gravitas that it should for many business owners. It's why positioning is now more important than ever – unless business owners see you as an expert in business, they won't be receptive to paying you for business-advisory work which, increasingly, is the only real future for accountants.

To summarise some of the key principles we've been discussing, I'd like to end this section with the winning entry for the AVN Practice Differentiation Award, in which Fiona Jones of Grant-Jones Accountancy describes some of the things they do which set them apart.

Winning Entry for the AVN Practice Differentiation Award: Grant-Jones Accountancy

"Our philosophy in Grant-Jones is: Show me the past and we will show you the future.

We understand the value of historical data as a means to plan for future growth and to build firm foundations. It focuses the firm, giving us a sense of purpose which we can use in all our interactions with clients and prospects.

We generate this future focus by using tools such as AVN's Performance, Measurement and Improvement methodology known as 'The Numbers.' We take clients through their past performance, their position in the market and their plans for the future. By walking them through this as a process, we help them to really consider where they want to go as a business and how they might achieve this.

Looking at their performance history shows them where they can improve and, via AVN's BenchMark tool, we can then provide them with insights into where they can gain a competitive advantage.

However, our focus on the future is not limited to the future of individual clients. We also contribute to the future of the world as, at the end of 2017, Grant-Jones became a B1G1 Business for Good. The idea is simple. B1G1 co-ordinate small donations from businesses all around the world and pass them on to 500 carefully screened projects that contribute to the United Nations 17 Sustainable Development Goals.

These small donations – which may provide pens and books for a child to support their education, or seeds and tools to a farmer to help them feed their family – are called 'impacts'. To date, they have made over 150million of them. We link our business services to these impacts – for every £1 we save for a client, we give an impact – and, as a result, it differentiates what we do from the rest. So far, we have made over 14,000 impacts – which means cleaner water for families, improved literacy for children and more food for everyone.

Earlier this year, we decided to go a step further by running a 'Get and Give a Million' campaign. This consisted of a marketing and a PR campaign, a free webinar, and an invitation for a free 90-minute meeting with Grant-Jones for attendees to identify potential savings.

Although the campaign did not directly generate much new business, it did provide good PR and raised our profile in the local area. The supporting social media campaign also raised awareness and has been generating more clients for us.

We now publish regular articles on LinkedIn and, with over 1000 connections, are reaching a wide audience.

Our activities have also created new opportunities. In March last year we were invited to contribute to the 2018 'Parliamentary Review' magazine, which involved an interview with and a feature on Grant-Jones and our vision for accountancy. This high-profile publication is read by politicians and senior policy-makers across government and our 1000-word article made the case for accounting firms to do more for their clients and the wider world. The editor-in-chief, former FT editor, the Rt Hon David Curry, told us he had never received such an inspiring submission.

More recently, we were interviewed for a video series produced by 'Collectively Camberley' as part of their independent business review of 2018 which featured on their Facebook page and website.

Our membership of AVN is pivotal to how we differentiate ourselves in the market. Through the tools and support provided, we are able to do more and go further in creating a better future for our clients and for the world."

29

The Perception Of Value For Money

With the rapid decline in the perceived value of compliance work, and the increase in automation of this core service, it's more important than ever to provide added value. In fact, these changes only appear threatening to accountants who refuse to adapt. Personally, I see it as a wonderful opportunity. Using technology to produce the core numbers leaves you time to better utilise your skills, by having meaningful conversations with clients about how making small changes to those numbers can make a huge difference to their turnover, profits and cashflow. As a result, they'll be able to invest in, and grow, their business.

When AVN help accountants improve the value they provide, we focus on three key areas:

1. **Value mapping** Enhancing the customer experience at every interaction, and adding additional interactions to increase the perceived level of professionalism even further.

2. **Adding value to core services** Taking time to analyse the accounts data, producing trends, analysing strengths and weaknesses, spotting opportunities and connecting that data to the aspirations of the business owner (both for their business and for their personal lives), having regular meetings and asking thought-provoking questions.

3. **Delivering added-value services that add value to the client's business** Promoting tools such as our 'Performance Measurement and Improvement Programme,' or 'BoardView' an AVN packaged service in which, in addition to playing a virtual FD role, the accountant also plays a strategic role within Board meetings.

First though, to return to basics, a question I'm often asked is: *"What is value?"* The simple answer is that it's subjective. If, in the eyes of a potential buyer, an item's perceived value outweighs its asking price, then you have a sale.

Adding value means you raise a client's perception of the value of an item or a service, ideally with minimal effort and cost. To give just one example of the many ways you can do this, let's take a look at car valeters, who are now so popular that you often have to queue, especially when, as well as a quick valet, some people also want the interior of their cars cleaned. This takes time and you usually need to sit outside. In fact, I've often used this service myself and on a sunny day have gone for a walk or sat somewhere nearby to read.

Recently, however, I've started to use a valeting company that's a little further away and a little more expensive. Why? Because they've kitted out the attached building that would once have housed a small convenience shop and sales counter (like many other such companies, they've moved into a former filling station). All they've done is add a couple of vending machines – one for drinks and the other for snacks – a few tables, some comfortable chairs, and installed Wi-Fi. But guess what? They now get far more business.

True, they may have had to make a small initial outlay, but the vending machines probably add to their profits and the cost of Wi-Fi and heating will be minimal. And, as a result, they can charge considerably more for their services and there's always a queue – which demonstrates that people value what they've added.

Little things really can add to the value experience.

Remember how, in the section on positioning, I described the importance of first impressions? Clients' perceptions of your value need to start high and – at the very least – be maintained, if not improved upon, with every single experience.

Another example of adding value is packaging. If you've ever purchased an iPhone, then you'll know that even opening the box is an experience in itself. The chances are that once you've checked your phone, the box will go straight in the bin. But people talk about the packaging and what a pleasurable experience it is to open it. It forms part of their kinaesthetic and visual experience.

Similarly, packaging your core services in a kinaesthetically tangible, visually aesthetic way (in other words, one you can touch and is pleasant to look at) adds credence to your solution. It's why our 'Performance, Measurement and Improvement' package, which – despite the general move to the Cloud – is presented in the form of a good old-fashioned binder (albeit one branded with each practice's colour scheme and logo), has a bigger take-up rate amongst the firms that keep it in this format than amongst those that make it Cloud-based. Our conclusion? Most of us still like to hold something – we feel we own it and therefore are more likely to buy into it.

Let's imagine that it's you who needs an accountant. In fact, right now you're looking to work with a different accountant because you don't feel you're getting value from your existing one. They're reluctant to embrace some of the new technologies you've heard so much about and you feel they're a little set in their ways. You know of a different accountancy practice in your area though, so one day you type their name into your search engine.

However, you find their website is pretty basic. It explains they do accountancy, bookkeeping, payroll and audits, so you decide to give them a call to find out a little more. The phone rings for quite a while before it's answered, and then it's by someone who almost sounds impatient that you've interrupted them. You explain that you'd like to know more about the practice and wonder if you could speak to someone. The person explains that no one is available right now but they'll get someone to call you back.

A day or so later, you get a call from one of the partners. They arrange a meeting and email you the address of their practice, but nothing more. When the time comes, you arrive on time but struggle to find somewhere to park. (Although the practice has its own car park, it's full.) As a result, you have to find a spot on the street and then run back to the office. By this time it's started to rain. As you're about to enter the building, you notice that the two spaces nearest to the door have a sign saying they're reserved for the partners. *"Charming!"* you think, as you shake the rain from your coat.

Inside, there's a reception hatch covered with a glass screen, behind which a receptionist – who doesn't even look up – is typing. You wait, a little uncomfortably, until they have finished their sentence, at which point they slide the hatch open and ask how they can help. You introduce yourself and explain that you're here for a meeting, but can't remember the name of the partner you've come to see.

The receptionist gives a small sigh and proceeds to call the partners one by one to find out which of them has a meeting booked. Once this has been established, they ask if you'd like tea or coffee (you'd prefer green tea, but go with the traditional variety in the lack of anything better) and then take you through to the meeting room. One side of this is stacked with boxes of books and client records. Although there are framed certificates of the partners' qualifications on the walls, the wallpaper is peeling and the carpet is a little the worse for wear with a fair few coffee stains. There's even a faint smell of damp.

Things pick up a little when the partner arrives, as at least they look smart and introduce themselves, and shortly afterwards your tea arrives. After a brief discussion, they give you a rough idea of the likely costs of bringing your accounts and bookkeeping to them. A few days later, you receive a formal-looking document by post that contains the proposal they've put together. However, you've now had a few days to think about it and have decided that your experience with them so far hasn't been great.

This time, instead of looking for a specific accountant, you use Google to search for accountants in your area. One of the names that comes up stands out because it has lots of reviews and a five-star rating. You click on the link and go to their website. This time, you're immediately impressed. Unlike all the other accountancy websites you've seen, this one doesn't mention accounts or bookkeeping. Instead, it tells a story and describes the difference they make to the clients they work with.

As you read, their words strike a chord because they exactly describe the challenges you're facing. You discover that not only can they meet all your legal requirements by producing your accounts work, but they share example after example of how they've helped businesses grow by using their skills with numbers to analyse this data. Their specific methodologies will help you determine the numbers in your accounts that – if changed in small ways – can have a significant impact on your business.

As well as numerous testimonials and case studies from satisfied customers, you notice they've also earned awards in business growth and customer service. By now, you're seriously interested, but are probably thinking that they're outside your price range. As you read further, though, you find that not only do they give a fixed price for their services, but that they're so confident in their abilities they offer a full money-back guarantee.

Although the price is a little higher than you'd originally planned, you think for a while. Are they really too expensive? Or might they be worth it? You remember, too, that case study after case study described how a client's profits had soared as a result of working with them.

You pick up the phone and give them a call. In just two rings it's answered by a pleasant-sounding voice. You repeat your previous query and, although none of the partners are available here either, this time the person who answered the phone gives you a quick run-through of how they operate: A client manager will meet you to gain a good understanding of your business set-up, then ask some additional questions to determine the best solution and to make sure you get a fair and accurate fixed price.

There and then, they offer to arrange a meeting at a date and a time that works for you and to allocate you a client manager. They even ask whether you'd prefer the client manager to come to you or for you to go to them. Impressed, you decide to go to them and a meeting is arranged for the next morning.

No sooner have you hung up then you receive an emailed calendar-invite with their address, telephone number and a link to a YouTube video to help you find their office. Intrigued, you click the link and the video includes a brief greeting from the practice receptionist who explains that as the office can be a little tricky to find, what follows is a time-lapse dashcam recording of someone exiting the nearby ring road and travelling to it.

The next morning you arrive for your meeting after a straightforward journey as per their directions and, in the car park, you see your name on a sign, reserving a space for you right beside the entrance. (Already you feel special!) As you enter the building, the receptionist smiles and greets you by name, takes you to the conference room and offers you a menu. This contains a list of drinks that, as well as tea and coffee, includes fruit and green teas, cold drinks, beer and even Champagne!

By now, you're really starting to wonder if the practice is out of your league. However, you settle for a green tea and the receptionist leaves you. (You've arrived slightly early.) On the table in front of you, next to your tea, is a folder, the front of which has a child's drawing and the words: *"These are the lovely words people say about my daddy."* Inside, all recently dated, are case studies and testimonials.

As you continue to look around, you notice that a TV is playing a slideshow. Each screen begins with your name, then goes on to tell you about the benefits you could expect from working with this practice. There are also quotes from clients, some sharing the improvements in profit and cashflow they've experienced, or the tax they've saved; others talking about how much more time they can now spend with their families.

There are also a number of posters on the walls that ask questions such as: *"If anything were possible, what would you do with an extra £1,000,000?"* or *"What's currently stopping you from achieving your business goals?"* Just as you're considering how you might answer these, the client manager enters, introduces themselves, and asks you exactly the same question. Perhaps slightly nervous by now, you reply saying that you don't really have any goals – you just have a small business and are looking for an accountant to take care of your accounts and bookkeeping.

You take a seat and the client manager – let's call her Jenny – sits next to you (rather than on the other side of the desk, like at the first practice you visited). She explains that it would really help if she understood your business so that she can provide an accurate fixed price there and then.

You begin to explain and Jenny listens intently and appears genuinely interested. After you've given a basic overview, she drills down even further with questions that go far deeper than simply ascertaining your number of transactions and turnover. Next, she moves on to asking about your role in the business, how it meets your personal needs and how many hours you work. As she seems genuinely interested, you start to open up: you're working a lot of hours and your relationship at home is suffering. In fact, even when you are at home, your mind is on the business and whenever your kids want to play you find yourself saying you're too busy because you're dealing with some work-related emails.

The client manager then asks why you set up your business and what your dream was. You're taken aback. It's not something you've thought about for a long time. But, slowly, you start to remember: You felt you could deliver a better solution than others you'd experienced. However, you realise you've fallen into the same trap as everyone else. You haven't created the business you thought you would.

Next, you're asked: *"If anything were possible, what would it look like?"* As you paint a picture of the vision you once had, you feel a sense of excitement that you haven't felt in a long time. Jenny asks how this ideal business would impact on your life. You think for a moment, then explain that you'd be able to deliver a better service, for a higher income, and without having to work quite so many hours. You'd no longer have to worry about where your next customer was coming from or how you were going to pay the bills. You'd be able to spend more time with your children – they're growing up so fast already that soon they'll be in their teens and probably won't want as much to do with you anyway. You get emotional at this because you know you'll never get the opportunity again, but, right now, your priority has to be putting food on the table for them.

Whilst you've been describing this, Jenny has been listening and asking questions. She then feeds back to you the vision you've just shared, both for your business and for the lifestyle this would give you. "Yes! That's exactly it!" you say, as you hear your aspirations described with an air of confidence that they're achievable.

She asks what you think has been holding you back. You explain that you find it difficult to price your services because there's so much competition. You struggle to get customers and, when you do, it takes longer to deliver the services than you priced for and you end up making very little profit or even a loss.

The client manager switches on her iPad and opens a piece of software called 'Time's Up!' She enters some of the information you've given her, takes out a brochure and places it on the table so you can both see it. She thanks you for being so open and honest and assures you that you've come to the right place because their practice can help you achieve your goals. On the first page of the brochure is a list of the problems they specialise in helping business owners overcome, and many of the phrases you've just used appear.

She turns over and the next page describes how their accountancy practice helps make the numbers that matter most to you, better. She explains how their business solutions not only deliver basic compliance services, but so much more as well. Then she introduces their nine-step solution: 'Performance Measurement and Improvement':

1. Decide what you want to achieve by gaining clarity on your goals both for your business and personal life.
2. Develop a plan by turning your goals into a business plan, forecasts and budgets.
3. Measure how well you perform each month through a combination of traditional management accounting information and KPIs (that way, you'll have your finger on the pulse of everything that matters) and then use this information to fine-tune your action plans.

4. Measure your annual performance by producing full financial accounts at the end of the year (as required by law).
5. Evaluate your performance by comparing this to previous years, so that the underlying trends are clear.
6. Evaluate your performance by comparing it to the rest of your industry, using benchmarking to identify your strengths and weaknesses.
7. Estimate how much your business is worth so that you can assess how well you are creating value.
8. Calculate how much more profitable and valuable your business could be through using everything you've learned about your own performance and that of others.
9. Develop a performance improvement plan (i.e. an action plan that sets out precisely what you're going to do to improve your performance).

She explains that while Step 4 is pretty much what all accountants offer, her practice believes in helping businesses to improve. *"Wow!"* you think. This is so much more powerful than anything you've experienced from accountants in the past.

She turns another page of the brochure and explains that they offer three levels of service: Five-star, four-star and three-star. The five-star package includes everything she's just covered in the nine-step solution, plus regular meetings and accountability to ensure that you maintain focus on carrying out the ideas and actions that arise from the meetings. (After all, she adds, your business will only improve if you implement these!)

She asks if that might be something you'd be interested in. You pause, then say that – given your current financial situation – you'd better see what the fee comes out at first. She smiles, grabs her iPad and selects the five-star option. The monthly investment figure that comes up is a lot of money, true, but – because the benefits it will bring have been clearly explained – you appreciate why.

You ask if she can talk you through the next level. She refers back to the brochure and shows you a chart detailing exactly what each level of service offers. She explains what you won't get in the next version down. You begin to feel that this will simply prolong how long it takes to get the results you'd like. You hint you'd love to go for the five-star option, but how can she be sure you'll get the results you need?

Picking up her iPad again, she minimises the pricing app and loads another piece of software called 'SSTW' (Simple Stuff That Works). She enters some additional information about your business and explains that SSTW will help you break down seven key sales drivers:

1. Pricing for maximum profit
2. Getting more leads
3. Converting more leads into customers
4. Getting customers to buy more from you
5. Getting customers to buy more frequently from you
6. Stopping customers from leaving you
7. Systemising for consistency.

Next, she explains how making some fairly small changes in your business to each of these will lead to a significant improvement in your profits and income. As she talks through each one, she shares a very simple strategy and you have a brief conversation about how you could easily apply it to your business. She also increases each of the drivers by just 1% or 2% from its current rate. By the time she's finished you realise that your business could easily generate several times more in profits than the fee she presented you with. Finally, she reminds you that they offer a guarantee and explains how this works.

You decide to go for it – after all, the benefits far outweigh the cost – and she returns to 'Time's Up!' to select the five-star option. She asks you to confirm your choice and then clicks an onscreen button to pull up the agreement. This specifies the service you've requested and details everything it includes in depth. For example, although unlimited phone calls are included, the agreement notes that if any of these lead to additional work, a fee will be agreed prior to it taking place so that you aren't presented with any surprise bills at the end of the year. In addition, there's a long list of all the other benefits you'll receive and a guarantee of your money back if you don't receive the value you expect.

Jenny talks you through every part of the document to confirm you agree – you absolutely do! – and asks for your bank details so she can set up a direct debit. (That way you can spread the payments rather than having to pay in one go.) You sign on the dotted line and feel really positive about the future. Finally, you think, you've found someone who understands you.

To finish up, she books you the dates for a year's worth of 'BoardView' meetings (included in the package you've chosen), and explains that these are like having a Finance Director attending your Board meetings. However, rather than purely reporting on the numbers, they'll explore strategic thinking around improving your business (in line with the seven sales drivers, eight profit drivers and cashflow drivers) and maintain a 'OnePage' plan for your business to track the KPIs that will keep you on target to achieve your business and personal goals.

As you stand up to leave, she asks if you enjoy a competitive challenge. Intrigued, you say, "Yes." She takes you to a room just off reception where you find a Scalextric and, on the wall, a leaderboard recording the best lap times. You smile at the childhood memories this brings flooding back and she asks if you'd like to try to get on the leaderboard. You have an amazing time – albeit for just a few minutes – and leave buzzing.

Outside, you find that your car has been valeted. The client manager, who's accompanied you, explains that they have an arrangement with a nearby company to give visitors' cars a valet as a gesture of goodwill. Finally, as she says goodbye, she hands you a welcome pack and explains that it gives a lot more information about the practice and the improvement journey you've just embarked on with them.

By the time you arrive back at your own office, you've received an email containing a welcome video from the practice and a digital copy of the proposal that you still have in your hand. Finally, as you open the welcome pack, a bar of chocolate falls out with a short note saying: *"Have a break and enjoy this snack whilst you read your welcome pack."*

You smile, take a bite, and settle down to read.

The scenario I've just described is not hypothetical. It's the experience of every prospect who visits an AVN member's office. Of course there are variations – I'm not suggesting each member should be a clone, and these aren't franchised practices – but each one has thoroughly mapped out their customer journey from start to finish to ensure the experience remains high from the very first interaction. (Additional reports, for example, produced for every meeting and each containing that extra 'wow' factor, help to maintain this).

Naturally, I don't expect you to adopt this exact approach, or to make overnight changes, but I do expect you to be aware of existing and prospective clients' experiences at every interaction and to explore ways in which you can make these better. To help, I'll break this scenario down in the following chapters so that you can replicate some of its key components.

30

Value Mapping

Above, we looked at the value-mapping process, at adding value to your core services and at situations in which added-value services are included as a normal part of your business. To recap, one hour before a client arrives the receptionist follows a standard system: a sign with the visitor's name is placed in the car park to reserve a space; the slideshow in the meeting room is modified to display their name on every slide; and the CRM system is updated with their drink preference and vehicle details. This means that should a client arrive unexpectedly, the receptionist should still be able to greet them by name and, when they hand them the drinks menu to say, for example: "Your usual preference is green tea, isn't it? Would you like that again or would you prefer to choose something else today?" We all feel special when someone remembers our name and our preferences, so these are simple (but highly valuable) ways of adding value to the customer journey.

To help get you started, grab a pack of Post-it notes right now and write one for each stage you can think of for the customer journey at your practice. Start from the point at which a prospective client has never heard of you and use a separate sheet for each of the current ways they might get to do so – whether that's searching for your website on Google, looking you up on LinkedIn or checking out your profile on Facebook.

In fact, this can be a great team exercise, so get some of your team involved. Ask them to also think about the stages. Not how to enhance them, or even how good or bad each one is, but simply to list them. Once you think you've covered all of them, collect the Post-it notes and stick them on the wall, shifting them around (this is why Post-it notes are so useful!) until they form a logical flow diagram.

Next, grab a differently coloured set of Post-it notes and get creative. How could you enhance the customer experience (and therefore their perception of value) at each stage? Write down as many suggestions as you can come up with for each one. And remember, it doesn't matter how nice your reception is if the doorbell doesn't work. Or how great a meeting you have with a prospect, if they then visit the toilet and it's not a pleasant experience.

As there's so much to consider, it can help if you focus on the five senses at every stage. Does your reception area stimulate all five senses of a visitor in a positive way, for example? Do you remember, in the first scenario, how one of the rooms smelt of damp? Our sense of smell has an incredible power to affect our experience, so the smell of fresh flowers would have had a much better impact. Is your waiting area comfortable or are the seats beginning to wear? What do prospects hear when they walk in? I've found a lot of accountants play the news channel in reception areas, but do you really want prospects being demoralised by bad news just before their meeting? Wouldn't videos of client case studies, or uplifting music, be better?

Next, move on to the meeting itself (that's probably what they've come for, after all). What happens before and after this? Do you send out a draft agenda before meetings and ask if there are any points that clients would like to add to ensure you both get what you need from it? Similarly, do you send out actions and notes afterwards?

Remember: The exercise of value mapping will help you to enhance the overall perception of value that your practice offers.

31

Adding Value To The Core Services

Adding value to your core services means offering additional benefits which may not take a lot of effort to provide, but do add considerable value. Examples I described earlier included offering a guarantee, fixed prices or unlimited phone support (whilst making clear that any additional work this leads to will be quoted for). To expand on that last point a little, although it may appear that you'll be opening the floodgates to endless calls, the reality is that customers are usually too busy to phone *unless* they actually need something else doing. And, if that's the case, if what they need doing is something you provide a solution for, it gives you the perfect opportunity to explain the benefits of your doing so and how much it will cost. Remember, many people will think twice before making a call they'll be charged for, so by charging, how much of this additional work might you be missing out on?

For many years, AVN members have used recording software such as 'TechSmith Camtasia' to video conversations around management or year-end accounts with the data on screen. Not only is it incredibly valuable to clients (who can use it to check something after a meeting), it also saves our members time. One accountant told me they'd put the video on YouTube (secured with a password, of course) and the client had replayed it five times. Imagine how many phone calls that saved!

Just as the previous exercise explored how you can add to the experience of each and every customer interaction, you now need to do the same for every service you offer. Start by examining the value they already bring, as most people fail to communicate this let alone explore ways to add more.

Communicating value can include everything from detailing the qualifications and experience of the people who'll deliver the service, to the exact process they'll go through to ensure clients get the outcome they need. In fact, you need to detail everything, even – or perhaps especially – those things that you and every other accountant take for granted, but which aren't necessarily appreciated by a business owner who thinks you simply click a button in a piece of software.

It can help to ask your best clients what they value most about you – and why. You can then use what they say, in their own words, to also communicate value. In this way, rather than sounding like you're blowing your own trumpet, you can say: *"Our clients tell us that what they really value about us is..."* and reel off the best points. (At first, you may feel a little uncomfortable asking clients what they value most about you and the services you deliver, but doing so will also reinforce this in their minds).

32

Providing Added-Value Services

Services that add value to a customer's business include the nine-step 'Performance Measurement and Improvement' system I mentioned previously. This is a packaged solution, each step of which is a strategic session oriented around important numbers in a customer's business. Focusing on these leads to quality conversations around improving them in such a way that the profits and success of the business also improve, allowing the owner to invest in additional help or automation which, in turn, enables them to spend less time working and yet allows the business to continue to flourish.

However good a packaged service is though, it can't sell itself. The key to clients signing up to it (and to your delivering it well) depends on your ability to communicate effectively, to build a relationship and rapport with each client, to understand them and their needs and to possess the acumen to see the impact and potential that certain numbers can have on their business.

How do you currently add value to clients' businesses? Are you guilty of giving great advice away for free? One of the problems with free advice is that's it's less likely to be valued and therefore acted upon. You also need to find a balance and to make a clear distinction between what you'll give away for free and what you'll deliver as part of a paid-for consulting session.

As an accountant, you possess a great deal of business knowledge. Even if you've only been established for a handful of years, you'll already have seen what works in the businesses you deal with and can apply that thinking across industries. The most important skill is the ability to listen incredibly well; the second is the ability to ask great questions that enable you to drill down and enhance your understanding; and the third is the ability to make connections to great strategies you've seen in other businesses or to strategies that you've learned along the way. Once you've done this, you can discuss these strategies with your client to explore how they might be applied to their business. It's then up to you to spark their creative thinking by saying, "This is what another of my clients does. I know your business is different, but let's explore how we might be able to tailor what they do so it fits."

To give you another pointer, do you remember the Scalextric? If you're wondering what the point of it was, in addition to making sure visitors have a fun, memorable experience, it also ticks many boxes from an NLP point of view. It's visual, kinaesthetic and auditory – in other words, it stimulates many parts of the brain. It gives visitors a reason to talk positively about the experience and to rave about your practice.

Imagine, for example, one of your clients is socialising with a business associate on a golf course. During the time they'll spend together, what do you think the chances are that they'll talk about you at all, never mind in an incredibly positive way? (I'm not saying they won't, of course, but is the chance high or low?) Now imagine the same scenario, but it occurs shortly after your client's meeting with you. Still buzzing from the fun they had, the chances are greatly increased. The conversation could easily go something like this: *"You'll never guess what happened the other day – I got third place on a leaderboard playing Scalextric! Haven't played it for years and I really enjoyed it. Can you believe it was when I visited my accountants? Actually, I think you'd get a lot from talking to them too, they're unlike any I've ever come across before…"*

Have you ever noticed how people talk about their bad or their great experiences rather than their satisfactory ones? By trying too hard to avoid giving customers a bad experience, many accountants fall into the trap of failing to make the experience outstanding. This, by definition, positions them right in the middle as average.

Remember: It doesn't have to be Scalextric; it simply has to be a reason to rave.

33

Packaged Solutions

On the whole, human beings don't like a lot of choice. Many of us don't even like having to choose from a menu if it's too long. We begin to worry about whether we might make a poor choice. In fact, we love it when the waiter recommends something since it shortcuts the decision-making process for us.

A common pitfall many businesses succumb to is to try to sell the pieces of the jigsaw separately, as features in their own right, rather than combining them to create a 'big-picture' outcome. Accountants are no exception to this. (Individual services they sell include accounting, payroll, bookkeeping, business consulting and exit-planning.) As they try to remember and to talk through these countless products and services, clients simply feel they're being sold to.

When you buy a car you don't start with a chassis and then buy each additional item – engine, wheels, tyres, seats, steering wheel – separately. You buy a solution. You may be offered some slight variations or bolt-on options but, ultimately, you buy a solution.

Do you remember I wrote about how most accountants' websites look, feel and express the same information in the same way? AVN members who've gone through the journey of improving how they position themselves and of formulating their packaged solutions, use their websites to promote these instead. And, in doing so, they significantly set themselves apart. People don't care about the nuts and bolts, they care about your solution. They care about the outcome: the time, tax and training saved; the mistakes (and the consequences of those mistakes) avoided; the profit lift; the reduced hours.

So how can you combine what you already do – and what you'd love to do – into a simple solution?

34

Efficient Capacity

The following winning entry for the AVN Business Advisory award, written collectively by the team at CPT Accountants, Darlington, summarises the 'Value' section wonderfully. The owner of CPT is Brian Thompson who over the years purchased the equity and a fair few challenges from what was previously a three partner firm.

After grading our clients, we discovered we had more A clients than we realised and, recognising the untapped potential, decided to select ten of these for our A★ programme – an evolving list of the practice's most valuable clients – with a view to maximising future fees, referrals and each client's personal objectives. We believe in the potential of these clients to transform our practice and their businesses.

From those ten A★ clients, below are three typical examples of how clients benefit from being in our A★ programme.

One client, a successful IFA, had been with us for many years. Historically, the records were brought in at the last minute, with limited bookkeeping performed at the client's end. As a result, we were tasked with a significant challenge in preparing the accounts in a timely manner.

The client's business is fast growing but by the time we were reporting on performance, the information was up to 21 months out of date and not much use other than to determine the tax payable, which was due by the end of the month!

We explained to the client that the status quo was unhelpful for all parties and hit home the importance of regular reporting of financial information, especially with such a fast-growing business. We quoted the client, using our three-tiered service quotes and with the assistance of 'Time's Up!', and the client signed up to the highest possible service package. This included bookkeeping, quarterly management accounts, various tax scenarios and planning opportunities both personally and for the company.

Based on the work carried out by CPT, the client now receives timely information on the company's performance and future tax liabilities. The client has been able to make critical business decisions, including the implementation of a share-restructuring scheme, based on this information. Without it, such decisions would have been incredibly risky and any potential tax savings would have been based purely on guesswork. In addition, the client would have continued the director's loan and dividend approach and suffered large personal tax liabilities as a result.

We were also able to advise the client that he was about to exceed the large company corporation tax threshold, so plans were put in place to make the quarterly payments once the threshold was breached. The client has potentially avoided incurring interest charges and reduced his risk of an HMRC investigation because of this.

Another client, a local painter and decorator, had been using our services for many years purely for compliance purposes. Whilst the client had been satisfied with our services, we knew this wasn't enough for his current needs and were mindful that we would lose his business if we didn't begin to offer the services he needed and deserved.

We started off by preparing timely management accounts, which allowed us to meet with the client on a quarterly basis and ascertain his 'why.' This being the amount of time he can spend with his young family, from here we worked together to allow him more time to do so.

We then used AVN's benchmarking reports to show the client how he was doing in comparison to his peers. This highlighted areas he was excelling in, but also those in which improvement was required. He then began tweaking his business model. We also advised the client that he should delegate more to his team and increase his prices. We gave him the confidence to do this by reviewing his quarterly figures and ensuring that any changes would not be detrimental to the business.

He has now been able to stop working weekends and the free time gained through the working week means he is now heavily involved in local business clubs, allowing him to grow the business, instead of working in the business.

We are also lucky enough to represent a high-profile, internationally renowned client who was referred to us by Brian's industry contacts.

We were initially engaged to overhaul their bookkeeping system, which was littered with aged balances and historic errors. Team members tidied up the data whilst Brian set up systems for the records and bookkeeping, so the client wouldn't find themselves in the same position again.

The client was so pleased with the work we performed that they invited us to quote for the virtual FD role within the organisation. We were successful with this and immediately took over the systems we had just set up.

The client is based around 100 miles from our practice so this was a key opportunity to embrace technology-based solutions, as is the CPT way. We moved the client over to a Cloud-based system, so any Trustee could review the financial position from anywhere; we set up bank feeds which connect directly to the bookkeeping package, so the client's team don't have to worry about sending over statements; and we linked up to their Dropbox, where all invoices and related documentation are uploaded regularly by the client's team.

The VFD role means we attend quarterly Trustee meetings to discuss the management accounts and answer queries. We also attend ad hoc meetings with key Trustees to discuss business strategy. The regular reporting of accurate financial information meant that we were able to identify a large looming deficit. On the back of this information, the client was able to take cost-cutting measures which saw a 40% decrease in the deficit the following year with the group breaking even – something which hadn't happened for many years.

Once expenditure had been reviewed, we turned to income. At a recent lunch meeting we advised the client on the impact of upping their fees, discussed alternative income streams and how to smartly select to whom they provide their services in a way which would maximise profit without affecting their reputation.

These lunch meetings are set to become a regular occurrence as they have proved invaluable to both parties by improving both business and personal relationships. Recently the Trustees declared to us that, thanks to our efforts, they are now able to sleep at night.

We've now covered the first three elements of the AVN roadmap: Clarity, Positioning and Value. I've described the chaotic position that many accountants find themselves in after developing their practice in an inefficient way, which means that as they take on more clients, they work harder and longer.

Typically, accountants who implement the principles I've described so far see a reduction in their hours, and an increase in their profits and enjoyment, because:
- They're now clear on who they want to work with
- They've put the mechanisms in place to attract them
- They've stopped working with unprofitable clients and with those that aren't even close to their ideal
- They've priced their services better and, to support those prices, have learned how to demonstrate the value they can bring.

Inevitably, however, they'll reach a point at which they're at capacity again. The point at which – if they want to continue to take on more clients – they either need to work more hours than they'd like or better leverage their time. (At least in partner-centred practices where, however large the team, the onus is on the partners to double-check and to sign off work, to hold meetings and to get involved in communication with clients).

Some, on reaching this point (a point at which they're earning a significantly better income than ever before and working only the hours they want) are happy to pause. After all, they've successfully achieved an extremely healthy work/life balance that enables them to spend more time with family, friends and on their health.

The two key stages in creating scalability are leveraging your time and embracing the most suitable technologies to enable efficiencies and automation. We deal with these in both the Gearing and Automation stages of the roadmaps.

A true business should work for the owner, not the other way around.
Any business should enable its owner to have choice about their role, including that of working purely 'on' the business rather than 'in' it. However, it's important to note that working 'in' includes delivering business-growth advisory services. (I say this because although I often notice that while accountants are happy to delegate compliance work to their team, they feel that they're the only ones who can deliver business advisory work. Of course, what this means is that they're still working 'in' the business, they've simply changed role. It may be that they prefer this, and that at first delegating compliance work will free up some of their capacity. There will, however, become a point at which it is once again filled).

Whether you choose to create a business that is capable of running without you – which, by the way, is the only true way to be able to scale up your business – or whether you simply want to delegate more while keeping the most high-level projects for yourself, is of course up to you. Either way, this section describes how to better leverage your time so that you can scale up as much as you want to. To do so effectively requires a certain mindset, one you may or may not already possess. If scaling your practice up so that it doesn't take up more of your time,

but does bring you additional income and enjoyment is important to you, adopting the right mindset is paramount.

Many accountants in practice believe that their customers are buying them and, as a follow-on to this, that their customers wouldn't want to deal with a member of their team. In their hearts, they also believe that no team member is able to deliver such a service as they do.

The reality is that this mindset restricts growth. When AVN members have surveyed their customers to ask how important it is for them to deal only with the partner of the practice, the results have been disheartening – at least for the partner! What clients really want is their work produced on time and accurately. Frankly, they don't care who does the work. (This isn't to say that they don't have a great relationship with the partner, just that they trust that they'll run a practice with high standards).

When you take your car to be serviced, for example, you probably always go to the same garage, but do you always know, or care, which mechanic actually carries out the service? I certainly don't! I simply trust that the owner of the garage has high standards and will ensure that everyone in his team delivers to those same standards.

Another common pitfall is for a partner to employ more team members but then double-check every piece of work before signing it off. This might allow you to leverage your time a little, but it doesn't free it up.

To avoid this, AVN advocate putting a client manager set-up in place, each with a team of their own. However, we often have to overcome members' concerns with this first. Concerns such as:

- What if they run away with my clients and set up in competition?
- What if they don't deliver to my high standards?
- They don't like talking to clients as it is
- They don't always interpret the numbers very well.

They're buying a solution

While such concerns are understandable – and admittedly, if you don't get this part right, some of them might prove to be correct – by adopting the right mindset and by developing a great culture and leading rather than managing your team, you'll be able to enjoy working with people who are as committed to your practice and its continued growth and success as you are. This will make scaling your practice considerably easier and enable you to transform your partner-centred accountancy practice into an accountancy business.

Do you have an exit plan? If so, what is it? It may be that you want to create a business that will simply continue to earn you an income when you step down from active involvement; or perhaps you'd like to pass it on to your children or sell it as a retirement fund.

Either way – and even if deciding still seems too many years ahead right now – it's important to develop your practice so that it can run without you. If you're not convinced, consider this typical scenario. A sole practitioner, who now wants to retire, has spent decades building up a client base and has five employees and a Gross Recurring Fee (GRF) income of £200,000. All things considered, it's not a bad level and, for many years, building up their GRF (as that's usually the sale value, give or take) has been the target for many people. In reality, of course, it's merely a block of fees and the baggage of a set of employees that's sold.

So now let's say that she's offered 1 x GRF for the practice, which – as is generally the case – comes with a claw back clause. What this means is that the buyer spreads the payments. Usually they'll make an initial payment of around 40%, followed by a further 30% on the first anniversary of the purchase, and the remaining 30% on the second. However, the subsequent payments are dependent on the fees that were originally purchased still coming in.

As a result of this, I've often seen accountants having to come back out of retirement because of a claw back clause affecting the amount of money they actually earned from the sale of their practice. Ultimately, this is because they'd built a partner-centred practice whose clients had bought them as the partner and now weren't happy with the new partner or the way they did things. In addition, the buyer will have had to try to integrate the team members they've taken on into their own way of doing things – something which is always going to be difficult.

So instead, what if the partner had built a great accountancy business? One that didn't rely on themselves – or indeed on any individual – to run it? In order for this to happen, a great team, committed to delivering a great service to its clients, must be in place, as well as systems, so that high standards are consistently adhered to.

This, then, would be a dream purchase for any buyer. They'd be buying a practice that would continue to run and to earn income for them from day one – all without the need to interfere or to change anything. Clients will continue to deal with the same team member as they always have and won't notice any change in service. The buyer will have the luxury of staging any changes they want to make – such as branding or introducing new services – over a period of time. They'll also be more inclined to keep the same team as they're delivering the service in its entirety and the business is generating a great profit.

Whereas buyers will pay considerably more for a practice they don't immediately need to become heavily involved in, partner-centred businesses that don't have systems or a great team in place usually sell for much less. Generally, the purchase price will be based on profit or EBITDA, with additional factors such as team culture, systemisation and reliance on the owner taken into account. At the time of writing the typical sale value of an accountancy practice has fallen to less than 1 x GRF. (This is due in large part to the growing number of accountants who have almost reached retirement age and are looking to get out as technology continues to evolve and to dominate. Making Tax Digital, for example, has scared a lot of people.)

I'm often asked why Gearing comes first and Automation second in AVN's roadmaps. Surely, they argue, the systems need to be in place before you can get your team to follow them? The answer lies in my more than 20 years' experience. Although AVN supply a ready-to-tweak suite of systems that can be applied and personalised to all aspects of an accountancy practice, the biggest challenge partners generally face is getting their team to follow them. To succeed in this, the culture has to be right and the team has to be made up of people who understand that systems are important for consistency. A second reason for Gearing coming first is that AVN members will have already received help to put systems (such as identifying quick-win systems that enable them to delegate work more easily) in place throughout their roadmap journey so far.

To build a great team you need to develop leadership skills. A team that's inspired to follow systems is much more likely to embrace them than a team who's told to follow them. What, though, if you're thinking: *"But I'm not a leader..."*?

What is a leader? Quite simply, it's someone who can excite others to follow their vision, to the extent that emotionally others want to do everything they can to make that vision a reality, rather than effectively being bribed to do so. (I'll be sharing more about the three categories of motivation later.) A great leader will also make sure they keep their team focused and challenge them with mutually agreed goals to keep everyone on track and so they can measure progress together.

I don't consider myself a natural leader. (After all, I was a software developer for many years, and the stereotype of a typical programmer is incredibly similar to that of an accountant!) I do, however, have a great team that I'm proud to be part of, and a vision that excites us all. I've also made a point of studying aspects of psychology to better understand how people communicate, how they behave and how they're motivated, and I can now adapt my behaviour to suit each individual rather than expect them to adapt theirs to suit me. I don't pretend I get it right every time (not least because my team will be reading this!) but, as with everything, I do make a conscious effort –spending regular, one-on-one time with each member to understand their wants, needs and desires – which is now largely habitual. (We all have a default, but the rest can be systematised.)

In the chapters that follow, as well as giving examples of practices leveraging their time through their team, I'll share some of the insights I've learned about people that I believe are important for you to be aware of. In giving you the knowledge you need to develop the right culture within your practice, my aim is to inspire you to begin to reduce your level of responsibility, confident that your team will assume the mantle with your same enthusiasm and desire.

Right now, of course, you might not have a team. Perhaps you're still a one-person band, trying to build your portfolio of clients sufficiently to justify employing one. Or you may have chosen to outsource – in which case you have a remote team. Either way, I recommend you continue reading not only because, once you are ready to take on a team, what you learn will be important, but also because I'll be sharing some useful advice around outsourcing (in itself another crucial way to leverage your time).

Let's start by imagining your car is stuck in first gear. Your foot's pressed to the floor in the hopes of getting it to move faster, but despite the engine working flat out, you're not going particularly quickly. In fact, the engine's unlikely to go on for much longer before it blows a gasket. Then, suddenly, you're able to change gear. What happens? The engine relaxes a little and the car begins to speed up. As you continue to change up through the gears, the engine's efficiency and running conditions remain optimal and you cruise comfortably along toward your destination – all without causing or suffering undue stress.

Now imagine that you're that engine and the car's your business. If you have a team, have you developed its members in such a way that they can now free up your time from the day-to-day activities in your business? In other words, are they allowing you to leverage your time or simply adding to your stress whilst you continue to work long hours?

35

Gearing – Leveraging Time Through Outsourcing

Although outsourcing isn't new – we've always tapped in to graphic designers and website developers, for example – there's been a huge rise in the number of people setting up as one-person bands, meaning the variety and accessibility of what's offered has increased.

One obvious benefit from outsourcing is that it's a variable or direct cost rather than a fixed one. As such, it can be easily turned off or ramped up or down as needed, whereas employing someone directly ties you to a fixed cost. (For some roles that might be important, for others less so.) In addition, outsourcing to an agency means you don't have to worry about sickness, holidays or even performance issues. The agency is responsible for ensuring that what you've outsourced for is delivered.

Fiona, an AVN accountant based in Camberley, geared up by outsourcing typical administrative tasks such as answering the telephone, which had the added benefit of ensuring clients and prospects always had a great experience. Then, as she appreciated the need to raise her profile, she engaged the services of a content-marketing expert who now takes care of her website, social media and marketing campaign needs, and is busy generating interest from her ideal clients. She's also outsourced her payroll and compliance services. In consequence, she's been able to free up her core team to focus on delivering business growth advisory, tax and management accounts, and has more time to spot opportunities for clients.

Not only has business increased – largely because she's now better leveraging her time through outsourcing – but Fiona's clients tell her that her practice is the most proactive they've come across. And, if you're concerned about the ethics of outsourcing client information, rest assured that Fiona (and every accountant we work with) is upfront with clients and explains that she ensures everything will continue to meet her high standards.

Another concern shared by many is that they won't feel in control if someone else is producing the work or handling the queries, or that clients will be unhappy to learn that someone external is dealing with their work. Of course, GDPR means that tighter sub-contractor agreements are necessary to ensure you're not breaking privacy laws, but these can be easily sourced and put in place whenever you outsource to anyone.

Another example of successful outsourcing is provided by Jonathan Vowles, of Vowles Charted Accountants in Bedfordshire. The following is an account by a member of his team of what happened.

"We faced a dilemma last year when we could see the shift in the accountancy industry towards advisory-led services. We knew this was the direction in which we needed to take the practice, but we had team members who were already beyond capacity dealing with deadline-driven compliance work. Their primary skills were basically technical and they weren't particularly client-facing. In fact, they were probably unsure about what an advisory conversation even looked like.

This meant that most of the advisory work in the practice was not being promoted by team members and only really delivered by Jonathan. In order to change the focus of the client managers, we needed to reduce their workload and to train them in a new advisory skill set, one which included having different, more proactive conversations and building relationships with clients.

We started by engaging an outsourcing company to do some of our accounts production. This has proved hugely successful – improving the turnaround time to around four weeks while maintaining the same high standards – and has also increased our profitability on jobs that were historically loss-making.

Although this has not been an easy process – the team have needed to change their mindset – after several months they can now see the benefits of reducing the turnaround time to the client and for their own job satisfaction. Our aim is to outsource around 50% of our compliance work within the next six months.

The next important stage was to regrade clients. We went through our entire database and graded clients according to a number of factors such as: likability, potential for/already having advisory work, profitability and the amount of services that they had with us. This has enabled the team to refine their approach to each grade. Lower-grade clients have their needs met through having their work produced by outsourcers, which means we can keep those clients' fees lower. Higher-grade clients are contacted more regularly by their client manager who, as a result, has a stronger working relationship with (and more knowledge about) them and what they are trying to achieve.

Our attention then turned to recruiting the 'right' people. We now have a real focus on recruiting people who we believe can 'think beyond the numbers' and provide insightful advice to clients that will help them to achieve their goals. This means that we've recruited people who are not only technically able, but who've also demonstrated their ability to explain and to find out what's happening behind the numbers. This has led to more experience and different approaches being available within the team, which in turn helps everyone to develop and to think differently.

All the team members are increasingly happy to attend networking events and we also hold our own annual event. All the team get involved by helping to organise it and speaking to existing and potential clients. The willingness to network and to create new leads has also been a focus when we recruit new team members.

Our quoting system enables the team to meet with potential clients and to provide a quote easily and efficiently without needing input from Jonathan or from other more experienced members of the team.

We've also introduced on-boarding meetings once a new client has accepted our proposal. The client is introduced to their client manager and bookkeeper/payroll person so they know who to contact with any queries. This removes their reliance on Jonathan as the only known point of contact.

In this meeting the expectations of both parties are discussed, and this has proven to set up a good working relationship from the outset, with both ourselves and the client clear on what will be delivered and when.

The team then own the relationship with the client and can fully understand the client's motivations and working styles which all helps to build stronger relationships.

We have encouraged team members to follow their interests and to develop specialisms, which has proved to be particularly successful in terms of job satisfaction and our ability to provide specialist advice to clients. For example, we've created new roles such as a 'Cloud Specialist,' who has specific knowledge on Xero add-ons and migration. We also have a Quickbooks Online Specialist who delivers training and technical advice on this software.

Through the adoption of these changes Jonathan's time has been freed up to concentrate on his own specialisms, which include tax planning, marketing and sales.

The team are becoming very good at converting technical questions that arise during a free meeting, to a chargeable meeting with Jonathan which is a far more valuable use of his time."

I hope the above has gone some way to convincing you of the benefits of outsourcing. However, an important rider before you start is that you need to be:
• 100% clear yourself about the outcome
• 100% clear that the person/agency you're outsourcing to fully understands your requirements.

Personally, I've used outsourcing for telephone answering, virtual PA services, graphic and web design and software development and in all cases I quickly became aware that even when the people I'd chosen were local – let alone overseas – regular communication and feedback were vital.

A telephone answering service is a great way to allow you and your team some focus time but, whether you use the service all day, every day or simply for short periods, it's important that whoever you choose answers the phone and treats your customers, prospects and suppliers in the way you want. Everyone claims they'll deliver a professional service, but is what they mean by this in line with your preferences?

For example, can you grant them access to your CRM system to log calls? Most systems are Cloud-based, so if you can, it offers a big advantage. Your customers might start to feel a little unloved if every time they call they're asked whether they're a customer, a supplier or someone making a new enquiry. I've known this to happen when multiple people are stationed at the answering service, but as long as they have access to your CRM, they can quickly type in the caller's name or in many cases phone-number matching can instantly pull up the name of the business for them. (Another piece of advice is to use a locally based service as the accents are similar!)

Fiona's telephone answering service once went above and beyond the call of duty when they talked a prospective client through the roads and streets of Camberley to reach her office whilst he was driving. The agency – Moneypenny – are a national firm and used Google Maps. When the client arrived he was astounded to discover he hadn't been talking to a member of Fiona's direct team. What a great example of outstanding service!

I also used a Virtual Assistant a few years ago. As I didn't need someone full-time, I tapped in to an agency and paid for 10 hours per month. My VA's work consisted of organising meetings, arranging my diary and keeping my emails under control by unsubscribing from and deleting obvious junk mail, sorting what was left, creating tasks and responding to emails to set an expectation as to when I would reply. Although her time was allocated to just half an hour per day, each morning I'd spend a few minutes on a video call with her going over what she was doing to ensure it was done exactly how I wanted. Admittedly this was time consuming to begin with, but it meant I could then trust everything would get done the way I wanted it to – every time. And it did.

When it comes to outsourcing compliance work, I'm sure you've heard some pretty horrifying stories of the quality of the work some accountants have got back. One of the problems here though isn't necessarily that the agencies weren't good, but that the quality of the information they were sent wasn't.

To unpick what I mean by that, often, when an accountant decides to test outsourcing their compliance work, the work they send is the pain in the backside jobs that they hate doing themselves. And the reason they hate doing it is because the books and records are in such a mess. In other words, they're sending crap in and therefore getting crap out. For a true test, try sending some of the better quality books and records and see what happens. If you like what they produce then continue to send them good-quality clients to work on, and in the meantime devote some of your time to helping the other clients to improve their books and records.

Whether you're on your own or have a team of people, I strongly recommend you consider outsourcing. By tapping in to outsourcing you'll free up your time to work on things that will increase your income. The most valuable use of your time is to have meaningful discussions with clients about the data produced by your outsourcers (as opposed to you sitting in your office producing it yourself).

A great example of how outsourcing can also improve your work/life balance is offered by Rennie Evans, of Prospero Accounting, who I visited a while ago at his home in Manchester. The conventional journey of a start-up accountant often starts from their spare bedroom. As their client base grows and their revenue increases they then progress to rented office space to give their practice a more professional feel for clients and prospects.

Rennie, however, was the perfect example of someone who'd gone full circle through that journey. His accountancy practice had grown to such an extent that he'd moved to a large office in the centre of Manchester. Not only were the overheads sky-high, but owing to congestion his commute had often taken him two-three hours each day. In other words, he was stressed before he even started work.

Three years before my visit, Rennie's landlord had given him notice to vacate which left him with a decision to make: relocate, or do what he'd been toying with for a while and set up a virtual office? If he chose the latter, he and his team could simply work from home. After giving the matter some thought, he decided to work from home. But why the virtual office?

If you've ever worked from home, I'm sure you'll have suffered the late night or weekend drop-ins when clients call by to give you their books and records and to run a few queries by you while they're there – as your dinner cools or your kids patiently wait to resume your interrupted game. I expect you've been on the receiving end of numerous out-of-hour phone calls, too.

Rennie certainly had, which is why he agreed with his former landlord that he could continue to use the same address for his business and that the receptionist within the serviced offices would forward his post and answer his calls, seamlessly putting them through to either his, or to his team's mobile phones. When it came to meetings, he and his team could either meet clients at their premises or, if that wasn't convenient, they could simply rent a room – by the hour – in his former office building. (Of course all his clients were aware of this, there wasn't any secrecy).

Rennie and his team now work from their respective homes. Rennie gets to relax by taking his dogs for a walk every morning and to appreciate the countryside where he lives. And working from home means his commute is now counted in seconds. (In fact, he's pretty much created an 'extra' day each week from the time he's saved).

He and his team meet at a mutually convenient coffee shop every fortnight or so and, in between, keep in contact via video conferences and messaging apps. Since the software they use is Cloud based, their system also allows everyone to record the status of what they're working on.

This virtual office costs less than a seventh of what he was paying for a physical office. In addition, he and his wife no longer need a car each. By using technology and outsourcing, Rennie has saved himself and his team considerable time and money.

What could you do with an extra day?

36

Leveraging Your Time Through Team

Another great approach to scaling your accountancy practice is to develop your team so they become client managers. Jo, based in Leeds, is a former AVN member who left us a few years ago purely and simply because she'd made such significant improvements to her business that she no longer required our help. However, when I saw that she'd won some awards I asked if I could interview her to see how she's doing. The video I recorded when I visited, captures her full story – from setting up in her spare room to leading what's now a fast-growing, profitable practice heavily focused on business growth advisory.

Key to the many improvements she's made along the way is that she's continued to grow her practice in a way that doesn't rely on her for the everyday stuff. She's still involved but - and this is crucial - she doesn't have to be. It's this that gives her the freedom to spend time working on her practice.

Like so many accountants, Jo - by her own admission - is a control freak. At first, even thinking about letting her employees loose on her clients was daunting. In her case though, she had little option. She was due to have major surgery and her team would need to run things without her for a while. And they did. In fact, they dealt with everything admirably. No clients were let down and the practice ran incredibly well. Why? Because she'd already put a lot of systems in place and had developed a great team culture. In reality, this final hurdle had been largely psychological. Jo simply needed to let go, to trust that her team would deliver and – perhaps even more importantly – that her clients would be happy to deal with someone other than herself.

Do you remember Paul, from Nuneaton? At the constant beck and call of his clients and his team, Paul was under so much stress he felt he had nothing to lose and agreed to follow our suggestion to hand over management of his client base to his team: no more meetings, no more double-checking their work. By splitting the client base between them and implementing a great strategy, he actually met very little resistance from clients. And, by freeing himself from having to deal with them all himself, he was able to take on the role of coaching those he'd recently appointed as client managers. Even better, once they'd been trained to deal with queries, it was a short step to their being able – in finding the answers to those queries – to start a conversation with clients about business growth solutions and opportunities.

Shifting to a client-manager structure must be carried out in a way that doesn't upset your clients or scare your team off. Paul's success was partly down to his process of introducing clients to their new client managers and to the client manager's back-up to reassure them that they had three points of contact. Then, every time a client phoned to talk to Paul, the receptionist would simply put them through to the client manager who would explain that although Paul wasn't available, they'd do their best to turn the query around quickly. Failing that, they'd get Paul to call the client back as soon as possible. In almost every case, they were able to help the client themselves and so the relationship between the two improved. On the few occasions they couldn't, rather than call the clients back himself, Paul would coach the client manager directly and/or identify a flaw in the information available to them and thereby improve the system.

(If you're worried that this sounds like the client managers were dropped in at the deep end, Paul made sure they were comfortable at every stage of the process. In fact, the support and coaching they received was of huge benefit to their careers.)

Once the foundations were in place, Paul was able to step back from client interaction completely. Indeed, his only interaction with clients now is social. If, for example, a client is waiting in reception when he passes, he'll say hello and pause for a quick chat before they head off to meet their client manager.

But what happens when the process doesn't go quite as smoothly as it did for Paul? Not long ago, for example, I visited Phil, an AVN member based near Cardiff, who was struggling to get his client managers to deliver to the standards he expected in client meetings. Despite being extremely competent accountants with great people skills, and being very switched on when it came to spotting opportunities for a client to improve their numbers, for some reason in meetings they weren't stepping up.

As I listened to Phil describe the situation, and drilled down to make sure I fully understood what was happening, my suspicions were quickly confirmed when

I invited the client managers into the meeting. Every time I asked either of them a question, they glanced at Phil before answering. Of course it's great that they looked up to and respected him, but the downside was that they didn't feel empowered to express their opinion without gaining his consent first.

It turned out that – with the best intentions in the world – Phil had been sitting in on client meetings. Although in his mind he was simply there in case his client managers were asked a question they couldn't answer, what was actually happening was that they were intimidated by his presence. In fact, to check they weren't saying the wrong thing, they would look at him for confirmation before they said anything. This, of course, made them lack credibility and the clients would start to direct their questions directly to Phil instead.

Phil had decided to sit in on meetings because he felt that clients' questions should always be answered there and then. But just think about that for a moment. While it's true that he may have had a few more answers up his sleeve than his client managers did, he couldn't possibly have them all. And, when he didn't, he wouldn't have thought twice about telling clients that he'd look into it and get back to them.

In the end, giving his client managers permission to use this same response was all that was needed for them to step up in meetings. Phil agreed he would no longer attend the meetings and his client managers agreed that if they couldn't answer a question there and then, they would compliment the client for asking a great question, write it down and say they'd look into it and get back to them. Furthermore, Phil would no longer simply provide the answers, but coach his client managers on the best way to discover these for themselves. After all, that was how Phil gained experience when he first set up his practice and it's probably how you gained your best knowledge, too.

Before we move on though, please bear in mind that there's a huge difference between delegating responsibility and abdicating from it. One accountant who attended our Masterclass was so excited by everything he heard about delivering more business growth advisory services and empowering team members to become client managers that he went straight back to his office and told his team about the changes he was going to make. However, hearing they were going to be renamed client managers and would be expected to deliver advisory services to clients scared some of them so much that three started job-hunting immediately and handed in their notice within a week of each other. For most of their careers, these employees had been involved in back-office compliance work with very little client interaction and zero business growth advisory. The thought of suddenly being expected to drop into this new role was too much.

Since client managers require additional skills to those of compliance, start by identifying which team members are right for the role. Some will need to be nurtured and developed more than others. Key to this is your approach – simply asking team members to step up to being a client manager should never be your first move.

Most owners set up their business because they have a particular ability, whether it's in accountancy or software development. As they take on more work, although nearly all of them will take on more employees as well, few will focus on developing their own leadership and people skills in order to bring the best out of their employees to allow scalability.

If you're concerned that you don't have the necessary people or leadership skills, in my opinion these can be developed. I certainly don't consider that I do. But I do strive every day to think about how someone with those skills would act and, to the best of my abilities, to replicate this.

37

Defining Leadership

When I was young I used to look forward to tuning in to BBC2 every week to watch 'Star Trek'. At that time (the 1970s), this consisted of repeats of the original series, but these were later followed by 'Star Trek: The Next Generation' and by the many other spin-offs. As I followed each new reincarnation, one thing that stood out was the difference in leadership style between the original series (created in the 1960s) and 'The Next Generation' (created in the 1990s). Disregarding any superficial similarities – we're talking about the military crew of a ship here, so obviously a hierarchy and command structure existed in both – in many cases the style of leadership had changed significantly. Whereas in 'The Next Generation', for example, Captain Picard would often request suggestions from his bridge crew before making a decision, Kirk, the captain in the 1960s series, wouldn't.

In one particular episode, Spock even reminded Kirk that he'd lose the trust – and command – of his crew if he were seen as vulnerable or perceived as less than perfect. Since all of the series are now available on Netflix, I decided it was pertinent research for this chapter and so I tracked down the episode to watch it again.

Throughout the episode, I noted that all the crew looked to Kirk for guidance, orders and decision-making. No recommendations were sought by him, but plenty of dilemmas were taken his way and he was expected to know the answers and to respond with the correct order. Although the episode was created in the 1960s, and although it was intended to represent a perfect future (including a perfect hierarchy of command), in reality it was the perfect representation of an outdated ideology. Today, even in the military, this method of leadership has been recognised as ineffective.

And yet it's still applied in many businesses today.

No one can know everything. If we tried, we'd simply sacrifice our strengths by focusing on making our weaknesses less weak. On the other hand, my team and I make things happen because we all have different strengths and play to them.

A good leader:
- Shares a vision that can inspire others
- Creates an environment in which everybody can become the best they can be at playing their part in helping that vision become a reality.

It might help if you think as a leader as more like a gardener. A gardener will develop a vision of what they want their garden to look like and the experience they want visitors to have of it. Next, they'll put in the plants and flowers that will help that vision come true, water and feed them, and keep any weeds at bay that might damage them or prevent their vision from becoming a reality. In short, they ensure that the environment for each plant and flower is exactly what it needs to flourish.

People are exactly the same as those plants and flowers. People need to be in an environment in which they're encouraged and are free to become the best they can be. One in which genuine interest is taken in them and their needs are met. If, despite this, they remain uninspired by your vision then they simply aren't right for your team and you need to find people who are. Once you have, encourage them to make recommendations and to use their initiative and judgement (more about this later). Get your team to step up and allow them to make the decisions that ultimately fit with your values and beliefs.

If flowers and plants fail to flourish it's usually because the gardener is either neglecting them or not sustaining the correct environment. Sometimes, of course, they've simply put in a plant designed for a different environment which now needs removing. If people aren't performing, there's a high chance their leader has fallen short in exactly the same areas.

Three things are crucial to create the right environment: equality, camaraderie, and a sense of achievement. Below is a brief insight into each.

Equality Although this includes fair reward, fair conditions and fair attention, I'm going to focus on the latter. Who do you spend most time on? We often take the best performers in our business for granted. Internally pleased that they're doing a great job, we forget to tell them or to express the gratitude they deserve.

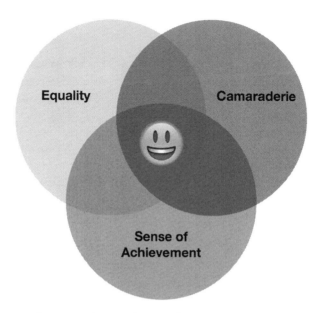

Conversely, we often spend most time on the people who simply aren't right for our business but, in our attempt to get them onboard and to do better, we simply demoralise the better performers. A good rule of thumb is: Great leaders hire slow and fire fast. I know I've been guilty of spending too much time on someone when, in my heart, I knew within a few days that I'd hired the wrong person. It's harsh but hiring the wrong people is like planting weeds in a garden. Unless you pull them up quickly they'll stifle and negatively affect the rest of the team and your overall vision.

Camaraderie A lack of camaraderie can inhibit performance. Create a buzz by setting goals. These are goals that everyone is involved in, but be careful they're not ones that cause your team to have tunnel vision and focus on achieving them at the expense of everything else. Carefully consider your goals, set milestones, and create camaraderie in achieving them. Celebrate every win, together.

Sense of achievement Help each member of your team to develop a sense of achievement. Is their workload realistic? Do they finish the day feeling they've achieved something or that they're only halfway through a list of jobs that was unreasonable in the first place? The latter will lead to stress and an ever-increasing list of things they need to catch up on. I often find that members of my team take on too much. In fact, I have to convince them to edit their lists down to the most important items so they feel they're achieving what they need to. Deciding what's most important and feeling comfortable with eliminating what isn't can be difficult to do alone.

Spend quality time with all your team. Make sure you understand them as individuals, and learn about their strengths and motivations. (You might be surprised at how rarely these are financial). Work with them to play to their strengths and to create an environment that motivates them.

Together, the above will help to create a high-performance environment that will inevitably take your accountancy business closer to your vision. Your job – as leader – is to be the gardener who works to ensure the environment is the best you can make it.

38

Kill The Staff...

Or, to be more correct, kill the 'staff' culture!

I've always hated the word 'staff'. It immediately confers an 'us' (the employer/manager) and 'them' (the employees) mentality. It puts people in their place. It harks back to an outdated chain of command and certainly isn't conducive to developing a team of people with a sense of ownership of the purpose of their business.

Here's an example of the difference, as I see it, between 'staff' and 'team.'

Staff One evening not so long ago I was with some friends at our local ten-pin-bowling centre when a group of people came in. One of my friends was buying a round of drinks at the bar and the barman seemed almost furious, grumbling to him about how he'd only just tidied the bowling lanes and now someone else had had the audacity to turn up expecting to play! Clearly he failed to see any connection between people coming in and him getting paid and keeping his job. In his mind, he's a member of staff. He has his duties – one's serving drinks, another is tidying the bowling alleys – and now he has to put additional effort in before the end of the evening. He's not happy and he has no qualms about letting other customers know that.

Team Earlier that same day, Tracy, an AVN team member, was in the process of organising one of our regular events. As it takes place over three days, two evening meals are included and we typically go to a local pub for one, and a local hotel for the other. (The hotel is more expensive, but it's nice to offer two different environments). On this particular occasion, however, the pub couldn't accommodate us, meaning we'd need to use the hotel for both nights. Tracy decided to nip across the road to the hotel to see the manager, whereupon she succeeded in negotiating him down on the price of the meals and drinks before coming back to share her success with me.

I'd like to emphasise at this point that Tracy has no accountability around this. Organising our events doesn't even fall within her remit, but she was happy to help out. Had she had a 'staff' mentality, she would simply have booked the hotel for two nights. But she didn't. Instead, she treated the business as if it were her own and looked out for its best interests.

Moving from a 'staff' to a 'team' mentality entails much, much more than changing one word, but making that change is a very good starting point. (If you're worried it might seem alien at first, I promise it won't be long before it starts to feel completely natural). In my mind, it's a crucial first step and one that will begin to change your and your team's mindset. As you continue to use it, your behaviour will begin to reflect the new reality it represents.

That's why 'staff' has always been considered a swear word within AVN. Make it one in your business, too, and you'll kill the culture it represents.

39

Getting Your Team To Step Up

Despite the title, I'm not a great fan of the expression 'getting your team to step up.' I've only used it because I'm so often asked: *"How can I get my team to step up?"* In fact, I believe everyone wants to deliver more and that often it's employers who suppress this. That's why the process I'm about to share focuses on reversing the damage done by many of them.

Let's look at a common scenario, one in which a customer reports a problem. One of your employees takes a call, makes a note of the problem and says they'll get you to call the customer back. (Does this sound familiar so far)? The employee then comes to you to explain the problem.

Perhaps you're working on something really important, but the complaint takes priority. As you listen, you feel the onus is on you to solve it and – because your employee has told the customer you'll call them back – the problem has now become yours to deal with.

Your employee leaves and resumes their daily routine while you're left fighting yet another metaphorical fire. After all, you're the boss and you have all the answers, right? But is that really true? Couldn't your employee have come up with a solution themselves that you'd have been happy with? So why didn't they?

The problem is that many people have been 'trained' not to think for themselves and that many employers are power-hungry control freaks who feel that unless they make the decisions things will go wrong.

This quells employees' enthusiasm almost as soon as they start their first job and the mindset – that they're paid to do as they're told, not to think – sticks. They'll continue to take any problems to their boss and to keep their heads down by doing what's expected of them and little more.

Not only does this suppress any spark of human ingenuity, but it means too much relies on you. So let's change things. Remember, the whole is not greater than the sum of its parts.

A Better Way

I'm privileged to work with amazing people who deal with any problems quickly, effectively and, in many cases, ingeniously. But it's not just about dealing with problems, they also suggest and implement great ideas to prevent those problems happening in the first place. (In other words, ideas for making the business better). At the same time, rather than continually being interrupted by the day-to-day operational stuff, I get to focus on the things I need to do that will also make the business stronger.

My team feel empowered to express themselves and – because of this – they feel valued and have a deep sense of worth. (And rightly so!) But, in case you're wondering, I didn't recruit them from a secret 'superhero' recruitment centre. They're ordinary people who do extraordinary things every day – and I'm going to share how you can develop your team to do the same.

Do it - Report Routinely

Do it - Report Immediately

Recommend

Ask

Go-For

Stepping Up in a Visual Context: The Initiative Ladder

The diagram left illustrates the different stages people can be at when it comes to using their own initiative. Many reside on either the lowest or the second-lowest rung. If they're a 'go-for' they simply wait to be told what to do: *"Go for this!"*, *"Go do that."* If they're an 'ask,' they might get on with the day-to-day routine stuff, but will bring anything outside of that to you. In other words, they're still not thinking for themselves.

The next rung, 'recommend,' is equivalent to: *"Bring me a solution, not a problem."* It's the first target rung, and, when I recruit people for AVN, I explain that it's the minimum level I expect. They need to take a few moments to think about the best way to solve (or at least improve) the problem and then bring their suggestion to me. Their recommendation won't always fit with our values, of course, or perhaps there's an additional factor that they're not aware of, but we can at least have a conversation and they'll leave with a greater understanding of the business and be able to offer better recommendations in the future.

To summarise, it's about breaking habits. For many people, it's a habit to ask rather than to think for themselves. The fear of recommending something that's wrong can also inhibit people. If that's the case, it's your job to encourage and remind them. Every time someone brings you a problem, ask: *"What do you recommend?"* If their response is, *"I don't know!"*, ask *"If you did know, what would it be?"* Reassure them that there's no such thing as a bad recommendation. Be patient and wait. Whatever their response, work with them on it.

Start by providing positive encouragement – it's great that they've made a suggestion. If you feel that their recommendation isn't quite right, ask yourself why before you respond. What would happen if you followed it? Would it really lead to a negative outcome, or is it simply a different approach to the one you'd take? If you realise that actually it could get the right result, then – as long it fits with your values and how you want your business to be seen – let them run with it.

If their recommendation doesn't fit with your values, explain why. Be positive and, where possible, work with them to develop it so that it does. If you're worried about negative connotations, give them the scenario: *"I wonder what would happen if…?"*
Help them to come up with a better solution themselves by asking thought-provoking questions rather than telling them the 'right' answer. The more you

work with them to make their recommendations fit how you want your business to be perceived, the more their recommendations will be presented in this way.

True, this takes patience, but there's no shortcut to building a great team. The rewards and benefits of taking the time to do so, however, are more than worth it.

Be the Support

Once you've agreed on a solution, let your employee run with it – after all, they developed it! Reassure them that you trust them to do so and that you'll support them. If things go wrong, encourage them rather than taking the task away from them. ('Recommend' may be the minimum level I expect a team member to be at, but it's also the maximum until I believe they're ready. I'll come back to this later).

Time to Trust

Sooner or later, members of your team will be bringing recommendations that – usually – fit. This means it's now time to take your trust further by moving them to the next rung of the initiative ladder: 'Do it – report immediately.'

To do this, you'll need to have a one-to-one conversation with each of them in turn as they reach this stage. Tell them that their recommendations are spot on and that you feel they're ready to move to the next level. Encourage them to trust – because you do – their own judgement and to deal with situations themselves. Ask them to have a chat with you afterwards about what happened and what they did about it.

Don't forget: No one's perfect and even good ideas can go wrong. Mistakes happen. If something doesn't work out, never chastise. Doing so will send that employee right back to the bottom of the ladder. Support them, but don't take the problem back. Encourage them to take responsibility for resolving the situation and support them every step of the way. Remind them that you trust their judgement and their original recommendation. This will make them stronger.

Provide Genuine Praise

It's easy to begin to take members of your team who are coming up with and implementing solutions for granted, but never forget to praise them. Everyone likes and needs to feel appreciated, and a simple but genuinely expressed 'thank you!,' 'well done!', or 'you're doing a great job!' goes a long way.

Time to Reduce Your Interruptions

Once you feel it's appropriate, encourage team members to move to the next rung, 'Do it – report routinely,' by reporting on what they've done on a weekly or monthly basis during team meetings. That way, not only will you show that you trust them, but you'll also gain more uninterrupted time in which to focus on improving your business.

Don't Let Fear Stop You

Sometimes when I've shared this concept, business owners have expressed concern that if they develop their team members too much they might start their own business in competition. Of course this may happen. (It may happen even if they don't). But in my experience it's incredibly rare. After all, starting a business is no walk in the park and many more people leave their jobs because they feel undervalued.

Creating an environment in which your team can express their creativity, make decisions for themselves and feel supported and appreciated will improve their loyalty, their sense of ownership and their commitment to the success of your business.

Time to Take Action

Talk to each member of your team about the initiative ladder. Describe the impact it has on you every time a problem is brought your way. Explain that you want to help them develop professionally and that their doing so will free up your time to make the business stronger. Remind them that, in the long run, this will benefit everyone.

40

Leadership vs Management

For me, the distinction between leadership and management is simple:

- **Leadership** seeks to inspire people with your vision and create an environment in which they can become the best they can
- **Management** seeks to control every action people take.

No one likes being controlled. Most of us live quite happily outside our employment without being supervised. We look after our house, our finances and our shopping. We organise our holidays, plan our weddings and bring up our children. Yet we come to work and all this suddenly stops. This control – i.e. this management – might keep people working, but it also makes them considerably less likely to go above and beyond their role or to bring forward ideas that could benefit your business. They turn up, do their job and then go home to where they feel free again. They look forward to the weekend and hate Mondays.

The key to developing a great team culture is to do your best to become a great leader rather than simply a manager. As I've said before, I certainly don't consider myself to be a natural leader, but I have learned some of their key traits.

Great leaders:

- Inspire others to want to help them achieve their vision and purpose
- Create an environment that allows each person to be the best they can be
- Take the time to understand others
- Adapt their approach to each individual in their team
- Accept that not everyone will follow them if they don't share their passion.

Notice that the word 'manage' didn't appear once. That's because I believe the only person you can, and should, manage is yourself. You can manage your mood, your behaviour and your communications.

Remember: manage yourself, but lead others.

41

The Values Of Your Team

One of the things I'm most passionate about is building a team that's truly committed. Many business owners try to mould their team and then wonder why people move on. They decide (wrongly, generally) that it's because they were offered a greater income elsewhere. They wonder why their team members can't think for themselves or why they seem to bring more problems than solutions and why they don't communicate with clients in the way they should.

I've been recruiting people for almost 30 years, to begin with for businesses I worked for then, later, for myself. Many, many businesses recruit based on an applicant's CV, but I've learned the hard way that unless you recruit people whose values are a close match to your own you'll be on a hiding to nothing. You'll end up wasting a lot of time trying to develop people who see the world too differently to you for it to work.

Do you recall how, in the Positioning section, I referred to Values? Well, let me finish that diagram for you.

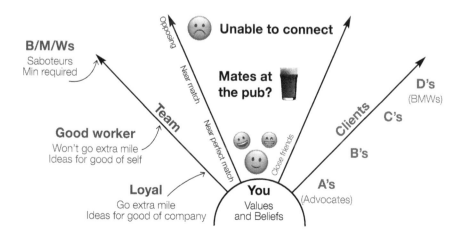

You'll find that those team members whose values are an almost perfect match to your own will be the most loyal. They'll be the people who are always willing to go that extra mile and to shed blood, sweat and tears for you. As they share your values, they'll often bring ideas forward that will benefit the company even if this means increasing their own role and responsibilities. They understand your vision and purpose, and they want to help you achieve them.

Next come those people whose values are a near match to yours. Although they're good workers, they won't necessarily go that extra mile and the ideas they bring forward will often be more for their own good – "Let's buy more comfortable chairs" – than for that of the business. They always make sure they finish at the exact time they're scheduled to and if something isn't complete, it just has to wait. They're open about the fact that they can't wait until Friday. They might be good workers, but they're not loyal, and they'll quickly move on if they get a better offer. (In their minds, a job's a job).

Last of all come the people whose values and beliefs are so far opposed to yours that they don't understand you or your vision at all. I call them the saboteurs. They complain about everything (usually to team members in the previous category as they're the most susceptible to their influence). They lower morale, but at the same time do just enough to ensure that it's difficult to part company with them based on their performance.

Alternatively, they might perform highly but completely destroy the culture within your team. You end up spending a ridiculous amount of time trying to get them to understand why you do things in a certain way, but as soon as your back's turned they're up to their old tricks again. Their toxic influence is compounded by the fact that you spend so much time trying to appease them that you have none left in which to show your appreciation to the most loyal members of your team. In consequence, your best people feel undervalued and start to move on.

We all need to feel that we belong and are valued. If you're losing your best people, you probably assume they're being poached, but in reality they could be leaving because they don't feel appreciated. And, once they've gone, what you're left with are the saboteurs and the people who used to fall in to the 'good' category but have now been seduced into the saboteur's camp.

It doesn't matter how much performance measurement you put in place either, as it's your team's morale that saboteurs ruin. (As I mentioned, legally it's difficult to part company with someone if they're performing). However, low morale leads to poor performance all round. Customer service suffers because there's a lack of genuine care, and before you know it your best customers are beginning to look for another accountant. (If you're lucky enough to have never experienced any of these symptoms you may think I'm exaggerating but, sadly, all too many accountants – and other business owners – have).

Of course, some team members may fit but aren't yet sufficiently engaged or they might simply have become demotivated and need to be re-engaged.

42

Discovering Your Values

Values go much deeper than guidelines. They can't simply be created by a team of people thinking up words that sound good, and neither should they be a set of rules that everyone has to follow.

So what are yours?

Unfortunately that's not always an easy question to answer. I like to think that values such as honesty, integrity and loyalty are a given – particularly in an accountant. Most people expect accountants to be honest and they won't choose you simply because you bandy the term about on your website.

When you're first asked to ascertain your values, your mind can go blank. In my own case, to avoid this, I was coached through a process and I strongly recommend you follow this approach rather than trying to go it alone. That said, you may find the following exercise useful.

1. Think of three people you really admire and of how they conduct themselves, how they always seem to do the right thing. (I'm not talking about celebrities or business magnates that you've only read about or seen on TV, but your family, friends, colleagues or simply people you know well and respect).

2. Next, make a list, as long as you like, of the qualities you most appreciate in each of them. (It doesn't have to be per person, or of qualities that they share). Here are some of the things I came up with:
    *   Doesn't just assume someone else will deal with a problem
    *   Won't go home until they've ensured a customer is completely happy
    *   Will argue their point if they believe they're right
    *   Will listen and consider other people's point of view
    *   Always positive
    *   Intelligent

- Interested in reading business books
- Team player
- Participates in fun activities
- Systematic
- Challenges my thinking
- Spots opportunities
- Wants to make a difference.

3. Once you've written your list, decide which of them are values and, of those, which are the most important to you. ('Intelligent' isn't a value for example. And although being positive is a great characteristic, sometimes we need people who are more negative. In my Board room, for example, there are some people who instantly see the downside of any idea. It's annoying as hell, but it does mean we have to think through every idea to make sure it will work).

4. Write down three to five items that encapsulate the essence of at least two of the qualities you've written down. My first draft included:
   - Has fun
   - Takes ownership
   - Gives more than takes
   - Challenges the status quo
   - Offers six-star customer service.

5. Provide three new bullet points for each of those items to explain what you mean by it. This is particularly important if you decide to use what I referred to earlier as a 'default value.' For example, for you, honesty may involve telling someone something you believe they should know even if it upsets them. (Other people might choose to be less forthcoming without feeling they're being dishonest). Explaining exactly what you mean by a value will help others to understand.

As you go through the above process, you'll probably realise that your first draft needs adjusting. Mine certainly did, but the values I eventually came up with were:
- Own it
- Make lives better
- Inspiring Wows
- Fun! with a serious intent
- Keep evolving

Simon Chaplin from GreenStones, an accountancy practice based in Peterborough, came up with a great way to explain exactly what he meant by each of his values. Once he'd developed them, he produced an example scenario and asked a client to help him create a storyboard to illustrate it. This storyboard is now on the walls of his practice and serves as an inspiration (and a decision-making guide) to each employee.

Of course, it should go without saying that the process doesn't end with putting a poster on your wall and/or your website. You also need to use your values as a filter to make sure you employ the right people within your team and that you work with the right clients and suppliers.

To reiterate: Discovering your values should not be a team exercise. If it is, by attempting to please everyone you'll simply end up diluting the finished product and neither you nor your team will buy into the generic set of values that results. In a multi-partner firm a degree of compromise may be necessary, but I recommend you carry out the above exercise individually first and then look for common values. If there aren't any at all, to be frank perhaps you shouldn't be working together.

Inspiring, Challenging and Supporting colleagues and customers to be the best they can be
GreenStones
Making it happen
Help each other
Share relevant knowledge
MORTGAGE
£29770
Seek enjoyable balance
Be honest
INDUCTION GUIDE
Be brave
PAS
EXAM

43

Why Financial Incentives Inhibit Quality Thinking

For a long time, most people believed that financial incentives and the promise of bonuses on reaching a certain target would inspire their workforce. However, while it's true that people might try to work faster in order to achieve a particular result, research has shown time and time again that this type of incentive produces a team that suffers from tunnel vision. Purely focusing on the outcome inhibits the brain's ability to think properly and actually leads to less accuracy and lower-quality work.

In fact, in one study in which two groups of people were asked to solve a puzzle (one which required them to think outside the box), the group that was offered a financial incentive consistently took more than twice as long to do so than the group that wasn't offered any incentive at all!

Studies also show there's a danger that financial incentives can permanently replace someone's natural desire to enjoy doing their work (and doing it well). In fact, one of these studies really stood out for me as it made me realise something I was doing very wrong with my children. Let me explain.

In this particular study[†], a group of children who liked colouring books were divided into three groups. (Most children enjoy seeing a black and white drawing become vibrant with the colours they've chosen, and how neat their care and attention can make it). The first group were told beforehand what they'd receive for each drawing they completed (a child-friendly equivalent to a financial incentive); the second group were given a surprise reward for each one afterwards; and the third group weren't given an incentive or reward at all.

---

† Conducted by Mark R Lepper, David Greene and Richard E Nisbett in 1973, the experiment was written up in Undermining children's intrinsic interest with extrinsic reward: A test of the "overjustification" hypothesis and appears in the Journal of Personality and Social Psychology, 28(1) 129-137.

Why Financial Incentives Inhibit Quality Thinking

As the results came in, although the first group produced more drawings it became clear that the care they took had reduced. In other words, they'd started to sacrifice quality for speed. Worse, in the weeks that followed, the researchers discovered that the children in this group no longer enjoyed colouring as much as they had previously. In fact, they now only did it if there was something in it for them. Their intrinsic motivation for doing it – enjoyment – had gone, as had their previous care to make sure they did a good job. Colouring had simply become a means to an end.

As I read through their findings, it occurred to me that I'd been doing something similar by encouraging my children to look for ways to earn money by washing up or doing the vacuuming. Instead, I realised, I should encourage them to do these activities simply to take pride in keeping the house tidy and in doing their fair share around it.

It's the same with your team. Never assume that a financial incentive is the answer – it might even have the opposite effect, as, in addition to destroying their natural tendency to want to do a good job, you may need to start micro-managing them. To illustrate what I mean, let's return to the children. Once their intrinsic motivation had been replaced by an extrinsic one, their accuracy was compromised. (In other words, they started to churn out more drawings just to get the reward). In the workplace, this would have meant that additional measures around neatness – keeping within the lines – would have had to be put in place. And what about any creative additions – perhaps some flowers – that they might have added? The quality between a task someone's completed through an intrinsic desire to do a great job compared to that of one they've completed simply to meet the minimum standard required to get a reward will be very different.

With extrinsic motivation, if the incentive stops the effort will too. Not only that, but such incentives usually produce diminishing results, as unless they continue to increase, they won't have the impact they once did. Eventually, a person may reach a point at which they don't need any more and so their effort will reduce – however tempting you make the opportunity to earn more.

Broadly speaking, there are three categories of motivation: extrinsic, intrinsic and altruistic. Each of us tends toward one (or a combination) of these and, by being aware of this when you talk to individual team members, you'll soon be able to ascertain which one's most important to them.

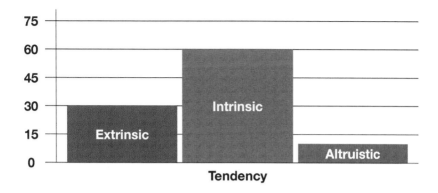

Extrinsic motivation, as the name suggests, includes external rewards such as money, expensive cars, trophies and certificates that demonstrate your success to the outside world. It can be a huge driving force. After all, just think how much pain some people will push themselves through in training to win a trophy in sport.

People who are extrinsically motivated will work hard and push themselves to achieve commissions and bonuses linked to their results. By setting himself the goal of buying a yacht within three years, for example, one accountant I know motivated himself to build the practice he needed for that to happen. However, extrinsic motivators aren't just limited to tangibles. For some people they include intangibles such as (public) praise and recognition – a standing ovation when they perform, perhaps – and they can also be negative: *"Do this or you'll get fired."*

For some roles – ones that include repetitive activities in which the only requirement is an increase in speed, quality and accuracy are easily assessed to ensure the minimum standard continues to be met – extrinsic motivation works well. It also used to be common in sales, although now recognising that it might encourage employees away from what's best for the customer, many used-car outlets have switched to a standard commission regardless of the cars sold. This way, the purchaser is more likely to get what's best for them rather than being encouraged towards a more expensive option simply so the salesperson can get a bigger commission.

Intrinsic motivation, meanwhile, is driven by a person's internal desire to achieve and to do a job well (and their reward for doing so is to feel good). Of course, they might still appreciate an external reward, but it should be in recognition of their doing a great job rather than a carrot to try to persuade them to do one.

Why Financial Incentives Inhibit Quality Thinking

This is why it's crucial to make time to listen to your people and to understand what's important to them. By doing so, you'll be able to reward them with a sincere "thanks" or "well done" and an occasional, personal surprise that you know they'll really appreciate – whether it's a small bonus, extra time off to spend with their family, or (if they have an anniversary coming up, for example) a meal-for-two gift voucher. Just make sure such rewards are irregular.

Finally, altruistic motivation is a person's desire to help others, often even at the expense of their own wellbeing. (Interestingly, research suggests that this could, to an extent, be underpinned by intrinsic motivation – a feeling of pride, guilt or shame – and/or extrinsic motivation – the desire for others to see and to recognise the good they do.) People who fall within this group are more likely to be motivated by you making a donation to a charity than a personal bonus.

Often, of course, we're motivated by a combination of all three. Someone who's intrinsically motivated toward achieving their objectives might still enjoy recognition for doing a great job and be pleased that their company gives back to the community in some way.

44

Behaviours And Communications In The Workplace – DISC

As it's a useful refresher, this chapter is taken from my book 'What's Next For Accountants – How to Make the Biggest Threat Facing the Profession Your Biggest Opportunity'. However, I know that understanding of DISC and its various spin offs is becoming more widespread, so do feel free to skip ahead to the next chapter.

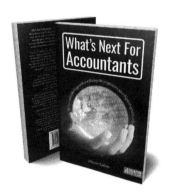

For thousands of years people have been trying to understand one another. In 1928 William Moulton Marston wrote a book called *'The Emotions of Normal People'*. In it, he described how although we all have very different personalities, formed by our unique experiences, values and beliefs, deep down there are many characteristics common to us all. He'd also discovered that these characteristics fall in to four main areas:

- Dominance (**D**)
- Influence (**I**)
- Steadiness (**S**)
- Compliance (**C**).

Each area forms a heading for a group of characteristics, and each characteristic contains a sliding scale of intensity. For example, 'Dominance' might range anywhere from 'Highly Dominant' to 'Highly Submissive.'

Although the four areas can't offer a complete personality analysis, a knowledge of them can help you understand what motivates people; how best to communicate (technical or big picture) with each person; and the type of work (leadership or sales etc) they might be best at. It's even possible to identify when frustration might arise and why.

I've used this type of personal profiling since 2008[†]. It's been useful in many situations – from making sure I recruit the right person, through to regularly profiling teams (to reveal any frustrations or to spark discussion) and customers (so we can tailor our approach and language to them).

It's important, then, to appreciate that not everyone can take on similar functions. Without going in to too much detail here, you can ascertain someone's profile by asking them to complete an online questionnaire which will produce a graph and report.
Below are a couple of brief examples.

High Dominance

- Goal-oriented and self-driven. Avoids failure at all costs – will happily work long hours and be incredibly resourceful to make sure jobs get done
- Unchallenged, may become bored and stir up trouble
- Not keen on detailed work, but will do it if necessary and as long as it's not repetitive or constant
- Outspoken and critical of those who don't meet their standards. Often hurts or upsets people without knowing. Can be explosive, but doesn't hold grudges.
- Not a 'people person,' but remains positive in antagonistic environments
- Once a project's challenge is over, prefers to leave the finishing-off to others.

High Influence

- Hates detail
- Incredibly positive – tends to get on with anyone and everyone
- Makes decisions based on summary analysis
- A 'people person', great at motivating and persuading others
- Loves to help others achieve their objectives – although as such, may fall behind on their own
- Motivated by public recognition – likely to display trophies and awards
- Strives to avoid rejection.

---

† Although there are many tools out there - including some free ones - I've found Thomas International **www.thomasinternational.net** reliable and their support and training incredibly good. (They insist you become accredited in feeding back results in a neutral, non-judgemental and conversational manner, which leads to better understanding). In my experience, free sites tend to provide 'canned' feedback, which risks pigeonholing people.

High Steadiness

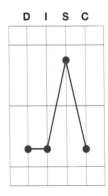

- Patient, kind and amiable. A great listener with a natural desire to help others
- If upset, tends to conceal it. If their frustration builds sufficiently, explosive. Can hold grudges
- Resistant to change, strives to maintain the status quo
- Family- and team-oriented. Uncomfortable away from their families
- Forms close-knit groups and strong bonds. Works best as part of a team and is a good organiser
- Completer-finishers.

High Compliance

- Task-oriented
- Technically minded; requires and gathers lots of information in order to take on a task or to make a decision
- Tends to be a perfectionist – a great strength as long as it doesn't slow down a project
- Always operates within standard procedures because rules are important to them
- Good at research – likes detail and wants everything they do to be 100% correct
- Naturally cautious
- Doesn't tend to be a 'people person,' but is loyal and adaptable (particularly to avoid conflict).

Although many of us, of course, belong to a combination of categories and are able to switch between them depending on our environment, we're usually more prominent in one. For each particular role, then, you should look for someone's preferred work profile. (Remember, however, that someone falling below the central line on a graph isn't evidence of weakness so much as a sign that they possess different strengths. Low-influence people, for example, tend to reflect on information rather than rushing in to make a decision straightaway. Similarly, low-dominance people tend to be accommodating, and hesitate to make a decision unless it falls within their expertise).

Each person's blend of attributes can also be illustrated on a graph. The one overleaf, for example, shows a profile of High S and C with Low D and I. The higher above the centre line an attribute scores, the more prominently an individual will display it.

Understanding people's strengths and playing to them will always get results. Giving a task that requires the characteristics of a High-Dominance person to a High-Steadiness one is likely to lead to frustration for the delegator, and discomfort – perhaps even inability – for the person to whom it's been delegated.

For a team to be successful – whether it's a project team or a Board of Directors – it needs to be comprised of all four personality types. The way a task is delegated should also differ according to the profile of who it's delegated to. Whereas a High-Compliance person will require lots of detail, a High-Influence one won't thank you for it. Similarly, if a High-Influence person is delegating to a High-Compliance one, they may not provide all the information the latter needs to feel confident in their role.

That's why I find profiling such a great tool. It helps you gain an understanding of how best to communicate; at which type of projects and roles an individual will excel; and how they're motivated. In terms of communicating, it serves as a great reminder that:

- **High D's** prefer you to get straight to the point, with no lengthy detail or chit-chat about the weekend (after all, that's in the past). Make a task challenging, keep your conversation short and sweet, give them a tight deadline – and then leave them to it.

- **High I's** love to talk about themselves, so start by asking what they did over the weekend. Once you're ready to move on to why you wanted to talk to them, they'll want to know you're asking them because of how great they are (and I don't mean on a superficial level). They want to know you're asking them because they're the right person). They enjoy recognition – and as much of it as possible in public.

- **High S's** are family- and team-oriented, so start by asking about their family. Next, as invariably saying 'yes' to work can mean they become overwhelmed, check their current workload. Once you're satisfied, move on to describe your expected outcome clearly and ask for their input. Let them know you're there to support them and that they should come to you as and when they need to.

- **High C's** are task-oriented and – like High D's – won't enjoy talking about the weekend or their family. Get straight to the point, but this time go into detail (and then more detail again). High C's need as much information as they can get. Talk through the task, describe the outcome and any guiding principles and rules. (High C's have a tendency to overcomplicate unless you set boundaries.) As they're great planners, let them produce an action plan but set a deadline and go through it with them before they start work. Also set up regular milestones. High C's are perfectionists and unless deadlines are – mutually – agreed they may keep working on tasks for longer than necessary.

As a high-dominance, high-influence person myself, I suspect I enjoy profiling because it helps me to get the best out of people, to motivate them and to get the job done. If you want to get the best out of people, too, I really do encourage you to learn more about it. It will help you appreciate that we all have different strengths, as well as the benefits of taking the time to understand the type of task you want to delegate and the type of individual you should delegate it to.

Communicating in the right way and understanding the type of language to use is crucial if you're to get the best out of your team. Remember, a great leader always adapts their style to get the best out of people rather than expecting people to adapt to theirs.

45

Accountabilities

Do you have accountabilities in place for your team? It's a question I often ask and the response is usually *"No"* or a blank look. So why are accountabilities so important? And how do they differ from conventional job descriptions?

Job descriptions usually detail all the tasks an individual will get involved in and/or be responsible for. However, as they're often extremely detailed, they can narrow an employee's focus and suppress their use of judgment. In addition, unless it clearly states a task, job descriptions can support an employee's argument if a situation arises in which you feel that they should have done (or be doing) more.

Do you remember how, when I explained the difference between leadership and management, I argued that management focuses on controlling people? Well, putting in place detailed, rigid job descriptions is a good example. A further problem with job descriptions becomes clear when you consider that every business has various functions. The function of answering the phone, for example, will likely fall to the role of receptionist. If you're a one-person set-up, however, you'll do it (switching from your MD/CEO role, to that of receptionist). Likewise, if you're having a conversation with a prospective client, you've switched to the role of salesperson or – since sales is a scary word these days! - to that of Business Development Manager!

Accountabilities are very different from job descriptions in that they simply set out the outcomes, the metrics and the purpose of the functions within the business, but don't micro-manage.

It's important to start by identifying the roles that exist within your business. All businesses, for example, require leadership, marketing, finance and operations, so identify the different roles (even if you currently fill them all) within each of these areas. Next, you need to bring clarity to these roles. For example: Who's the first person someone speaks to when they enter or call your office? If you have a receptionist, have you written down what they're accountable for when greeting visitors and callers?

Below is an example of the accountabilities that AVN has in place for our receptionist role. (Although I prefer the term 'First Impressions' to 'receptionist,' since effectively that's what the person who fills the role does on our behalf).

ACCOUNTABILITY

Role: First Impressions

Accountable to: Head of Finance

Purpose: Wow our visitors and everyone who communicates with us by ensuring that every interaction they have with us is amazing.

Systems for this Role can be located in: System Builder

When using judgement, be guided by our values:
- Own it
- Inspiring 'wows'
- Fun, with a serious intent
- Keep evolving
- Make lives better

Accountabilities:
- Answering the door with a welcoming smile and directing guests as appropriate
- Ensuring that customer information is accurately stored in our database so all new and existing customers are up and running quickly and we're able to use the inputted data to wow them
- Answering the telephone politely and seeking to understand and help the caller as much as possible before escalating the call
- Processing of all inbound email boxes, acknowledging receipt of emails instantly and aiming to resolve each query within a maximum of 24 hours
- Helping out with administrative tasks – from helping with outgoing and incoming postings to preparing for, tending to and tidying up after events.

At AVN, we've found that detailing - and even laminating - the accountabilities for each role reminds each person of what performing it looks like. Notice, too, that each accountability starts with a word ending in 'ing.' In other words, they describe ongoing occurrences, not ones that stop once a target is reached. And each has to be dealt with either reactively (answering the phones) or proactively (helping out with admin).

The precise way each accountability should be conducted - the 'How To' - is then described within the system for that role. I'll go into this in more detail in the Automation section but, for now (and simply to whet your appetite!) the system for answering the phone provides a script such as: *"Good morning, Bloggins and Co, Lucy speaking. How may I help?"* along with guidance such as remembering to smile when answering (listeners can tell whether someone is smiling or frowning) and to answer on the second ring (research has shown that earlier than that can startle a caller, while longer gives them the impression that their call isn't important).

Remember to consider the role and requirements before you consider the person who might currently be in it. After all, your business needs to reflect what you want for the future rather than choices you've made in the past. So take humans out of the equation, detail the accountabilities of each role, and then find the right person to fill it. Imagine that each role is like Cinderella's glass slipper. It won't fit everyone but, when you do find the right person, they'll bring the role to life.

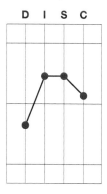

There's also a number of other factors to take into account. To remind you of what we learned in the previous chapter, as I want someone with good people skills for this role they'll need to have a high I and S profile. And, as they'll need to approach each query in a systematic way and be meticulous in maintaining our database, a high C profile (although not necessarily as high as their I and S) is important, too. To capture this, I created the DISC graph below and then listed the most common characteristics a person with it is likely to have.

- Detail-oriented
- Systematic
- Methodical
- Organised
- Friendly

- Accommodating
- Kind
- Communicative
- Patient
- Thorough
- Tenacious
- Supportive
- Dependable
- Compliant
- Loyal
- Sincere
- Non-antagonistic
- Precise
- Steady
- Asks "why?", "how?" and "who?"

This process needs to be replicated for each and every role in your business. Some roles might not require a full-time person, but each should still be kept separate and contain clear outcomes. When a person takes on that role they can then see what they need to achieve to fulfill it successfully. If someone is given multiple part-time roles, you also need to make sure they understand how to prioritise their time between them. If, as your business grows, one of the roles gradually becomes full-time, the role itself won't change, you simply need to give it to another person.

Some roles – such as a Client Manager, marketing or salesperson – lend themselves to metrics. If so, indicate these clearly below the accountabilities. In the case of a Client Manager, for example, the accountability of producing a set of accounts in itself isn't sufficient. If only one set is produced in a week, this is unlikely to be profitable. The measure may not be turnaround time either. Instead it may be Gross Recurring Fee income, together with other important metrics for the year.

In a great example of removing the restraints and creating an environment that allows teams to flourish, some AVN members whose Client Manager roles include acquiring new clients have metrics around their own Gross Recurring Income. In addition, rather than paying them on a typical nine to five basis, they've implemented 'ROWE' (Results-Only Work Environment). In other words, as long as clients are happy that they can communicate with their Client Manager and that work is turned around in line with their preferences (and within government deadlines, of course) the partners don't mind which hours their Client Managers work, or where they work from.

A metric around Gross Recurring Income involves setting a figure over and above the Client Manager's salary to ensure they're delivering a profit to the business and that the onus is on them to take on customers or price existing ones at a 'value-priced' rate. If they don't, they'll have to work with a greater volume of customers to meet the target. If, however, they do price effectively, they can work with fewer customers (and therefore less hours) per week to achieve the same outcome.

A word of warning though: If you remember my discussion around selective attention, you probably realise that having just one metric in place might lead to tunnel vision. That's why you should balance Gross Recurring Income with 'Client Happiness,' for example.

It's also important to note that the above discussion applies equally to outsourcing. Be clear about what the role looks like and how it should be conducted. That way, when you come to outsource, you're much more likely to get the results you want.

46

Giving Feedback
(Difficult Or Pleasant)

Everyone needs feedback. We all want to know if we're doing a good job or not. And yet feedback - either positive or negative - is rarely given quickly or regularly enough.

Neglecting to give positive feedback can lead to your team feeling demotivated and unappreciated. Their 'over and above' effort will stop and at some point they'll move on. On the other hand, neglecting to give feedback around negative behaviours allows these to become habits and, as the line continues to be crossed - generally further each time - handling the situation becomes increasingly difficult.

Admittedly, it's not always easy to give positive or negative feedback. (Ironically, positive can be just as difficult for some of us). It's why our default position is often: *"Let sleeping dogs lie!" "After all"*, our reasoning goes, *"they're only doing what I pay them for, so why should I tell them they're doing a great job? Especially when they might want a pay rise!"* But, as I've explained, whether we're motivated intrinsically or extrinsically, we all like to know we're doing a good job.

The key to giving both positive and negative feedback is:
Be timely; be specific; be genuine. If, for example, it's positive:
1. Talk to the person instantly
2. Describe exactly what happened
3. Ask why they did it
4. Describe how you felt about it
5. Describe the impact doing it might have on others (customers, team, quality etc)
6. Encourage them to keep doing it
7. Say, *"Well done!"*

If it's negative:
1. Talk to the person instantly
2. Describe exactly what happened
3. Ask why they did it
4. Describe how you felt about it
5. Describe the impact doing it might have on others (customers, team, quality etc)
6. Encourage them to recommend a better way(s) to do it next time and agree on one
7. Say, *"Well done!"* to them for coming up with a better method.

As you'll notice, in both cases the process is almost exactly the same. In addition, both scenarios end positively, and limit conversation to the event and to the thinking behind why it happened and what led to a particular outcome, rather than making it personal.

To illustrate what I mean, here's an example of giving negative feedback in the wrong way:

You: *"John, I heard you answering the phone the other day. You sounded very grumpy and were clearly in a bad mood. It's not good enough – you need to be more cheerful on the phone."*

Or even positive feedback:

You: *"You're doing a great job, John. Keep it up!"*

In the first example, not only did the speaker wait for a few days (which makes remembering a specific incident difficult), they also failed to make any attempt at conversation or to understand the situation. They simply told John off. Meanwhile, in the second example, their praise was superficial. What – specifically – is John doing a great job at? Making tea?

Here's how that first conversation could have taken place:

You: *"John, I heard you on the phone just now and you didn't sound very cheery. Is everything alright?"*

John: *"Yes, everything's fine. It's just the way I speak!"*

You: *"Right, well I'm glad you're okay, but. you sounded a little grumpy, I thought that if that was me on the other end of the line, personally I'd feel like I couldn't talk to you. So it might mean that a customer – or even a prospective customer – doesn't feel welcome. Does that make sense?"*

John: *"Well, I'm not sure what I can do about it. It's just my voice – I'm not great on the phone."*

You: *"Alright, well, this is really important, so let's discuss some ways you can sound a little more cheery on the phone because when I speak to you normally you sound fine. What is it about speaking on the phone that makes you uncomfortable?"*

[You then discuss this together and both agree that if John takes a deep breath prior to answering, smiles and pretends he's talking to his mother, he'll come across much better].

You: *"Thanks for being so open to improving on this, John. I think what we've agreed will have a great impact on our customers. Well done!"*

As you can see, the issue has now been addressed but in a conversational, non-confrontational manner and, rather than feeling disgruntled that he's just been told off, John's feeling positive and has himself been involved in coming up with a solution.

Remember: Giving negative feedback doesn't have to be negative in itself. Treat everyone as though they're genuinely trying their best and seek to understand why something has happened in the way that it has. You can then work together on how best to overcome it or to prevent it from happening again.

Now, here's how the example of giving positive feedback could have gone:

You: *"John, I just heard you on the phone with that customer. It sounded fantastic – I thought you came across as really cheerful and enthusiastic. What was it that made you sound so great?"*

John: *"I don't know. It's just my natural phone manner – and winning personality – I suppose!"*

You: *"Well, I really liked it. You sounded really welcoming and represented the business really positively. I imagine the customer felt a real connection and as if they could discuss anything with you. You'll have left a real positive mark on them so do please keep it up. Well done!"* 🙂
(Yes, the smiley face is a reminder to smile as you say this!)

Follow my suggestions above, and both parties will feel positive going forward.

47

Dealing With The Child Inside

Have you ever been in the middle of a conversation with someone, perhaps about their performance or behaviour, when they suddenly:
- Burst into tears?
- Respond aggressively or have what can only be described as a tantrum?
- Go really quiet and then sulk for hours – if not days?

If so, as well as feeling really awkward and guilty, you may have responded by trying to soothe them. You may even have changed tack completely, perhaps softening your initial concern and becoming a little more encouraging. However, as long as you've been conducting yourself in a professional manner, presenting the facts and keeping to a specific event or behaviour rather than making it personal, my advice is that if any of the above does happen, then don't react in the way I've just described.

As children we develop mechanisms – such as crying, having a tantrum or sulking – that help us to get our own way or to make our parents feel guilty when they've told us off. If our parents allow these to work, then such tactics stay with us into adulthood.

In the case of tears or tantrums, my recommendation is to explain to the person that you're suspending the meeting for a few moments to allow them to compose themselves, and that you'll then resume it. Once they realise their response isn't going to mitigate the reprimand, they'll start to amend their behaviour. It may sound a little unsympathetic at first, but responses such as those I've mentioned above – by making it personal – simply allow the employee to divert attention from them having to face up to a shortcoming.

48

Radiators And Drains

I'm sure you've heard the expression about people being like radiators or drains? Some people are like radiators – radiating positive energy, they're happy and bouncy and instantly make you feel more positive, too – and others are like drains. The drains are the people who always seem to be down in the dumps; they're forever insisting on sharing something negative that's just happened to them (it's always to them) and sap the energy from a room as soon as they walk in.

So who do you want to surround yourself with? With radiators or drains? And – even more importantly – which of the two are you?

A good friend of mine, Jonathan, is the retired partner of a five-partner practice and used to speak at some AVN events about his journey with us, and about how it had helped his practice to grow and transform its service delivery. As well as talking about how his practice had been transformed though, Jonathan explained that he had been, too.

It's probably fair to say that most of us don't stop to think about how we convey ourselves until we're asked (or forced) to. But, as good leadership is key to running and growing a successful business, we cover it a lot in our training – which meant Jonathan finally had to face up to his behaviour. In fact, he realised that he'd been a drain for many years. As he stood on stage, he'd admit to the room that in the past he used to arrive at work most mornings looking stern and - annoyed after his commute or simply focused on the day ahead - barely greeting a soul. His employees would have most likely thought, *"Hmm, he's in a bad mood again. Better keep my head down."* The atmosphere would have become subdued and morale with it. In other words, his behaviour set the tone for the rest of the office.

But we don't have to bring our bad mood to work with us, do we? It's a choice. After all, I'm sure there'll have been occasions in your own past when – just after an argument with someone or after you've been upset by something - you've bumped into someone you haven't seen for years and instantly put on a smile and greeted them warmly (rather than bombarding them with your problems). Whether, after they've gone, you choose to fall back into your previous mood is, of course, up to you. My guess though is that you probably don't - or not to the same extent, anyway, since the mere act of smiling (however hollow it may feel to begin with) usually makes you feel better.

In our events, Jonathan went on to describe that, once he realised the effect he was having, he made a conscious decision that (no matter what he actually felt like) on entering his practice he would take a deep breath, smile and take a few minutes to greet everyone; to ask how they were and to listen to their response. (In other words, to be genuinely interested). And, he explained, the difference this made was profound. Not only did it make him and his team feel great, but when your team feels great, their performance increases, customer service improves - and your financial performance does, too. (In case you need a further reason to smile!)

The culture in your practice, begins with you. If you're a drain, be aware that you'll soon end up surrounded by similar people since the more positive ones will move on.

But what if, although you do your best to be a radiator, you have people who are drains in your team? I've certainly experienced this and have seen the impact they can have on team morale. (As you'll have noticed, I value having fun in the office. After all, we spend so much time away from our families, that office life ought to be fun - albeit balanced with still getting things done, of course!)

Over the years I've had many conversations with 'drains' who, when I ask if they're aware of their impact, answer that they have problems and that no one can be expected to smile every day. (Of course, while that's true, failing to smile 365 days a year is still impressive!) I've also learned that there are many reasons for their behaviour. Some 'drains,' for example, thrive on the attention of the carers in the team rushing over to ask, *"What's wrong? Tell me all about it."* Others are simply not right for your practice and, by continuing to work there, will affect its culture negatively. In my experience, no matter how closely you work with someone to try to make them fit, if the culture is alien to them the attempt will be futile.

Another reason for their behaviour might be that they simply don't enjoy their current role. If you honestly believe that they fit your values and culture, but aren't playing to their strengths (or simply feel unfulfilled), explore the possibilities together. If you can offer them a different role, great. If not, help them to find a job that's a better fit.

Of course it's also possible that they're genuinely suffering from depression, which isn't something to be taken lightly. It's only by talking to people who are drains though that you'll discover the reason for their behaviour. In the case of depression, it may be that by talking and genuinely listening you can encourage them to seek help. (If you do discover that someone in your team is suffering from depression, I also suggest you seek professional advice on how you can best support them).

49

The Winter Blues

Following our conversation at the end of the previous chapter, I have to confess that when I was younger I didn't understand depression. I thought that everyone was capable of choosing how they felt and that they should simply 'snap out of it.' As I've grown older, however, I've learned more about it and about how sometimes our bodies simply stop producing the 'right' chemicals, leading to an imbalance that can affect us in many ways - including depression.

There is also what I call the 'winter blues.' You may, for example, assume that someone in your team has turned into a drain when they're actually suffering from this - perhaps without being aware of it. While seeking professional advice is always the best option, I hope the story below will at least help you to identify it should it ever affect any of your team, your family, your friends - or even yourself.

When I hit my mid-30s, I noticed how I regularly began to struggle to be positive. I would see the negative in any situation or decide that an idea simply wouldn't work. This would last for perhaps two or three weeks and then I'd come out of it. However, it took me a few years to realise that this always coincided with the clocks changing in October, just as the longer nights and shorter days began. My negative state would kick in from that point and gradually get worse until the winter solstice, when, as the days slowly began to get longer, I'd begin to feel better.

A little research quickly brought me to SAD (Seasonal Affective Disorder), but - out of sheer stubbornness - I decided not to see a doctor. (In my mind at that time, resorting to tablets felt like losing a battle). I knew that exercise helped with depression and, since I didn't do very much of it at that time, as October approached I committed myself to running regularly. And it worked. That winter I stayed positive. *"Great!"* I thought, as I set myself an annual reminder to start running regularly each October, *"I've cracked it!"*

A few years later though, running stopped having any effect. I assumed my SAD was getting worse and – because I was aware of the impact it had on my team, in Board meetings, and at home – this bothered me. A little more research suggested that I needed more light, so I made sure I got out of the office at lunchtime to go for a walk, and bought a special SAD blue-light box. Again this seemed to work for a few years, but then had less and less effect. I also discovered that our bodies need daylight to create vitamin D, so off to the shop went my wonderful wife to buy me some of those, too.

Should you or one of your team, family or friends ever find themselves in a similar situation, here's a list of what I've found most helpful:
- Blue light – preferably shining in my face whilst I'm having breakfast
- Vitamin D tablets – again, with breakfast
- Exercise – preferably at lunchtime, as it's still light
- A wake-up light – it helps me to wake up naturally
- Booking a holiday somewhere sunny when the clocks change.

50

Finding The Right People

Once employers have determined the role to be filled, most will list the day-to-day tasks required and then either use an agency to recruit or advertise directly using the various online and offline platforms available. Once CVs start to arrive, they'll filter them down to around five and then invite the chosen candidates for an interview where they'll be interrogated about their work history. The person with the right qualifications and references, who comes across as the most positive or who's best at selling themselves, then gets the job.

The successful candidate starts and is shown the ropes, learning about the business (or at least as much about it as they're told), and getting to know the other members of the team. In the early weeks, they make a big effort to create a good impression and to pass their probation period. Bit by bit, though, they begin to relax and to act 'normally'. However, even if they're a high-performer whose normal is still high, it doesn't necessarily mean that they're right for your business. As I mentioned in the Values section, if their values aren't in line with yours, they're unlikely to connect with what you're striving to achieve. In fact, they can easily start to affect the culture you've fought so hard to create, or even poison it with their comments or 'jokes' about the way you want to do things.

Before I fully understood why values are so important and how best to recruit people whose values match your own, I'd certainly been on the receiving end of this. It's why now, when we recruit at AVN, we use a process that we've developed over many years, one in which we consider DISC profile, attitude and ingenuity. (I want people who can figure things out for themselves).

Don't forget though that simply asking candidates if they agree with your values isn't going to cut it. You'll need to check by asking them to share stories of how they dealt with certain situations in the past.

51

Focusing Your Team On The Customer

As you can no doubt tell, leadership and recruiting the 'right' people is a subject I'm passionate about. But, once you've created a great environment in which people can flourish and become the best they can be, how do you ensure they think of the customer (spotting opportunities and becoming more commercial when looking at the numbers in their accounts) in everything they do?

Frustratingly, many accountants get used to producing accounts as if they were working on a production line, without ever really taking the time to analyse them or to discover trends that might reveal problems. (For example, if the business owner is gradually working harder for less, or cashflow's getting worse). It might seem obvious, but I've heard too many examples of qualified team members failing to make the connection that poor numbers can herald disaster. They simply keep churning them out.

Similarly, others may have focused on function for so long that the word 'client' no longer means anything to them. The client may be a parent with a family depending on them, or have hobbies and interests they'd like to pursue (rather than spending every waking moment in their business), but too many qualified team members (and some practice owners, too, sadly) have lost this human connection. It's almost an irritation when a client phones with a question and meetings often become a tedious round of going through their accounts demonstrating that they've dotted the I's and crossed the T's.

While I hope I've painted a much bleaker picture than the one that exists in your practice, do you remember how, in the Value section, I described a customer's experience of phoning and visiting two different accounting firms? Which experience do you think customers and potential customers have when they call or visit yours?

Do your team members walk through reception and ignore anyone who's waiting there because it's not them they're there to see? I've certainly been on the receiving end of this. Over the years I've lost count of the number of accountancy practices I've visited in which, even though the receptionist is pleasant, other employees have walked past without even the faintest of acknowledgment of me. How did it make me feel? Not very welcome, that's for sure. (I've also entered buildings in which the paint is chipped, the wallpaper's started to peel off and I certainly haven't been brave – or foolish – enough to use the toilet).

As I explained, simply telling your team to think more about the customer won't work. If you really want to make a difference, you need to engage them in exercises to think through the whole customer experience and to come up with ways to improve it. Personally, I involve my team every time we look at improving the customer experience. Even if I have my own idea, rather than share it with them I'll start by explaining the concern(s) I hope to overcome.

For example, if I feel that customers are having to make more effort to book themselves onto one of our events than they should, I'll encourage the team to put themselves in the customer's shoes. If they were busy, would they be more likely to persevere or to simply give up? If so, what are the repercussions of this? (Questions like these help them to understand the situation from the customers' point of view). Once they've done this, we'll map out this part of the customer journey together, put each stage on the wall, and then brainstorm ways to improve the experience at each.

Involving the team in this way means they buy in to the concept – after all, they're their ideas. We then agree which of the (hopefully many) ideas we'll use and divide up the responsibility of making them happen. Finally, we check back with weekly progress reports and agreed deadlines.

52

Conscious Leadership

I use the term 'conscious leadership' as a reminder that most people aren't natural leaders. Instead, we need to be consciously aware of how we behave and interact with others in our communications and demeanour.

I know that I've focused a lot in this section on what you may consider to be the more psychological aspects of understanding what makes people tick. It's because I strongly believe it's crucial to appreciate that we're all different and that, rather than switching off when someone thinks or communicates in a different way to us, we view their input as something incredibly useful that otherwise we might not have considered.

To return to DISC profiles, there's a good chance that a high-I individual with low C won't appreciate detail, while a high C needs a lot of it if they're to fulfil their role which can, by the high I, be seen as 'information for the sake of

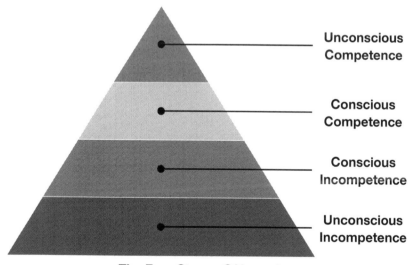

The Four Stages Of Learning

information.' If this happens (and it often does, in fact I've been involved in such debates) compromises have to be sought. With a little discussion and some give and take on both sides, solutions can always be found. Adapting your approach doesn't mean you lose control or compromise on standards, it simply means you spend time seeking to understand first, then to be understood.

I mentioned earlier that I don't consider myself to be a natural leader, but I do know what good leadership looks like and I make a conscious effort to replicate it. And, as I do so, those habits gradually become my own.

If you're aware of the four stages of learning, you'll know that they start with 'unconscious incompetence.' In other words, we habitually do things that aren't right without even realising it. Sooner or later though, something happens which makes us realise and we move on to 'consciously incompetent'. (An improvement, as at least we now know that we need to improve!)

The next stage, 'conscious competence' comes when we learn a better way to do things, but it still takes a lot of effort. I liken this stage to the early days of learning to drive: you know everything you should be doing, but you still have to concentrate on which gear you're in, how high the revs are and how fast you're going. In fact, there are so many things to consider at the same time that it can feel overwhelming. Gradually, however, most of the tasks become habitual and you're able to do them almost without thinking, leaving all the work to your internal autopilot. At which stage – congratulations! – you've reached the stage of 'unconscious competence.'

I recommend that you apply the above thinking to your own leadership skills by recognising ('conscious incompetence') when you've dealt with a situation poorly or avoided dealing with it at all. To remind you of my gardener analogy: You need to nip any issues in the bud. If not, however trivial they may seem at first, they'll be harder to deal with in the long term. If you're faced with a problem, take a breath and remind yourself of my recommendations in the feedback section.

As long as you have the right team in place, they'll take feedback on the chin and strive to implement the agreed outcome.

53

Award-Winning Gearing

I'll end this section with the winning entry for AVN Firm of the Year 2017, from AVNExcellence 6-Star accredited firm MDH, based in Croydon. MDH also won our 2019 Customer-Focused Team award. Incidentally, the entry was written by a member of owner Michael Hemme's team...

"If time, resources and exceptional team members were in limitless supply, running MDH would be a breeze. The reality is, it's a continuous juggling act between how best to use our time – be that to develop systems, provide training and development for our people, or find new ways to deliver an exceptional service. Even writing those words makes us wobble a little – it really is one of the biggest challenges every business has to face, but we think we're winning. Here are a few of the things we've learned, or been reminded of, in the last year.

Successful businesses invest in their team. Not just in external training (and we do plenty of that), but in them as individuals. Nobody arrives at the office and leaves 'themselves' at the door – we are who we are, and no amount of training will change our underlying personality. We can all work to improve ourselves, perhaps to be more open to change or more tolerant of other people, but our basic human characteristics remain – which is why we believe it's best to acknowledge what these are, to understand them and to work with a person's 'true' self rather than trying to mould someone into something they're not.

We start with a 'Talent Dynamics' assessment (similar to DISC) to dig into an individual's natural disposition: where their strengths lie, areas they're less comfortable with, and their innate lean towards specific styles of communication or thinking. For example, are they detail-orientated and precise, or creative and more chaotic in their thought process? No trait is right or wrong, but they do impact the way we can work together.

We share this information with the team. It enables us all to communicate more effectively. We know what the person sitting opposite us needs to perform at their best and we take responsibility for ensuring that they have this.

We seek out new team members who bring a different way of thinking to the table. People who have natural skills which suit the needs of the team – perhaps someone has all the natural characteristics of a great salesperson, but has never sold a thing in their life. If so, that's alright. We're happy to teach them if the basic skills come naturally to them and they have a desire to learn.

This process helps us find the right people to occupy the seats at our table. The seats around our table are continually changing. As the team grows, both in numbers and personal achievements and development, responsibilities are passed on and redistributed. There's no strict hierarchy, it's about fitting the right task to the right person and ensuring that everyone is contributing in equal measure to our overall success.

We monitor our team capacity monthly. Data from personal one-page plans, which includes current jobs and tasks outstanding, income targets and personal development achievements, are fed into our Gross Recurring Fee plan. It shows us instantly if the team is over-capacity (e.g. their tasks outstanding are growing), which triggers the process to recruit.

It takes time to find the right people to join our team. We look for the person, rather than the individual with the right qualifications. This means it can take longer for the person to receive the training and guidance to deliver our service in an exceptional way.

This is why we monitor our capacity so frequently and act quickly. We don't wait for the 'storm to pass' – we aim for our team to be best-positioned to delight our customers.

Everything we do at MDH is built on the foundation of our values: honesty, heart, focus, being action-orientated and inspiring. We apply these principles both to our work internally (in developing best-in-class systems and delivery) and externally (helping clients to become the best that they can be). Although lots of companies have a list of values, they're usually written by a marketing team because they 'sound good.' Ours are different. We choose them as a team. They're part of who we are, and they guide us in decision-making and delivery.

Here's just one example of that in action:

A client rang in when Michael was away and asked, *"How can Michael leave his business unattended?"* Natalie, a client manager at MDH, could have simply explained that Michael was on holiday and uncontactable, but she saw an opportunity to deliver on our value promise.

Natalie was honest with the client and explained that the business needed Michael to take time out as, without this vital downtime, he couldn't operate at his best. She went on to explain the amount of investment Michael had made in the team to ensure that delivery was first class, even without him being in the office. Natalie took ownership of the client's query and provided a complete solution. In fact, she went even further and took the opportunity to inspire the customer in how he could achieve the same and get a much-needed break from his business. This is just one example of our values in action.

As a team, we have proved that we can operate without Michael working in the business. When Michael goes on holiday he has minimal contact with the office, he even leaves his mobile phone behind. We have a team member, or in most cases several team members, who can handle 98% of enquiries.

As the members of our team develop and take responsibility for a wider variety of tasks, including sales and marketing, more and more of Michael's time is given over to the strategic planning for the business. This has helped to propel our growth to the next stage.

Michael is spending more time on quality control, using secret shoppers and customer feedback to hone our delivery. He never comes in to 'fix' things himself. It's about training the team to be independent and to deliver above expectation.

Personal development is probably the biggest differentiator to being part of MDH, but that doesn't mean we overlook technical training or industry knowledge.

The team regularly attends events such as TAG, AVN events and Xerocon. It's important for us all to learn about the tools in our industry and to help keep MDH at the forefront of business-growth accountancy."

54

Automation

As a child (or perhaps even recently!), did you ever try going up a down-escalator? Every footstep sinks back to where it began. True, some additional effort might allow you to ascend, but it's so much more effort than it seems, and if you relax for even a second, you'll soon start going backwards again. (Of course, if the escalator were turned off, every step you take would be on solid foundations).

It's the same with a business – it takes effort to establish and to grow. In fact, even to maintain it, since there's always the churn rate to consider and the business relies on you for decisions and input. If you take a holiday, for example, you still need to make sure you're available in some way otherwise your business will begin to slip backward. (The irony is that you work so hard you really need a holiday, yet there you are, working from the beach unable to either relax or unwind).

Unless you stop what I call the 'reverse-escalator syndrome,' your business will never work for you, or be very saleable either. You need to ensure that each step you take toward your goals is supported by a firm, solid structure, and that you don't need to take the same step over and over again.

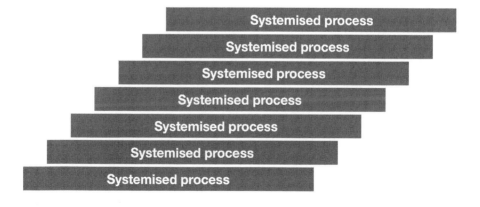

Systemised process

Systemised process

Systemised process

Systemised process

Systemised process

Systemised process

Systemised process

That's why this section will look at building the systems and tapping into the technologies able to provide the solid infrastructure you need if you're to progress (rather than to feel you're stuck on am escalator). After all, we're privileged to be living through exciting times during which there's been a remarkable explosion in technology and, whilst it's true that this will replace some jobs, it will also create opportunities for new ones.

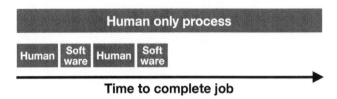

Time to complete job

When AVN works with an accountant to improve their practice, typically we help them put systems in place. That way, even if they don't yet have a team, they can use those systems as a reminder of the extra steps needed to deliver additional value to clients and, of course, as they do develop a team those same systems will enable them to delegate more effectively and to ensure that the extra bells and whistles are maintained and the customer experience remains outstanding.

In this section, I'll address the power of systems and look at the impact of automation and how technology can replace human intervention, thereby freeing people up to carry out higher-level cognitive functions. As technology continues to improve, we can either resist it (which will most likely result in our business failing) or embrace it by letting it take care of the lower-level tasks and using what it produces as human touchpoints.

Although we've now reached the fifth stage in our AVN roadmap, when working with members we certainly don't ignore systems until we reach this point. In fact, right at the beginning of their journey we identify time saving systems which will enable them to delegate more easily (whether to an employee or by outsourcing). And, as they continue their journey, we gradually identify more systems they can adopt.

But, you may ask, if that's the case why do we wait until so late in the roadmap to focus more deeply on systems? Because in reality this part of the process:
1. Identifies the gaps (which areas still require systemising)
2. Revisits the systems already in place to see how they can be enhanced and made more efficient by combining them with the technologies available.

55

Your Way

I've mentioned before that accountants are often perfectionists and even (forgive the term) control freaks. Over the years I've lost count of the number of times I've heard one say that although they have a team of people, they still feel the need to double-check everything to ensure that it's perfect and meets their own high standards.

It's one of the reasons it can be so difficult to grow your practice as, the more it grows, the more burdened you become. If you're not double-checking one member of your team's work, then another one is consulting you about something else. Why? Mostly, I'm afraid, because you've created an environment in which people feel they have to run everything by you because you insist things are done your way. (And no one really understands what that way is because you keep it stored in your head).

I remember one AVN member saying that they were just going to have to let go and give up control. My response was: *"Absolutely not!"* It's your practice, so of course every piece of work and every interaction should be delivered in a way that reflects the reputation you want it to have. Letting go doesn't have to mean giving up control. It simply means putting mechanisms in place to ensure that everything is delivered to the standard you expect every time and – where human initiative is required – decisions are made in line with how you'd want.

I'm sure you already accept that you can't do everything, but I suspect that if you stopped to think about it for a moment you'd find that you're actually doing far more than you should. I recommend that you start by diarising everything you currently do and look for the things that can or should be delegated.

One of the biggest frustrations, perhaps, can come when you start to grow your practice. When you start to build a team by employing already qualified accountants in their own right, you find that each of them comes with their own way of doing things (generally one they've learned from another practice).

This isn't to say that they don't produce great work, but the challenge lies in the inconsistency it can create as each person will have nuances in the way they produce and present data and results.

If you've previously tried to put systems in place, you may also have met with resistance, or been accused of insulting your team's intelligence by trying to tell them how to do a job that not only are they qualified to do, but that – in their eyes – they've been doing successfully for years. (To return to DISC, many accountants are high C's which means they strive to get everything right and hate getting things wrong. If the system you want to introduce is different to how they do things, they'll consider it to be wrong).

However, as systems are key to appeasing your internal control freak and learning to let go, they're both a necessary and an important way to grow your business. If each member of your team produces accounts, conducts meetings, prices for work and even answers the phone in different ways, from a client's perspective it'll be a lucky dip as to whether or not their experience is good and it makes them feel special.

The following may be a commonly used example, but there's a reason for that – it's because McDonald's is such a great illustration of a systemised business. It's what allows them to franchise at least one restaurant per week somewhere around the world. Every time you walk in, whichever country you're in, you're greeted in the same way and the uniforms are, well, uniform! The decor's the same, the way the food is presented is the same, and even the order in which the sauce, lettuce, and gherkins are placed on your burger is the same. Crucially, of course, this is what ensures your experience is the same every time, too.

While we're on the topic of food, the BBC programme 'MasterChef' often features very experienced chefs, some of whom already have their own restaurant, who know how to produce great-quality food and do so every week throughout the series. However, at one point, they have to demonstrate how they perform under even more pressure by being placed in a busy Michelin Star-rated restaurant and tasked with producing one of its signature dishes.

You've probably noticed how this involves them being trained on a system for producing each dish (even if it's something as apparently straightforward as chicken and chips!). The chef has a certain way of doing things and – no matter how much experience the contestants have – the orders are based on exactly the same process. (The chef knows that customers are ordering a specific taste and visual experience and that it has to be produced consistently every time). The chef takes the time to show each contestant, step by step, exactly how long they should cook their dish for, at what temperature, and even where to place each decorative dot of sauce. They're not allowed to start until the chef is satisfied and even then it's checked every single time to ensure consistency. (In the real world, of course, as they gain experience the checking would gradually reduce until it reaches the level of ad hoc quality-assurance checks).

Your clients could have chosen to work with any accountant, but they chose you – which means that the style of work you produce must be replicated by everyone in your team, every time. And it's crucial to explain this to them, to emphasise the importance of consistency so that your clients can be confident that everything will be produced in the way they've come to expect.

Remember, consistency will help you to build the reputation of your practice.

56

Are Systems Robotising Humans?

I think it's fair to say that in many industries the most repetitive, low- to medium-level cognitive jobs are rapidly being replaced by computers or even robots. I'm also fairly confident that if a basic and repetitive role in your practice is currently being performed by a human, then it's 99.9% likely that a £20 - £200 p/m piece of software exists that could perform the same job in a fraction of a second. The result of this – however harsh it may sound – is that employing people to fulfill this role is unviable, unprofitable and inefficient.

If you like to have toast for breakfast, the chances are that you also have an electric toaster. Each morning you simply pop in a slice or two of bread, push the lever down and – hey presto – a couple of minutes later up it pops, toasted to your pre-set preference. If, however, you use a grill, the experience is probably considerably less consistent; partly, at least, because as human beings we're easily distracted and can lose track of time when we try to multitask. (I'm sure I'm not the only person to have burnt my toast because I decided to pop the kettle on or load the dishwasher at the same time). In short, our brains simply don't cope well with multiple tasks and it's easy to miss an important step in a process.

That's why, whenever I prepare a webinar, I use a system to ensure that I structure the content in a specific way that enables the audience to understand the principles it contains in the best way possible. Otherwise, I might rattle on for an hour about something I consider important, but which – without the necessary structure in place – quickly loses the audience.

The reason I started to do this is because during the first few webinars I ran, I used to see a drop in audience numbers as it progressed (which, I have to say, hurt). To try to improve matters (yes, I'd reached the stage of 'conscious incompetence!'), I got in touch with an excellent presenter I know and asked him to watch a recording of one of them. The feedback he gave was incredibly helpful, as rather than focusing on the quality of my content, he drew attention to problems with its structure. Afterwards, I created a system based on his feedback so that every time I developed a presentation in the future I could follow the same structure – and it worked perfectly. (Same content, better structured, better received).

The same applies to marketing. Whether you're writing an email, a letter, a social media post or even creating a video, there's a structure that works and then there's a set of rambling words … And the beauty of using a system to create your structure is that whenever you learn something new, you simply have to tweak the structure rather than having to try to remember to implement the new step every time.

A friend often uses a technique in his presentations that plays on Gestalt psychology (in other words, on our brain's need for completeness). For example, if I were to say *"1, 2, 3, 4"* and then stop before it sounded like I'd completed my sentence, you'd most likely complete it for me by saying *"5"* in your head. (McDonald's cleverly used the same technique a few years ago when one of their ads played a short, catchy tune which then continued into song with the lyrics 'I'm lovin' it.' After a while they dropped the song part, but stopping after the tune simply forced our brains to sing 'I'm lovin' it' for them – and, in the process, to reinforce how much we love McDonald's!)

However, my friend uses the technique to engage and retain his audience. At the beginning of each presentation, he'll begin telling a story but then, at a crucial point, say: "I'll come back to that later." Next, he'll deliver some content around points that he wants to get across, then begin another story, unrelated to the first (even, in some cases, unrelated to his content at all). This succeeds in keeping his audience totally engaged –they don't want to risk missing the end of his stories – until, at the very end, he wraps up by finishing them all.

None of us can remember everything we need to, let alone when we need to. Often, we're likely to remember something we need to add to the agenda of an important meeting whilst we're in the middle of a film in the cinema the night before! That's why systems are essential. They help us to remember the really important things – even if it's simply remembering to smile before we pick up the phone.

57

The Power Of Mistakes

Everyone – even perfectionists – makes mistakes, but it's what you choose to do with those mistakes that makes a profound difference to the success of your practice. All too often, many of us try to cover them up, preferring not to admit to them for fear of being seen as incompetent. Or, we might vow to learn from them as an individual by never making them again. But what happens when someone else in your team makes the same – or even a different – mistake?

In my younger days, I've certainly been on the receiving end of bosses telling me off when I made a mistake, but all such an approach does is to encourage a cover-up mentality. Not only do mistakes happen, you should consider each one a great learning opportunity – both for the person who made it and for the entire team. (After all, if one person made it, it's likely others will). As Eleanor Roosevelt said: *"Learn from the mistakes of others. You can't live long enough to make them all yourself."*

It will take courage and an open-minded team, but imagine a culture in which each member shares mistakes they've made without fear of judgement. Or one in which, after they've done so, instead of making them feel incompetent the whole team focuses on identifying ways to make sure it can't happen again.

Although such a system would be an excellent way to ensure that everyone learns from each other's mistakes, now imagine that you employ a new team member. Unless you've built avoidance mechanisms into your checklists and the steps in your systems, all that group learning will be lost and the process will have to start all over again. As a useful illustration, at one point the medical sector were sending out an average of 7000 white papers a year in an effort to help doctors learn from mistakes that had been made across the country. But trying to read 7000 documents a year on top of doing their day-to-day work simply wasn't possible. Instead, it was decided to send the documents to a dedicated team whose role was to build error-avoidance mechanism into each system or checklist.

What if team discussions around mistakes not only prevented them from happening in the future, but also stimulated creative thinking that led to better methods being implemented overall – whether tapping into new technologies or a new way of processing jobs? Creating this type of environment though has to begin with the partner(s). Otherwise it might suppress openness by making it appear that only junior members of the team are expected to volunteer mistakes, and senior members will feel that the more senior they are, the more infallible they should be.

Ego may get in the way but, if so, I implore you to swallow it. Personally, I find that my team really get behind me when I'm open about a mistake and are incredibly supportive in coming up with great ideas to make sure it doesn't happen again. Show that you're human by sharing your mistakes and opening up team discussions for improvements. Put mechanisms in place that invite team members to share their mistakes (anonymously if necessary) and those of others, as well as their solutions. Although at first this may look as if you're creating a 'tell-tale' environment, avoid this by encouraging impersonal, fact-based reporting and through keeping conversations positive and based around eliminating similar problems in the future. Welcome all ideas – there's no such thing as a bad one, since even these may lead on to a better one.

I recommend that you hold these meetings regularly – whether weekly, fortnightly or monthly – and ensure that each one leads to a specific action(s) to improve the system or checklist concerned, rather than stating, *"Let's all just be more careful in future."* Set clear rules, too. No one should try to find out who made a particular mistake, for example, or prohibit any negative discussion around how it could have happened in the first place.

If, after the fact, it seems impossible that a certain mistake was made, it's usually because the person who made it was under pressure, overwhelmed or distracted. That's why it's important to determine the root cause of what led to a mistake rather than looking at it in isolation.

58

Their Whole Set-Up Stinks

I vividly remember visiting a certain accountancy practice many years ago. Although I visit many practices, this one really stands out – and for a very wrong reason. Upon arriving I was greeted incredibly pleasantly and shown to a waiting area, after which I had a wonderful conversation with the practice owner who then offered to buy me lunch before I set off back to the train station. Never being one to turn down food, I gladly accepted. What happened next though instantly – and permanently – damaged my experience of the visit.

You'll recall that in the Value section I talked through the customer journey and how every single interaction point affects a visitor's perception of your practice, and how each point is as important as the next. (Rob Walsh of Clear Vision, who contributed to this book in an earlier section, often talks about the importance of the doorbell. Does it work or is it hanging off the wall? Is it clean or grubby-looking? Would someone actually want to put their finger on it? After all, it'll often be a visitor's first impression of your practice).

I also discussed the importance of appealing to all five senses – because of their connection to our memory – and that the most powerful memory 'tainter' is smell. Going back to my visit, then, my overall experience was ruined because just before we set out for lunch I nipped to the toilet. I'm sure I don't need to elaborate at this point, and I'm also sure my host would have been mortified if he'd known but, at the time, I chose not to mention it. (Although in hindsight I should have, as that way they could have put precautions in place – perhaps asking the receptionist to always check the toilets before clients arrived – to avoid it ever happening again).

Whether someone visits your practice for 30 seconds or a few hours, if they use your toilets, make sure their lasting impression isn't: "This set-up stinks!"

59

An Inspiring Example Of Systemisation

Throughout this book I've included real-life examples of accountancy practices much like your own, which by implementing the concepts I'm sharing, have seen for themselves the great results and returns this can bring.

Below are two more such examples – and please note that both were written by team members who (despite any fears you may have around resistance) are proud of the systems their firms have put in place. Furthermore, each of them is a fully qualified accountant and client manager.

MDH Chartered Certified Accountants – Croydon

"We want our business to run like clockwork, but without losing our personal connection with clients. We don't expect our people to be machines, but it's vital that our service is consistent – regardless of the team member providing the delivery.

A vital component of our success is trusting that when we're away from the office the process continues without us. The principal example of this is when Michael, the owner of the practice, goes on holiday. Although these are real breaks – he even leaves his mobile phone in the capable hands of the team, knowing that they'll take care of all client queries – it wasn't always like this.

Like many business owners, he rarely switched his phone off. Both his family-time and holidays always had the shadow of work – the odd text and call would lead to a chain of emails. Any business owner can relate to this (and many team members, too). Automation was a key component of tackling this infection. Robust, tested systems enable you to step away, confident that the process will work without you.

When we asked Michael how he felt the first time he went on holiday without his mobile phone, he told us, "There was a range of emotions. Control being one: 'How could the business run without me?' And shades of guilt, too: 'How can a business owner go on holiday and be successful?' 'Will the business operate without my passion?' Now, I genuinely relax. I can't say I don't wonder what's happening or have the occasional pang of guilt, but this is minimal. In an emergency the office can reach me – which has only been necessary twice."

As a team we give 100% when we're at work, but we also give ourselves 100% when we're away from it. It's our systems that have given us this freedom.

We've found that merely developing systems is not enough though. You need systems to monitor the systems and have quality-control checks in place, too. Let me explain ... We're fortunate to have a wealth of new technology at our fingertips. Software such as Xero and QuickBooks provides instant wins for both our clients and ourselves. They make streamlining bookkeeping and management reporting simple. However, as with all systems, if you put garbage in, you get garbage out. So it's not enough to simply have the systems, you need training, processes, procedures and someone monitoring all of these to ensure they're adhered to and improved over time.

It's a big job and one we don't underestimate. The rewards of embracing new technology are huge, but the investment needed to squeeze maximum value from them is high too. We start with team training. Every process we use, including soft skills many people take for granted (such as answering the phone and conducting meetings), to typical client tasks such as entering purchase invoices and preparing year-end accounts is documented and – most importantly – the documented process is followed. A team member is trained in every process on a one-to-one basis and then continues to follow the documentation once they're 'flying solo.' A senior team member reviews their work and provides feedback and guidance on learning points.

There are benefits beyond that of consistent delivery, too. Our team can grow quickly thanks to the simplicity of systemisation. A new team member, or outsourced service provider, can follow the system and deliver, on time, every time. We know how long processes take, so we can budget effectively and protect our margin. A further, huge benefit is team stability. We're ensuring that every team member is set up to succeed, by providing them with all the tools, resources and training they need to excel at their work.

The efficiency we achieve through consistent delivery of compliance services gives us more time to work with clients, engaging with them on their goals, direction and more. There are some simple systems that help us achieve first-class service delivery. For example, we train at least two, usually three, members of the team to handle any enquiry. This ensures clients get the answers they need, when they need them, even when team members are on holiday.

Clients, both current and prospective, can expect prompt communication. Calls are returned within 24 hours and emails responded to on the same day during business hours.

Accounts isn't always about number crunching. It's about helping clients through stressful and confusing changes in their business – and we help them best when we can see them. Body language and expression is essential in helping us understand if a client is happy and comfortable with the solutions we recommend.

We don't restrict this to meetings at their offices or ours though. We use Zoom Meetings to connect online through video. This helps us to respond faster, get a clear understanding of their needs and deliver solutions quickly."

Another great example of the importance of systems comes from **Wood and Disney Ltd – Colchester**

"Sometimes it's difficult to appreciate the changes Wood and Disney have gone through in automating the business so that the directors can focus on working on the business – and enjoy the numerous holidays and family-time they've been able to take in the past 12 months. At least, that is, until we actually sit back and reflect on the astonishing amount of changes we've all undertaken as a team.

To begin with, although we were all inspired by the various conferences, webinars and blogs we'd watched and participated in, we found it difficult to set time aside to do anything about them. As a result, the directors decided to engage the whole team so we could start putting plans into action.
We had a general idea of where the directors wanted the business to go, and what our ideal client 'niches' were, but there was something so much more solid about having this agreed in writing. We started with our vision of why we chose our particular business industry and why our clients would want to trust us with theirs; who our main clients were; the services we wanted to provide; and where our directors wanted to be in five years' time. We finished by describing exactly how we planned to streamline our business to become the business we all strived for.

Now, with our vision of where we wanted to get to, we were able to re-evaluate everything that we did, what the directors wanted, what we used and the outcomes we were receiving. Introducing software, providing new services and working on the business takes valuable time and to ensure the high level of services our clients were used to receiving was not compromised, we first needed to work on freeing up time.

We started by creating system processes on everything from accounts reviews and filing accounts to changing a VAT stagger group. To date we have over 50 new system processes and are continually creating more. This has given the Wood and Disney team the ability to complete different tasks, avoiding any bottlenecks and ensuring consistent output. The admin team are also now able to complete additional tasks by following the systems with the result that the partners, Peter and Brendon were able to take a step back from working in the business and concentrate on it instead.

With these systems in place we have been able to outsource 75-80% of the bookkeeping and accounts work. We created a thorough checklist and checking-in process so no set of accounts is started without all required information being available. This drastically improved turnaround time and the client's expectations. With the team's time now diverted from compliance processing, we are able to concentrate on more advisory services such as updates on the company and its key numbers, spotting potential areas on business growth, and tax savings. It has also allowed team members to start delving into the AVN tools and to start preparing for the AVN Performance, Measurement and Improvement folder - The Numbers, which originally would have been a task for Brendon and Peter.

Time-billing and being paid after the work is done is becoming a thing of the past. Also, whereas we'd started to introduce pre-agreed fees paid monthly with our chosen direct debit system before the accounts deadline, on review the method and software weren't working to the standard we desired. However, with their new-found freedom the directors were able to test pricing software. This was then rolled out within the team and all amendments (which are consistent) are suggested and actioned by various team members as we are the ones who predominately use the software and engage with clients.

All new businesses and renewals are provided with a bespoke package calculated by the software based on a number of parameters, which ensures pre-agreement of fees collected by direct debit. The change in style and software has helped the business remarkably – not only because we no longer require pre-approval by the directors, but also because admin demands have significantly reduced with recurring payments.

As the monthly fees are now included in the month's billing, monthly targets are no longer a wish but a reality. All fees are seamlessly managed by the admin team, which enables the team to complete additional work. This has resulted in six consecutive months of our highest billings ever recorded.

Cloud accounting has been a massive focus for our business. Recommending Xero and QuickBooks Online, we made the decision to off-board any clients who weren't willing to migrate onto the Cloud because they obviously didn't hold the same vision as us. The team now undertakes all the Cloud onboarding and training – which means the directors have effectively made themselves redundant in this area!

Continually looking for ways to improve our skills, we started using feedback forms in our client review and training meetings. This not only helped us to identify areas that required work, but also to discover additional work opportunities that clients perhaps didn't even know we offered! This has alleviated the pressure on the directors to hold most, if not all, client meetings, and the impact of this simple addition has been even more successful than originally anticipated. With more team members participating in meetings, the client relationships have grown to the extent that the main point of contact for most clients is now one of the team rather than one of the directors.

To ensure the systems are followed and remain current, we have regular catch-up meetings and if new changes are to be introduced, the system is amended (or created), tried and tested. To make these updates easier to announce and discuss we have just introduced the use of Slack for all internal conversations. An idea or amendment is suggested, discussed, tested and actioned with emojis to confirm success.

Our next mission is a brand-new Cloud CRM system which will combine the workflow tasks so that everything can be stored in one place and is easily assessable by the whole team.

On review of the changes we have undergone over the past 12 months, we see these as the main path to everything we are all striving for."

60

Where To Start With Systemising

Every business, be it large or small, has many functions (even if, to begin with, one person is filling all the roles). In his brilliant book *'The E-Myth'*, Michael Gerber describes these roles and asks, 'if you wanted to create a franchise of your business to replicate it in different cities around the world, would you be able to?' If your answer – along with that of many owners – is 'No,' it means your business is too reliant on you. To make sure it's a 'Yes,' you need to adopt the mindset of making your business franchise-able. (As we discussed in Part 6, the increase in value and appeal of a business that doesn't rely on its owner is also considerable).

The first step is to stop believing that customers are buying 'you' personally, and to realise that they're actually buying into the solutions your business can provide. However, even once you've achieved this, systemising your practice isn't an overnight job. All AVN members gain access to a full suite of ready-to-tweak systems which saves them thousands of hours in identifying and developing systems, checklists, forms, scripts and agendas etc, but they still need time to integrate these into their practice. (Saying, *"I've written a system for 'X', go follow it!"*, simply won't work).

Start by recording your daily activities in a journal and then, after a week or two, look through it to identify the most common one that also requires the least of your skills. Once you've done so, grab a pack of Post-it Notes and write down all the steps and elements (one per sheet) that are important to you about that one item.

As an illustration, let's return to the apparently simple example we used earlier, that of answering the telephone. At first glance it may appear that anyone can carry out this role: whoever it is simply picks up the phone, tells the caller the name of your company and asks how they can help. However, perhaps one of the items on your daily activity list is that calls that someone else could have dealt with are often put through to you. Or perhaps you don't yet have a team and it's one of your – many – roles to answer the phone. If so, and as I've mentioned, more and more practices (whether they have a team in place or not) are tapping into a professional telephone answering service as it's such a huge time-saver and improver of productivity. However, the effectiveness of outsourcing a service like this – or, indeed, of having a team member fulfil it – is largely dependent on the systems that you have in place around it.

For example, what script should they use when they answer? If you're in a meeting, do you want clients simply to be told that you're unavailable? Or that you're in a meeting? Unless you make the script explicit, you're not in control of what's said. (And remember how annoying it will be for a client if it sounds like you're in the office, but don't want to speak to them – which can easily be inferred if the message is conveyed incorrectly).

AVN member Paul, who you probably remember from Part 3, shared a great example of the importance of getting the script right with me. After he had gone through the process of appointing client managers in his practice, a letter was posted to each client introducing them to their new client manager and explaining that although Paul – as the owner of the practice – would still be around, they now had a dedicated client manager to look after their affairs in the event that he wasn't available. Next, Paul instructed his receptionist not to put their calls through to him.

However, the first version of the script – *"I'm sorry, Paul isn't available right now. May I put you through to your client manager, John?"* – didn't work because clients would simply say, *"No, it's alright. Please ask Paul to call me back when he's free."* In response, Paul decided to tweak his script (as I hope you're beginning to realise, one of the advantages of these systems lies in how easy they are to tweak and then to measure the effect), so that in future, when a client asked for him, the receptionist would simply put the call straight through to their client manager who would answer and use a script along the following lines: *"Hi Roger, I'm afraid Paul isn't available right now, but I'm John, your client manager, and I'm 100% up to speed on your affairs as I've been dealing with them behind the scenes. If you tell me the nature of your enquiry, I'll do my best to help you right away. If not, I can pass the message on to Paul, but I know he's not going to be available for quite some time."*

Obviously the client manager didn't reel all that off without pausing for breath, but generally the result was that the client would tell them their query (albeit sometimes with a little hesitation) and nine times out of ten they'd be able to deal with it instantly. Furthermore, on the rare occasions they couldn't, rather than return the call himself, Paul would coach them to come up with the answer so they could call the client back themselves.

The outcome of this was to increase clients' trust in their client managers and, almost overnight, Paul was able to transfer their care to his client managers. After all, the golden rule of customer service is 'speed stuns.' And most clients simply want their queries answering as quickly as possible.

As I hope the above example proves, even a seemingly simple system such as answering the telephone can form a crucial link in enabling you to delegate tasks. By doing so it can free you up to work on your business to make it stronger, and to develop your team to deliver to the standard you expect.

What currently takes up most of your time? And what simple system could you create as a starting point? If you free up just a few minutes with your first, and then a few more with your second, you'll soon start to see a snowball effect. It often only takes a few minutes to create the first version of a new system, so do it and then get it out there. Don't fall into the trap of building, tweaking, modifying and re-thinking it before it's even been used. Avoid being a perfectionist. Systems will never be perfect until they're in use when you'll be able to tell what needs tweaking.

61

What Needs To Be Systemised?

The aspects in your business that can be systemised fall within seven key areas:

1. **Leadership**
   - How we create and structure new systems
   - How we set goals
   - How we run leadership meetings such as those of the board
   - How we report on targets and metrics.

2. **Finance**
   - How we produce the management information
   - How we report expenditure
   - How we price our services
   - How we prioritise paying creditors and chasing debtors
   - How we chase creditors
   - How we set up direct debits and/or credit card payments.

3. **Marketing**
   - How we capture testimonials
   - How we capture case studies
   - How we create email campaigns
   - How we structure blog content.

4. **Operational**
   - How we present our accounts pack
   - How we deliver powerful client meetings
   - How we present tax returns
   - How we deliver business-advisory services (yes, rather than trying to play it by ear, remember this is a system too!)

5. **Administrative**
   - How we structure email

- How we process incoming emails
- How we organise webinars
- How we organise seminars.

6. Customers
- How we answer the phone
- How we deal with complaints
- How we get feedback.

7. People
- How we deliver career development reviews
- How we deal with grievance procedures
- How we store employee information.

62

The Automated Systems

As I've mentioned before, a growing number of applications exist that will enable you to automate and to shortcut many of the steps in each of your systems. The technology is, however, changing so rapidly that although I'll be naming a few products below, bear in mind that they're likely to have been superseded by the time you read this. The key purpose of this chapter, then, is to help you consider which areas in your business can be streamlined and made more efficient through the use of technology. (And don't forget, just like the rest of this book, the points that follow are as relevant for your clients as they are for you).

Capturing Enquiries

Imagine a business owner, frustrated with their current accountant, is trawling the Internet looking for a new one. Following my advice in Part 4 of this book, you've invested a lot of time in your website, and it now describes your vision for how you want to help business owners to improve their profits and achieve the work/life balance they want. It also displays several case studies from satisfied customers describing how their business has improved because of you.

Our business owner is intrigued. Suddenly, a pop-up chat box appears with the message: *"Thank you for visiting our website. I'm John, part of a 24-hour support team, and I'd love to help you with any queries."* Impressed, the business owner types: *"It's alright. I'm just taking a look at different accountancy practices in the area."* John immediately types a response and a conversation begins, during which John asks a few pre-determined questions to ascertain whether or not they're the type of client you've specified you want to work with and, as they are, because he has access to your diary, John's able to organise a meeting for them with you there and then. He also emails some additional literature about your practice and asks permission to add the business owner's email address to your records.

Despite John not being an internal member of your team, he's been able to set up an appointment and capture a new lead. You may feel that the business owner would have got in touch with you anyway – but maybe, maybe not. Maybe they'd have had every intention of doing so, but, when they got to work the next day, they were met with an urgent call and it simply slipped their mind.

My first technology tip is to tap into a live chat box control. Not with a view to you or a member of your team monitoring it, since this would only cover nine to five each day, but with a view to outsourcing the role. (I also strongly advise this because most users will only wait a few seconds before moving on, so imagine if the member of your team whose role it is had just popped to the loo!) Most external services will go through a detailed FAQ exercise with you to make sure they understand your desired outcome from a chat with a prospect and a client – and remember, they don't need to have technical answers to every question, Simply being able to arrange a time for a mutually convenient call is often best.

E-commerce

The moment someone decides to do business with you is also the best moment to agree payment terms. Getting paid afterwards can lead to disputes, to the need to chase, or to have an impact on your cashflow. Most accountants now take monthly direct debits and, rather than fees for any additional work arriving as a 'surprise' bill, they're agreed in advance and either paid for there and then using a credit card or a one-off additional direct debit payment, or are spread over the remaining months of the client's current fee period.

Is your practice maximising on this? Are you helping clients to put these types of payments in place? Does your system ensure that every client conversation which leads to work over and above the original requirement, also include the agreement and payment of a fee upfront?

CRM

A good-quality Customer Relationship Manager tool – one which can do everything from monitoring the warmth of leads to storing vital customer information – is essential to any business and accountancy is no exception. (In fact, as I discussed in Part 5, you can even log a client's preferred drink option!)

Imagine the impact you could create, if by logging that the last time you talked to a client they told you it was their child's birthday, the following year you send a birthday card. Or, just as importantly, if you record a client's nut allergy. Logging such things means that clients don't need to repeat the same information each time and plays a vital role in building relationships.

CRMs that have been specifically created for accountancy practices are often called Practice Management applications and frequently include additional areas of technology – such as client portals, secure storage, online signing facilities and project management. I'll be expanding upon this below…

NB: It's important to mention that following GDPR you need permission to store client information, although you can easily build a request for this into their letter of engagement, for example. And bear in mind, too, that if a client leaves, some of their data will also need to be deleted.

Project Management
Measuring exactly what progress is being made on client work is important in any business and most CRMs/Practice Management tools provide a project management module. How effectively you use this will help with efficiencies, as many can be configured to send out emails when an item has been progressed to a relevant stage, for example – or to send out alerts when it hasn't.

One possibility is to configure the software so that each stage can only be progressed when a checklist has been completed showing that all the information required has been received. That way, a member of your admin team can chase the client for any information that's still missing, and an accountant doesn't need to be involved until work on the accounts can actually begin.

Many tools also incorporate a portal so that clients can see the progress of their work and what they need to send in either via the portal or (surely not!) carry bag.

Client Portals
A client portal is an incredibly convenient and secure way of receiving and sharing documents with clients. Clients can read, amend and digitally sign documents, you can track any changes and even restrict certain parts from being changed at all. You have complete control and clients have much better clarity. (A portal can also help with client onboarding as engagement letters can be uploaded for signing).

Client Communications

A whopping 55% of our communication comes from our body language; 38% from the tonality of our voice; and only 7% from the words we actually use. Now, think about that for a moment in terms of how we usually communicate these days, which is largely via the written word in emails, instant messenger or – more rarely – a letter.

In other words, in most cases we typically lose 93% of the effectiveness of our communication. And have you ever sent an email – either internally or to a customer – with the best of intentions, only for it to be misinterpreted? I know I have. Telephones, of course, introduce tone of voice, which improves matters by raising effectiveness to 45% but, even so, nothing will ever beat a face-to-face meeting if you really want to build rapport and reinforce relationships.

The problem is though that it's rarely convenient to trek across town – or even the country – to convey a five-minute message. This is where video-based technology comes in. Surprisingly, however, although such technology has been at our fingertips for many years now, very few of us take advantage of it. Very few, that is, amongst a certain generation, as at the time of writing, my 10 and 12 year old children have grown up using FaceTime to talk to me, my wife or their grandparents. (Indeed, if I call one of them in any way other than on FaceTime they think it's odd!)

In fact I've joined them, as increasingly, even on the phone, I feel that a vital element of communication is missing – from me and from the person I'm speaking to – which is why, for face-to-face meetings, I now use live video-conferencing technology. (In my case, the free version of . The fact that it limits calls to 40 minutes and visually counts down the last five is fantastic at keeping meetings to a fixed time and focusing your mind on making a decision!)

Sometimes, of course, a live meeting isn't necessary. Perhaps I simply want to send someone a personal thank you, or to answer a quick email query so, for this, I use a video messaging service called BombBomb. In fact, both tools are fantastic and I highly recommend them. (I know many people find being on video uncomfortable at first, but the reality is that everyone else is used to seeing you and hearing you anyway).

Reports and Dashboards

When we drive, our cars don't present us with a list of figures that specify the exact quantity of fuel remaining, the exact temperature of oil and water, or the exact speed and revs per minute. Instead, a quick glance at the dashboard gives us the key figures.

Similarly, in business, a visual representation of trends and numbers can give an at-a-glance understanding of the metrics that are most important to us. (And remember, whilst most accountants are by nature detail- and numbers-oriented, most business owners are big-picture thinkers and considerably less keen on looking at documents filled with figures).

Take AVN's BenchMark tool, which our members use to benchmark the performance of their practice to that of others in the UK. Amongst other things, it provides a One-Page Performance Improvement Plan which presents the key metrics in a colour-coded bar chart: red if compared to others where you're low in an area; amber if you're similar; and green if you're strong. This allows both the owner of the practice concerned and our Practice Growth team to identify any specific areas which can be improved.

BenchMark is also used by our members with their own clients to do exactly the same. In fact, since 2004 (its first iteration), it's been embraced by an ever-increasing number of accountants who use it annually with their clients, and it now has a vast range of industries within it specific to SIC codes. By comparing two years' worth of data against an industry, a business owner can see, perhaps, that their business is charging less than their competitors, or is in a worse debtor position.

One Page Performance Improvement Plan — AVN INSPIRING ACCOUNTANTS

Where are you now		Where you want to be	How you get there
Your key numbers	**Which ranks you**	**Your targets**	**Your action plan**
Sales growth	14.3%	**Sales** – What would you like your sales growth and margin of safety to be? NB: improving your sales growth to match the upper quartile – i.e. to 25.0% – will add £37,108 in extra profit.	**Sales** – As a first step calculate the impact of working on each of the key sales drivers, i.e. getting more sales leads, converting more sales leads, keeping customers for longer, selling more to each customer and selling more often.
Margin of safety	30.0%		
Gross margin	35.0%		
Operating margin	10.5%	**Profit** – What would you like your profits to be? NB: improving your gross margin to match the upper quartile – i.e. to 79.9% – will add £109,600 in extra profit.	**Profit** – As a first step focus on pricing – since pricing is often the biggest single factor driving the profitability of many businesses. Look at the sales mix by carrying out gross margin analysis by customer and/or product group. Review costs control. And investigate process inefficiencies.
Net profit margin	10.5%		
Growth in net profit	50.0%		
Sales per £ of employee costs	£2.14	**People costs and productivity** – What would you like your average employee costs, sales per employee, sales per £ of employee costs and profit per employee to be? NB: improving your sales per £ of employee costs to match the upper quartile – i.e. to £2.46 – will add £21,309 in extra profit.	**People costs and productivity** – Systems are the key to productivity and efficiency. Review the systems and processes. Identify areas of waste and inefficiency. Map out more effective systems and document them. Involve the team in creating better systems. And then train the team in following the business systems and processes.
Average employee costs	£46,750		
Sales per employee	£100,045		
Profit per employee	£10,500		
Asset turnover	4.04	**Assets** – What would you like your asset turnover, debtor days, stock days and debtors to total asset ratio to be? NB: improving your asset turnover by 10% – i.e. to 4.44 – will add £24,000 in extra profit. Improving your stock days to match the upper quartile – i.e. to 5.1 days – will add £14,271 to the amount of cash you have in the bank. And improving your debtor days by 10% – i.e. to 1.7 days – will add £28,208 to the amount of cash you have in the bank.	**Assets** – As a first step, identify ways of getting paid on time, in full, every time. Then create the operational and financial systems you need to reduce debtors, work in progress and stock.
Stock days	5.62		
Debtor days	1.92		**Cash and gearing** – Explore refinancing options, and consider invoice discounting, factoring and asset finance. Also, review your credit control systems and processes for paying suppliers, and renegotiate the interest paid on borrowing. And avoid nasty surprises by producing regular high quality cash flow forecasts.
Debtors to total assets	2.12		
Current ratio	3.83		
Quick ratio	3.17		
Interest cover	0	**Return on investment** – What would you like your return on investment to be? NB: improving your return on investment to match the upper quartile – i.e. to 49.1% – will add £94,678 in extra profit.	**Return on investment** – Much of the above will have a big impact on your return on investment. What else can you do?
Return on investment	42.4%		
Return on capital employed	45.2%		

In addition to BenchMark, there's a plethora of other reporting tools within the accountancy profession that can produce visually appealing reports. By mapping the trends of previous years, many can instantly show that, over time, X is gradually getting worse. (However, as you're aware, viewing numbers in isolation only reveals half the story). A rapidly increasing number of accountancy-specific dashboards, reporting tools and systems are also designed to connect seamlessly with non-accountancy tools. For example, you can now monitor how well online posts have been received – through likes, comments and shares – and how much traffic your website has received over a given period, and on the same screen, how much this has impacted on sales enquiries and revenue. (So you can tell whether the time you've invested in social media is paying off or not).

Although it's easy, these days, for clients to experience 'analysis paralysis,' tapping into reporting tools such as those I've outlined above makes presenting the numbers that really matter to them – and in an easily understandable fashion – quick and easy. This, in turn, means you can have better-quality conversations about what they mean and any underlying trends they reveal.

Internal Communications
On any given day our inboxes are filled with emails from existing and potential suppliers, newsletters, auto-responders, junk emails and emails about upcoming events. And that's before we even mention enquiries from clients and prospects. In fact, it can be a full-time job simply staying on top of them.

That's why, long ago, I decided to delegate the processing of my emails. Any emails that come in are now filtered by my admin team, with those that can be dealt with by other members of my team forwarded on, and only those that no one but me can deal with forwarded to me – which just about keeps it manageable!

Sometimes, though, internal communications compound the problem: a team member pings you a quick email with an apparently simple query, you ping a response back, they respond to check they understood what you meant and – before you know it – you're playing email ping-pong. (Or, worse still, you're not even part of the conversation at all, but the instigator of it CC'd you in and you're now caught up in a two-way conversation that's needlessly filling your inbox).

The above scenario is why, at AVN, we try to keep emails for clients and suppliers and instant messaging (we use Slack, but there are other tools out there) to communicate as a team. Slack allows us to have one-to-one chats or one-to-many, and to set up a project-specific channel so that everyone involved in the project can confer and all the dialogue is stored for future reference. It's also great when someone's working from home (or when you outsource), as it shows a participant's status ('online,' 'offline' or 'busy') which means you know whether you can expect an immediate response or not.

Of course, while most technologies are advertised with the promise that they'll be able to shortcut key parts of your processes, it's important to remember they all come with pros and cons. I've seen many people subscribe to a product, then spend hours setting it up only to find it doesn't quite do everything they want. They immediately start to look for an alternative. To avoid this, I recommend you set a deadline that gives you a sensible amount of time to compare products, read the reviews and post questions on any relevant online groups you're part of. (But be specific, explain what you want to achieve and ask whether X product can do it. If you simply ask if X is better than Y, chances are you'll get just as many replies that recommend X as Y).

If you still have reservations about a product you're leaning towards, run them past the supplier and ask for a demo. In some cases, the product might have been upgraded or the supplier may be able to tell you whether it's a feature they're looking to add in the future – and, if so, when.

Once your deadline has been reached, make your decision and commit to it.

As a Practice Management package will quickly become the hub of your prospect and customer information, switching and changing it too often will impact on the performance of your team and practice. My recommendation is that you keep up-to-date with how other such tools are developing and monitor that the performance – and price – of yours is keeping in line with them. If they're not, talk to your supplier first. Migrating to a new system is considerably more than a data-transfer exercise; it also involves fresh training and introduces another change to your team.

63

A Winning Technological Formula

The actual technologies you choose to implement in your accountancy business will be very specific to your wants and needs which is why, for the most part, I've shared insights in to the types of technologies to investigate and kept specific product naming to a minimum.

Jackie Hooper of JDH Group based in Abercynon, South Wales won the AVN Award for AUTOMATION. Here's her entry where she describes the changes she's implemented. Of course, whilst the products Jackie refers to may not suit your accountancy business, the act of challenging the status quo in terms of the technologies and providers used has led to improvements in productivity and efficiencies in expenditure. In addition, there are some pretty sound procedures Jackie and her team took in terms of cyber security and data protection.

"We wanted to streamline our systems to free up time to make more changes. This is what we did.

1. A review of and change in general of all of our software providers resulted in having access to better cloud-based packages with more licences and users at a fraction of the cost that we were paying. Now, we can all work at the same time. This has improved our productivity and efficiency.

2. We set up Go Cardless and linked it with Sage in order to have more control. This is better than standing orders, where the client has the mindset that the fees will never change. So direct debits are more flexible. We can email direct debit mandates and request payments. We have a card payment system too which means we can collect money for yearly or occasional work. This saves us 3 days a month debt chasing and our bank balance is higher than it has ever been. We also don't accept cheques either, so we don't waste time taking cheques to the bank!

3. Auto Text saves us time when chasing for paperwork. It was cheap and easy to set up and we could import our client database, so it didn't take long to do. It's a quick and easy way to chase for deadlines.

4. Transferring to Sage 50 accounts software for our client database allows me to set up a user for each member of the team and lock down what they would be able to access. All can access the customer base so client's details can be updated immediately. Now we have everything in one place, and the work is not duplicated.

5. Implementing online payslips for clients has freed up time – no clients asking for re-prints.

6. Sage 50 Bureaux Manager has enabled us to have all our payroll clients on one dashboard, where we can toggle back and forth between clients for reports, without having to log in and out using Sage 50 Payroll.

7. Sage Pensions Exchange is a new tool that uploads pension data quickly and efficiently. (It does depend on what pension provider is being used).

8. Sage One cloud has been implemented for smaller clients ready for Making Tax Digital. Clients find this solution quite cost effective. We set up bank feeds to streamline it and ensure clients get some training and then monitor it.

9. We started to use the Nominal Link in posting payroll to accounts. This works for more complex postings too, including departments and costing centres.

10. Sage Drive was recently adopted in our business. We can log in and work at the same time as the client. Now the client doesn't need to wait for us to finish our work and there is no risk of the wrong backup being used and we can access the system whenever we need to.

11. Iris Open Space gives us a place to securely upload documents for digital signing and approval. Some of our clients might be too busy to come in for an appointment but they can approve documents/tax returns for submission. This saves time.

12. We use Mail Chimp to email clients helpful information, e.g. Trigger List. We can keep in touch with our clients and alert them if they need to tell us of

any business changes. We sent out the GDPR brochure that AVN kindly provided and reminded our clients of their obligations.

13. One of my team researched GDPR and collated lots of useful information. Here's what we have implemented:

A. We now use Bit Locker Drive Encryption on all portable storage devices so that data cannot be leaked.

B. Clients either get password protected payslips via email or use online payslips. Reports are uploaded to Iris Open Space, rather than sent by email, which could get hacked and data leaked.

C. We bought a business mobile phone to keep in the office and set up all our clients with HMRC log ins using this mobile for the access code.

D. We set up Dashlane for Business on each PC. No passwords are written down. Passwords need to be complicated but Dashlane fills in the box for us. It will audit the information and tell us whether a password is strong enough.

E. We have ensured that our sub-contract bookkeepers will be compliant with GDPR.

F. We checked on our storage facilities and asked to see their policy on storing our client's data.

G. We have completed a GDPR audit, which made us think about our systems and processes, with a view to improving our security system.

H. We have created a new GDPR opt in form, which lists how and where we store client data.

I. We have data cleansed our old clients, ensuring that we have backups and reports if need be, going back 7 years. The older clients have now been removed and their working paper files have been shredded. We have been through our HMRC portal and deleted old clients.

J. We have MFA (Multi Factor Authentication) on our email system for extra security.

K. My home office has become part of the main office network and the special router and static IP address will ensure that there are no network problems. This is a more secure system.

L. In our main office, we changed our Wi-Fi password and set up a guest Wi-Fi log in. This is on a physically separate network, so our system remains secure, whilst allowing our clients to access the internet.

M.We will to get the Cyber Essentials Plus certificate. This is a full audit of our system to ensure that we are fully secure and compliant. It will be done every year and is another layer of security. It's worth it to know that our business is both compliant and safe.

N. We pay for Cyber Insurance. Our IT support team told us that we are the most secure business of all their clients. They wished that other accountants took security as seriously as we do. We want our clients to know that their data is safe with us.

All these changes have strengthened our business and prepared us for a future in the technical world we find ourselves in."

64

Why You Must Raise Your Profile

Earlier I described how, if you have in place a 'reason to rave,' a client might start to talk about their experience and highly recommend your practice when they're playing golf with a business associate.

Once, of course, such a recommendation might well have been enough to convince their associate to pick up the phone the following day and call you. In line with the whole argument of this book though, that world is changing. In fact, we have in our pockets an oracle to which we refer for advice and insight before every decision. (As well as to find out what we've seen that familiar-looking actor in before). Yes: Google.

Research, conducted by Google itself, has revealed that our buying trends and habits have changed significantly over recent years. (You can check this research out for yourself by typing 'ZMOT,' which stands for Zero Moment Of Truth, into Google). ZMOT revealed that people now carry out far more research before they're ready to buy and – because there's so much choice – making a decision has become increasingly difficult.

In fact, most of us worry so much about making the wrong decision that we procrastinate over making one at all until we feel we've explored all possible options. ZMOT also provided insights as to how potential customers build up sufficient confidence before they make a decision to buy.

To return to our golfing scenario, if your client's business associate hasn't previously heard of you, instead of just calling you, the most likely outcome is that they'll check you out by typing your name – rather than the name of your practice – into Google. The second most likely outcome is that they'll start their research on LinkedIn (again, by typing in your name); and the third is that they'll search using the name of your practice.

Have you ever tried Googling your own name without including that of your accountancy practice? It's an interesting exercise and often quite a wake-up call. To illustrate what I mean, I'd like to share a personal story.

Although AVN was originally founded by Steve Pipe, Mark Wickersham and I were partners in a separate business that worked very closely – and eventually merged – with it. Despite being part of AVN from very early on, then, and being heavily involved in creating many of its resources and its strategy, I was quite happy to remain in the background and to lead the team rather than to get up on stage as Steve and Mark both enjoyed doing. In fact, not only were they up on stage a lot, they also embraced every opportunity to publish content online in numerous accountancy publications and had each written several books. In short, they were incredibly well known, liked and trusted within the global accountancy profession.

Meanwhile, despite being Managing Director of AVN, I wasn't its 'face.' (Not that I had any desire to be. As an introvert and an extremely private person, I didn't enjoy being on stage nor did I see the need to be). In 2015, however, both Mark and Steve made the decision to gradually step away from AVN to focus on their other passions (more of this later). At first I was confident that – having already been around for 17 years – AVN's reputation would allow it to carry on exactly as before, but I quickly discovered that this wasn't the case.

Attendance at our events began to plummet and it soon became apparent that 'people buy people' and I simply wasn't known within the profession. I even received emails from accountants that AVN had been marketing to successfully for many years, saying I needed to establish a relationship with them before I began marketing to them! It was a bit of a wake-up call to say the least.

Reading the ZMOT research (luckily, a colleague thought to suggest this) was one of those penny-drop moments. I Googled 'Shane Lukas' to find out for myself what accountants we were marketing to would see if they looked me up. The results were horrifying. Despite being presented with thousands of results, not a single one on any of the pages was about me. In fact, the third entry on the first page was a news headline about a Shane Lukas – based in Brazil – who'd been found guilty of a horrendous crime. (And be warned: sometimes, even if it's obvious that a result isn't about you, it can still taint your name by association).

I quickly realised that 'my' Shane Lukas needed to dominate the first page of Google (after all, very few people ever get beyond that!) so that in future, whenever anyone received something from me, they'd be able to find out more about me quickly and easily – and avoid any negative connotations.

What might potential customers find if they Googled your name? Or, if a business owner was looking for the answer to a question around areas such as bookkeeping, payroll and tax, would Google suggest links to your practice?

Of course, as well as your own profile, you also need to raise that of your team. Remember, to build an accountancy business, you need to make sure it doesn't rely on you as an individual, which means that my advice around how to dominate the first page of Google also needs to be followed by the key individuals within your team.

I'll also be sharing how you can build a relationship with those love (but difficult) to get clients. That way, even if they're not quite ready to switch to you right now, when the time comes, you'll be top of the list because they already know, like and trust you. (In other words, you already have what I call the 'KLT factor.).

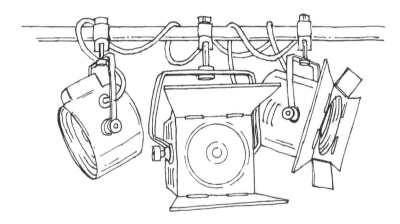

Before we start, I appreciate that even the title of this chapter will appear daunting to some people. Raising your profile can feel very much like shining a spotlight on yourself. *"Look at me!"* it seems to shout. After all, many accountants are natural introverts and certainly don't relish forcing themselves into the limelight.

To overcome this, it's important to understand that it's less about shining a light on yourself, and more about being a light-bearer (or light-bearers in the case of your team). As such, you'll be able to shine that light on the things that are most important to clients and prospects and, once they identify you as the person shining this light, they'll begin to know, like and trust you.

It's also important to remember that any content you share – whether online or offline – should be insightful and helpful. Too many people use social media (or other platforms for audience engagement) as a means of self-promotion – which simply puts people off.

65

Google

Personally, I ask Google heaps of questions every day: from finding a website that I can't remember the specific URL for, to confirming some legislative detail, or checking out reviews on the latest Cloud technology bolt-ons – and that's just at work! In exactly the same way, business owners will use Google to answer their accountancy-related questions.

Of course, it's not really Google that answers their questions. Google simply looks for articles and blogs that do and then presents these in its search results. To do so, it uses a number of factors:

- Keywords (ones that closely match those in the user's query)
- Time (the more recent the better, otherwise the answer might be out of date)
- Location (again, for accuracy, one close to your own is preferred).

The key to populating those all-important first pages of Google is to write articles that answer the types of questions business owners are most likely to ask – and to do so regularly. (And don't forget: Google also loves videos, which is why if you were to 'Google' my name, you'd find video clips and images of me as well as articles I've written).

As, where possible, Google prefers to take data from multiple sources, if you 'Google' my name you'll also notice that every result leads to a different website – including the AVN website, my personal LinkedIn profile, my YouTube channel, my Facebook page and Amazon (some of my books are listed on there), as well as my personal blog site (**www.shanelukas.co.uk**) which I created specifically to ensure yet another source. In addition, I regularly post articles on various online accountancy publications, such as AccountingWEB. Together, these resources not only raise my chance of showing up on Google when someone enters my name, but also when an accountant is searching for solutions relating to challenges their practice is facing.

I don't claim be an expert in social media – in fact, I honestly don't believe you need to be. Often, through fear that they might get it wrong, I've seen a practice owner tap into the knowledge of an outside expert, only for this to fail. Remember, the best person to get content out there is you. It isn't a huge burden and there are plenty of tools that can help you to automate your regular postings. Too many so-called social media experts are guilty of posting generic, self-promoting articles that not only fail to answer questions or provide solutions, but also fail to reflect either your personality or what your accountancy practice stands for. (If you do insist on outsourcing your content writing, then I strongly recommend you record the information you wish to convey and create a set of branding guidelines that includes your purpose, values, beliefs and preferred tone of voice. That way a copywriter can help you to capture these, but the key points remain your own).

If you're not producing content already, start now. Make it as helpful as possible and don't worry about giving away free advice – the more you're seen as the person who provides the answers to people's questions, the more you'll build your KLT factor and your chances of working with them in the future.

Ensure that your accountancy practice website has a blog section and get writing. After all, your clients regularly ask you questions, whether by phone, email or in person. In future, keep a note of these, together with your answers and, when it's time to write your next blog post, simply write one of them down. It doesn't need to be long. 300-500 words are sufficient, especially if you don't want to bore people or get bogged down in too much detail! Simply provide an overview and then add that for an answer tailored to their specific circumstances, readers can get in touch for a free initial consultation.

Another useful tip to remember is: *People don't care how much you know until they know how much you care.* So make an effort to connect with your audience, but without making your article generic in an attempt to suit everyone. Speak directly to your ideal client. The more targeted your content, the more it will connect and resonate. Finally, avoid keeping the content dry. Let your personality shine through.

Be helpful rather than trying too hard to sell your services. Give before expecting to get. I recommend that you create a personal blog and post your articles there, too. In addition, every time you create a new post, make a point of conveying exactly the same content to video. Simply prop your smartphone on your desk – or invest in a small stand – press record on its built-in video-camera, smile and start talking as if you were talking to your favourite client. Make it short and sweet and don't worry about the occasional 'um,' 'erm,' stutter or fumble. Think of these as showing that you're human; not worrying about them will also enable you to create more content rather than doing take after take in an attempt to get each one exactly right.

Once you've created your blog post, pop it on your website, add a copy to your LinkedIn profile and company Facebook page and, for videos, to your YouTube channel as well. (If you don't yet have one, then you should.) Make sure you choose titles as close as possible to the questions that may be asked, and use additional keywords within your post to capture possible variations on these. In the case of videos, add the text of your post or article to its description – to ensure that Google presents this in response to queries – and populate the keywords, too.

Finally, come up with some suitable teaser text – a short, enticing sentence or two to tempt people to view your post (*"Want to know how to…?"* is often good) – and a link such as *"Check out my blogpost at…"* to use on Twitter, LinkedIn and Facebook. (Many tools allow you to add these just once, and then schedule them to go out on multiple platforms as often as you wish).

Personally, I aim to create at least one article and one video per week. At first this felt like an enormous amount of pressure and as soon as I sat down to write my mind went completely blank. To overcome this, always carry a notepad or have an easy-to-load app so next time you're asked a question, you can simply jot it down or press 'record' on your phone and use this as the basis of your next post. I promise it's as simple as starting with: *"Here's a question I'm often asked…"*

Finally, don't expect immediate results. It takes time to build your profile. Do, however, regularly test your progress by typing your name or any questions you've recently answered into Google to check that both yourself and your articles come up. (I'll come back to how you measure effectiveness later).

66

Social Media

A few weeks before I wrote this chapter I spoke to a businesswoman in her late twenties who, when I explained what I did, instantly recalled a bad experience she'd had with accountants. She explained that after establishing her business (teaching business owners how to use LinkedIn), she identified five local accountants on LinkedIn and sent them an invitation to connect. Although they'd all accepted, only one had sent a follow-up message enquiring as to her reason for connecting and asking if she'd like to arrange a chat. She found it exasperating that none of the others had taken the opportunity to get in touch.

Remember: If you're registered on a social media platform, use it or lose it.

I imagine that most of you are already registered on LinkedIn. If so, what's your strategy for ensuring that new connections are made to feel welcome? Do you make the effort to greet each of them and to understand their reason for connecting?

Although new platforms are springing up all the time, at the time of writing – and despite what the younger generation may think! – LinkedIn, Facebook, Twitter and YouTube are still the most popular. However, it's crucial to understand which platform your ideal client prefers. The profile you've drawn up of them should already include a detailed breakdown of various key elements, so type 'Social Media Usage Demographics' and your country into Google and see which platform(s) match those which your ideal clients use the most.

Finally, don't spread yourself too thinly. As the style of post often varies substantially between each platform, it can become very time-consuming to create (or even just to tailor) content for each. Pick a manageable number that works for you. Even if that number is one, it's better to use one platform effectively, than many ineffectively.

67

Presenting Your Knowledge

Even before social media, AVN understood the need to build relationships and to increase your KLT (Know, Like and Trust) factor. It's why we've been encouraging members to present what we call BBFs (Business-Builder Forums) and since the early 2000s provided them with everything they need to run these in the most effective manner.

In short, the purpose of BBFs is to build your KLT. To do this, members invite around 20 existing and prospective clients (or their representatives) to their practice, or if they aren't able to accommodate that many, to an alternative venue. Once all the participants have arrived, our members deliver a 45-minute presentation on a business topic, followed by a 45-minute discussion forum. (This can either be about the topic that's just been presented or other challenges that attendees are facing, as it enables them to tap in to one another's knowledge and experience).

In fact, some AVN members are now using video-conferencing platforms such as to host these forums in the form of webinars. A word of warning though, as whilst it's a great way to extend your reach and accommodate more people, webinars will never be as powerful as a physical forum because the moment they finish, the connection to the audience is severed. (Compare this with a queue of people staying behind to talk to you – or to each other – in a physical forum).

BBFs, then, are a powerful way to build relationships on a face-to-face level. However, the biggest hurdle is that at first many accountants don't feel comfortable with public speaking. However, once we've helped them to overcome this, they're able to deliver great BBFs and through them build relationships and trust, leading both to additional work from existing clients and new work from prospects. Why? Because they've positioned themselves as experts in business.

68

The Most Powerful Business Card

The most powerful business card you can offer a prospective client is a book that demonstrates your knowledge and ability to help business owners grow their business by applying strategies that work.

Putting in the time it takes to write a book may seem daunting. You may also wonder whether it's worth it. If you are, wonder no more! I've lost count of the number of AVN members we've helped to produce their own book over the years and each of them has told us that it's been an absolute game changer. So why does writing a book help you acquire better-quality clients, more quickly? In short, because it positions you as an AUTHORity.

Rather than about making lots of money through book sales (which is highly unlikely to happen anyway), it's about impact. Earlier, I shared how little I'd once done to raise my personal profile within the accountancy profession. Despite both Mark and Steve regularly encouraging me to write a book, I felt I didn't have anything to add to what they'd already said. I eventually realised, however, that this simply wasn't true. Although my experience, passion and learning were similar to theirs in some ways, in others they were completely different. One of my particular passions lay in coaching in its purest form: in understanding people through their behaviour, motivations and psychology. My experience in developing team cultures in different businesses and my interest in technology also meant that I was one of the first to recognise the impact this would have on accountancy. My first book, *'What's Next for Accountants'* published in March 2017, contained all this knowledge and experience and, in consequence, quickly rocketed to become a No.1 best-seller on Amazon in the UK. (It also came incredibly close in the USA and Australia, despite the fact I hadn't marketed it in either country).

Never underestimate, or forget, how much knowledge and experience you've gained from working with so many different businesses and their owners over the years. During countless conversations you'll have learned what works in business and what doesn't. In fact, writing a book often makes you realise just how much knowledge you do have.

Before you start, remember that writing a book requires a lot of perseverance and discipline. I hope that doesn't sound condescendingly obvious, but I've seen many people start only to fail to finish. Everyone hits writer's block at some point along the way, which is why I've likened writing a book to completing an Ironman Triathlon: You start off swimmingly, there's a few ups and downs as you cycle through the middle chapters, then a long hard slog as you run towards the finish. But, when you do reach it, I promise the sense of achievement is huge and the benefits massively outweigh the effort.

To help get you started, here's the process I follow:

1. **Set a target date.** (If you don't set a deadline to complete your first draft, you'll never finish it!)

2. **Create a block of time – preferably daily – in your diary.** During this time, only work on your book. (Personally, I set my alarm an hour earlier than normal and work in the kitchen whilst the rest of my family are still asleep).

3. **Start by writing a brief bio of around 300-500 words.** This should answer the question, *"Why me?"* and include your experience, qualifications and the outcomes you've helped people to achieve. This will demonstrate to readers why they should read your book.

4. **Decide what question your book will answer.** If, for example, I buy a book on getting the most out of LinkedIn, it's because I've been asking myself *"How do I get the most out of LinkedIn?"* Think about the big questions your ideal clients might ask or need the answers to. Unless they're asking the questions your book answers, why would they bother to read it?

5. **Brainstorm everything you know that answers that question.** When I sat down to write my first book I hadn't come up with a key question. In fact, I was even struggling to come up with a list of things I felt I could write about. Focusing on the central question I wanted to answer made me much clearer about all the ways I could do so and I was quickly able to commit these to paper.
(Incidentally, as I'm a big fan of mind mapping, I use an app called iThoughts which allows me to use the keyboard to dump my thoughts and

then drag and drop them when it comes to structuring content. The other great thing about it is that as fast as I type in one idea and press 'enter,' a new branch appears ready for my next one, which makes brainstorming as rapid-fire as it should be. It's vital not to overthink things at this point, just keep typing ideas – three words max – then press enter and type the next one).

It's also important to give everything when you're brainstorming. After all, if someone's going to buy your book, it's only fair they should get value from it. (If you're worried about this, don't be. I tend to find that many readers go on to ask for your help in making what you've written about happen).

6. **Structure your ideas.** Once you've ended up with a fairly large mind map (or whichever method you choose to follow), it's time to begin grouping your ideas together and putting them under chapter headings. Move the groups around so that your chapters follow a logical flow.

7. **Think about stories, case studies, anecdotes, images and illustrations.** These will help to support and enhance each chapter.

8. **Make your big promise.** To encourage potential readers to pick it up, tell them what they'll gain from reading your book. What outcomes can they expect if they implement its learning?

9. **Get writing.** Aim to write a specific number of words during each writing session. (I commit to 1000 words per hour). Remember, our brains love trying to answer questions and solve puzzles so, if you do get writer's block, type out a question. Just looking at what you've written will help to reactivate your brain.

It's also important not to worry about how nicely it reads to begin with, just get your first draft completed. Once you've done so, you can read through it again to tidy it up. Then ask someone else to read it and to give you feedback, so you can make any necessary adjustments.

The next part of the process gets a little more expensive and complex. You could send your draft off to book publishers, but personally I'd recommend self-publishing. (Remember that the purpose of your book is its thud, wow and positioning factors). If you're happy to go down this route, send your book to an editor (you can find one online) who edits the type of book you've written and who understands your style. If you want your sense of humour to shine through, for example, make sure you find an editor who appreciates this. (Otherwise they might remove it).

Whilst they're working on your book, identify other authors you admire and who are known to your target audience, and then connect with them to ask if they'd be happy to provide an endorsement. (A high-profile endorsement is a great way to add credibility to your book). If they are, send them the draft and – as an additional courtesy – a synopsis to help them decide whether they want to read it or not.

You'll also need to find a graphic designer to create a cover design and, once you've received everything back, a typesetter to prepare your book in a digital format ready for print. When it comes to print run, I recommend you aim high as not only does each book work out more cost-effective, it also means you have plenty of copies to give away to prospective clients.

Finally, you can use your book to generate leads from your websites by offering a free download in exchange for someone's email address. Many AVN accountants, for example, harvest new addresses in this way, which they can then market by using auto-responders to drip-feed insights.

69

Getting Press Coverage – For Free

Many potential clients amongst your target market who don't yet know you read newspapers and trade magazines (online or offline), listen to the radio or podcasts and watch TV, but advertising in any of these can be expensive. However, there is another way you can feature in them that's absolutely free. (Free, that is, apart from a small investment of time; but the rewards far outweigh this in the boost to your credibility, to positioning you as an expert and to attracting new clients).

As journalists are always looking for stories that offer interest and value to their audience, the answer is press releases. Budget day, for example, offers a great opportunity as many journalists might not understand the implications of its announcements. In fact, sending a newsworthy report in a timely fashion almost guarantees its inclusion. (One real-life example is: "Accountancy practice doubles in size overnight." The story was actually that a one-person practice had recruited its first employee, but the press liked the way the story was written!)

To give you some more ideas, below is a press release around an office move:

Moving in the right direction: A new era for ambitious local accountants
Local practice Bloggins & Co. is taking a major step forward by relocating their Chesterfield office to Sheffield. Although their new location is just seven miles from their current office, it signals the firm's intent to continue to support their clients and represents the progress they've made in recent years.

Having been based in Chesterfield for three years, the possibility of moving the practice to a more central location has long been considered by the firm. With the move set for [the date], everyone at the company is fully aware of the benefits associated with moving to the city, as director

John Bloggins explains:

"The crucial thing for us is that our location is suitable for the most important people: our clients and our team. Ultimately, we feel we've outgrown our current set-up and couldn't miss the chance to own such a great new office.

"Centrally located and offering excellent access to clients and other business associates, the new premises seemed the most logical place to establish our new base. We already have a number of excellent clients in the area and are looking to expand on this by helping more businesses in and around the city."

Many other businesses in the area have acknowledged the high-quality and prestige of the new offices at Sheffield, as John Bloggins goes on to explain:

"We've been contemplating this for a long time as it was becoming increasingly clear just how outdated our former offices were. Our new premises, however, are modern, purpose-built and far more accessible.

"Naturally, we were apprehensive – particularly about transferring all our equipment and files to the new space. However, everything's gone without a hitch and there's no doubt in any of our minds that the move will have fantastic long-term benefits for Bloggins & Co. as a practice, and that it will improve our already strong relations with clients."

With a growing presence in the Sheffield area, Bloggins & Co. is making positive strides in the region despite the difficult economic climate. To mark the opening of their new office, the ambitious accountancy practice is offering the opportunity for local business owners to join them at an open evening on [the date], when they will have a chance to look around the new offices, meet the Bloggins & Co. team and network with their peers amongst the local business community.

If you're interested in attending the open evening, please contact Freddy on: 01234 XXXXXX.

What stories could you send to journalists? Perhaps how a client has turned their business around or is set to expand after receiving your help?

70

Leveraging Your Time To Nurture Those Love-To-Get, Hard-To-Get Clients

So far in this section we've looked at ways to build your KLT (Know, Like and Trust) factor by:

1. Creating content on social media to:
   - Get your name recognised by Google
   - Increase exposure to your target market
2. Delivering presentations to a room full of clients and prospects
3. Writing a book and putting it in the hands of prospects
4. Using press releases to feature in local and even national news channels.

Each of the above will result in an increase in enquiries, which means that the more specific you can be about the type of client you love to work with in your communications, the better the quality of those enquiries will be.

Remember, though, that not everyone will be ready to work with you immediately. For some businesses, the timing simply may not be right. They may not be experiencing sufficient frustration with their existing accountant, or be clear enough on the benefits of going through what they probably consider the upheaval of changing accountants. That's why it's so important to maintain a relationship with businesses you'd like to work with in the future, as that way you'll be able to tell when the time is right to strike up a conversation about working together.

ZMOT – the research I referred to a few chapters ago – reveals how long it takes (on average) before we're ready to put our faith in working with or buying from new people and the answer comes in the form of three key numbers: **7, 11, 4.**

Seven is how many hours' exposure someone needs to have had of you, whether in person (perhaps hearing you speak at a seminar, or meeting you on a one-to-one basis at a networking event), in the form of reading material or through a video. Seven hours probably sounds a lot, but how long have you spent reading this book so far? (Another good reason to write one yourself!) Add to that the delivery of regular presentations and those hours soon start to clock up.

Eleven is the number of touchpoints. (How many times someone comes across you, your name, or your accountancy practice in a positive way.) Social media postings help with this and I strongly recommend putting in place auto-responders, too. If the term's new to you, an auto-responder is a series of emails that goes out to an individual automatically over a period of time from the moment you first capture their email address. To return to the example I gave in the previous chapter, if someone wants to download a free copy of your book from your website, make sure they submit their email address and – to make sure you meet GDPR requirements – agree to receive additional email correspondence first.

If you have an auto-responder in place, their doing so will trigger a series of emails to be sent to them at regular intervals – such as day 1, day 3, day 6 and day 12 – which you can configure as appropriate. (Be careful though, too frequent and you may cause them to unsubscribe). These emails will provide value in some way – perhaps by providing a strategy for improvement – and act as a regular touchpoint to keep bringing the prospective client back to you.

Four relates to the number of locations in which someone may come across you, such as: a post on LinkedIn; an email; presenting a seminar or at a networking event; and a video on YouTube.

To give you a flavour of those numbers in action, here's how AVN makes use of them in order to build our KLT factor with accountants through our pipeline. (A pipeline – or sales funnel – is the process of understanding where prospective clients are in terms of their readiness to buy from you and of continuing to nurture them until they're ready to do so.)

If you acquired this book from our website, the chances are that you downloaded a free copy of it in digital format and opted in to receive email correspondence from us at the same time. Doing so will have automatically enrolled you onto our free online training course, 'ImproveYourPractice,' a series of videos I created to share tips, ideas and strategies you can implement in your practice to guarantee immediate wins and results. (If you haven't registered yet, you can do so now at: **www.improveyourpractice.co.uk**)

In addition, you'll be invited to our regular webinars that are packed with powerful content which we – or rather our CRM – carefully monitors to record who attends. Our CRM automatically applies a weighting mechanism to each accountant in our database and increases this each time they attend a webinar or watch a video until the weight reaches a set point, at which we'll attempt to strike up a dialogue. (On our pipeline this is known as 'Dialogue,' as until this point a prospect's interaction with us has been one-way, through passive learning).

At this stage we'll contact you to arrange a phone call, and during the conversation that ensues, offer some tips as well as a more tailored set of recommendations based on that conversation. (Each with the genuine purpose of building trust and delivering value.) After this call, we'll nudge you a little further along our pipeline by following up to see how you're progressing with our recommendations – all the while continuing to gauge whether or not you're the kind of person we'd like to work with more closely and whether or not you fit our ideal client profile. Then, once we're sure you're right for us, we'll invite you to attend one of our workshops.

This may sound a time-consuming process, but in our eyes it's crucial. Not only do our webinars and training videos aid large numbers of people in ways that are important to us, they also ensure that we only work with accountants who fit the profile of our ideal clients. (We know that those people who reach the end of our pipeline are the ones we really want to talk to.) And please note that most of the work is leveraged until the later stages, so make sure your CRM package has the functionality to replicate the technical aspects of the process I've described.

I imagine, however, that some of you will be questioning whether you need such a complex system – particularly if you have no problems acquiring clients, or if it doesn't take you '**7**, **11**, **4**' to build enough KLT for a fairly cold enquiry to choose to work with you. Remember, though, that the **7**, **11**, **4** principle is an average. It may be that the clients you'd really love to work with aren't ready to begin working with you as quickly as others are. The process I've described is simply a way of leveraging your time so that you can begin to attract a greater number of warmer prospective clients. Doing so will then allow you to filter them down and be more selective about those you'd really like to work with.

71

The Longer Game

At least some (if not all) of the ideas I've written about in this section you may not be doing or even see the point of doing. However, even if they're out of your comfort zone at first, the methods I've described will all help to build awareness of you in the marketplace and generate new business in the future. To prove it, below are three examples contributed by real accountancy practices who recognised the need to raise their profile and were brave enough to overcome any inhibitions they had about doing so.

First, Fiona Jones of Grant-Jones Accountancy, based in Camberley.

"We've made a significant investment of time in raising our profile. With the support of our 'content alchemist' (who manages our content) we've refreshed our website to bring it up to date, developed a marketing strategy and plan, and run several high-profile campaigns.

We've produced several brochures, a book, a regular blog on LinkedIn and daily social media activity, all aimed at raising our profile in the local marketplace.

In the early part of this year we ran a 'Get and Give a Million' campaign. This consisted of a marketing and PR campaign, a free webinar and then an invitation for a free 90-minute meeting with Grant-Jones to identify potential savings.

Although the campaign did not generate much new business directly it did provide good PR for us and raised our profile in the local area.

The supporting social media campaign has raised awareness of us as a business and, over time, has been generating more clients for us.

In March we were invited to take part in the Parliamentary review. This involved an interview and a feature on Grant-Jones and its vision for accountancy. Published at the end of the year, we will feature in this high-profile publication that's read by politicians and senior policymakers across government.

Our 1000-word article makes the case for accounting firms to do more for their clients and the wider world. The editor-in-chief of the Review, former FT editor, the Rt Hon David Curry, told us he had never received such an inspiring submission.

More recently, we were interviewed for a video series being produced by Collectively Camberley as part of their annual independent business review which has been featured on their Facebook page and on their website.

We are currently preparing a series of video training courses to release as 'Third Thursday Knowledge' – sharing good-practice financial management skills with small business owners. The first of these – on cashflow management – will be released in the next few weeks. We're also planning to launch Business Breakfast Forums later in the year."

The next contribution comes from Steven Carey - Numbers UK Ltd, based in Plymouth.

"We have much more influence than a practice of our size should. One example of this is 'The Numbers' folder that is currently on display in AVN's Head Office. ('The Numbers' folder you may recall from the Value section of this book is the physical representation of the AVN nine-step methodology known as Performance, Measurement and Improvement that AVN members can license the use of and brand in their own way).

Another is our appearance in Shane Lukas and Steve Pipe's book, 'The World's Most Inspiring Accountants.'

We are starting to develop strategic relationships with key partners, most of whom have come into contact with us via LinkedIn.

How are we making sure we are known, liked and trusted?

Our main effort has come through LinkedIn, where we post regular content and comment on the stories and posts of others. I spend about one day a week posting on LinkedIn or meeting up with contacts made on that platform.

Recently, we've agreed to provide business valuation services to a niche lawyer specialising in the sale and purchase of businesses, and I've been invited to speak at a regional event held by our marketing agency.

My co-director offers property tax appraisals to a large firm of local mortgage brokers.

We've held regular Business Builder Masterclasses in Plymouth and have just started to hold larger-scale events in Exeter. As part of that, we're bringing in outside speakers who are key partners of ours.

Our marketing agency has just finalised some 'get to know us' videos for our website, and these are being cleared for publication by our brand consultant as I write.

My LinkedIn posts tend to be content marketing, rather than pure promotion, and this builds on my years of experience writing a regular column for a local, free-distribution newspaper.

My co-director has recently been named as one of Accountancy Age's 35 under 35 – people who are changing the face of the profession – and has also been a panel member on Xero's regional partner roadshow.

I was one of the founder members of the AVN Strategic Development Group, which will be bringing some exciting new insights to AVN members over the coming months and years.

We have livestreamed our coverage of the budget speech for several years now, beginning just one month after Periscope was launched by Twitter, which made us the first accountancy practice to do so.

Measuring the Effectiveness

We've received client referrals from mortgage brokers, and we note the referral source on every new client form. We write and thank every referral and enclose a bar of chocolate in the thank-you letter. Last year, our main referrer asked us to stop sending chocolate, so we discounted his fee instead!

We're designing and implementing a mobile-based net promoter score survey, using one of our target clients! It's hoped that as they see our proactivity they will come on board as our client. Once established, we'll be using push notifications to further enhance our customer/client communication.

Future Plans

We intend to develop more video guides to put on our YouTube channel and our website. Topics are being drawn up, but we're using the Business Breakfast Forum themes/titles to start us off.

I will also devote more time to the development of strategic partnerships and standard documentation to deliver the services we offer through these.

Since I really enjoy meeting people, and developing solutions, it's unlikely that I'll ever give this up!"

The final example comes from Val Wishart at Beyond The Numbers in Edinburgh. Val had already won AVN awards two years in a row when I wrote this book; in fact, winning the first was the catalyst to the personal improvement which helped her win the second.

"Winning the AVN Award for Clarity gave us a real confidence boost but at the same time scared Val to bits as she had to go up on stage and be interviewed!

The event turned out to be a real catalyst for change as winning the award gave us the impetus to start to work on raising our profile within the business community in Edinburgh.

Val decided that she was going to face up to her fear of public speaking, learn how to do it properly and then embrace it as a way to raise the profile of the firm.

As is often the way, once the wheels are set in motion the momentum picks up, and all sorts of opportunities to raise our profile started to arise.

Telling the Beyond the Numbers Story
Val was asked to speak about what Beyond the Numbers had achieved in the past year at a strategic planning day event for 100 Scottish business members of the Action Coach community. This was an ideal opportunity to talk to business owners looking to grow and develop their businesses about who we are and what we do differently from other accountancy firms.

Although it was a real 'shaky-voice' experience for Val, immediately after the talk she was approached by three attendees who were so impressed by what they'd heard that they wanted to speak to us there and then about working with us and they have subsequently signed up as clients.

Ambassador for a National Networking Organisation
Val was then asked to become an executive team member and ambassador for WeDO Scotland, a prestigious support, networking and knowledge-sharing organisation supporting entrepreneurs in Scotland.

She was asked to sit on the judging panel for the WeDO Scotland awards and presented the award for the Young Entrepreneur of the Year at the awards ceremony.

Educating Business Owners
A few weeks' later Val's local business coach. Alan, asked her to present a seminar to his clients on understanding the numbers in their accounts to help them with their business growth. She used the AVN Business Builder Forum PowerPoint presentation on 'How to Interpret the Numbers in Your Accounts' and it was a real revelation to the business owners attending! The feedback given was all excellent and Val has since become the go-to person in the group for help and advice.
Two new clients are in the process of coming on board as a result of this seminar alone.

Given the success of this seminar, Val and Alan, decided to set up a business club for business owners to come along, learn and network in a very relaxed, supportive and fun environment. They decided to call this 'The Really Good Business Club.'

Next, they spoke to some friends who are experts in their chosen fields and convinced them to join as the core group of members. Each of these has also agreed to give a talk about their own area of expertise.

The core group spreads the news about the club and the various topics being presented and brings along their own clients and prospects. The club meets once a month and has a different speaker and topic at each session so it's always fresh and varied. Everyone is able to share their own knowledge, get to know other business owners and do business with each other – oh, and make some good friends!

Some of the topics we've covered include 'Creating the Right Environment for Your Team'; '12 Top Tips to Keep Your Website Tiptop' and 'How to Choose the Right Business Model for Growth.' None of these topics are about accountancy!

Through this we've met new clients, and helped educate them alongside some of our existing clients. We have also spread the news that we're more than number-crunchers as we help them with all areas of their business.

All of this has involved Val facing – and overcoming – her fear of public speaking by just doing it.

AVN Conference Speech
When Val was approached by Shane to give a talk at the AVN conference one year after winning the Clarity award, she decided that the sick feeling in the pit of her stomach caused by his request meant she had to get some help if she was to overcome her fear once and for all.

She decided to engage a public-speaking coach to help her overcome her fear of standing on the stage and telling her story. Val has been working on her speech and learning some new techniques to overcome her nerves and to get her message across in an engaging way.

The results of her hard work will be seen at the conference, which will be the culmination of a very active year in terms of profile-raising for Beyond the Numbers.

Social Proof

We've actively sought out reviews from our clients and this is bringing us a lot of interest through our website.

We're very active on LinkedIn, partly due to the Really Good Business Club and WeDO Scotland, but also through our own blogposts which aim to help business owners with tricky questions.

We received an enquiry last week from a business owner who'd asked three people who they'd recommend and they all recommended us!

We intend to continue to raise our profile through giving help, advice, information and introductions to business owners in Scotland and look forward to Val's talk at the conference!"

To end this section, I'd simply like to add that over 150 accountants were in the room to listen to Val at our conference and the average score she received on the feedback sheets was 'Excellent.' And rightly so!

72

Making A Profound Difference To Your Clients' Lives

It may seem odd that the seventh stage in the AVN Roadmap is 'Purposeful' since from the very beginning of this book I've been conveying how strongly I feel that accountants can, and do, make a profound difference to their clients. And, perhaps to add to the confusion, it's at the third stage – the Value section – that we help accountants to identify the tens and hundreds of thousands of pounds' worth of potential financial improvements in the businesses they work with which will positively affect the lives of those clients.

In Value, we equip AVN accountants with tools, resources and training around specific strategies that are proven to improve sales and profits and strengthen cashflow, which in turn enables deeper investment and the possibility of recruiting more people to lighten the burden. However, challenges in a business can of course stem from issues far deeper than sales, profits and cashflow, which is why I see many accountants making the natural transition to delivering a deeper level of help through coaching, mentoring and consulting their clients.

Everything we've gone through in this book applies to any business owner. You can use what you've learned to help clients achieve improved clarity around their vision and what's important to them personally, and then help them to reverse engineer their goals into a strategy, better position themselves in the market so their price isn't set by their competition, add considerably more value to their prospect and customer journey, scale their business through gearing, systemise it through automation, and finally raise their own profile in the marketplace and become far more purposeful themselves.

It may seem a daunting prospect to be able to help businesses in these ways, but it's something I've seen even the most sceptical and fearful achieve. In fact, my book *'What's Next For Accountants'* is a complete guide to becoming a business advisor. It will help you to understand and hone the skills that you

301

most likely already have and to structure sessions with clients so that they get maximum value. It will also help you to craft consulting programmes in which the focus of each session moves to a different element that's key to a business. It includes a step-by-step guide to discussing these programmes with clients and prospects to promote and sell them in a low-risk, low-resistance fashion so that it's not uncomfortable, and it also provides some very specific strategies to cover with clients that are generic to any business.

I recommend that you make *'What's Next For Accountants'* the next book you read, since by building on the business advisory aspect, it will help you generate more income and become even more purposeful to your clients.

Below are some more real-life examples contributed by accountants who are making even more of a difference to their clients and changing lives…

The example below was written by Michael Hemme's team at MDH Accountancy and Business Growth Specialists in Croydon

"Our own success would be meaningless without the success we help our clients achieve. We're lucky to have a very low churn rate of our client base, which surprises many as our service offering, fee structure and delivery have changed dramatically over the last four years. Our clients have seen the positive impact our guidance and advice have on their businesses and they embrace the changes that we help them to implement.

One client in particular stands out. He started out in 2011, mid-recession, selling and renting homes in Surrey. From the outset we knew he was our kind of person – customer service is at the heart of what he does. Despite huge competition from major accountancy firms, he chose to work with MDH.

Michael, owner of MDH, works with the business owner to give him support on developing his business. As the owner explains, "We meet twice a year and it's just helpful to speak to someone who isn't involved;" going on to add, "Michael's gone through everything I have, shared experience and given me advice."

From a standing start the business has grown every year, but some significant milestones have been reached in the last 12 months. The business owner has achieved their big goal of a personal balance sheet exceeding £1m, they've increased their profit, increased their team and taken more frequent, longer holidays. The client said, *"I'm confident I would have achieved this position at some point, but Michael and the team have helped me accelerate the process. I'm enjoying the rewards sooner than I expected."* He went on to say, *"I'm looking forward to the next chapter."*

The business owner's success is not a stand-alone story, it illustrates how continual steps towards your goal is a winning strategy.
MDH has also supported one company from its inception in 2011 – when, like so many new businesses, it started from the kitchen table of the entrepreneur behind it. What started as a quick-turnaround VAT return has now evolved into a business advisory relationship that has helped the business owner towards their personal success.

It's not just about the business numbers, but the individual's goals. Very few people set about a new business venture just to 'start a business.' They have a personal goal in mind. MDH works hard to give a rounded service that also meets the needs of the individuals.

This particular business owner likes how we offer advice and practical guidance to support what he's looking to achieve in both business and personal terms – and the fact that we proactively raise ideas for him to consider on everything from tax planning to financial planning. After all, with business success comes personal wealth, and we want to be sure our clients are making the most of everything they earn.

We provide other added-value benefits too. If there's a complementary service that we don't provide, the team can be relied on to recommend someone who does – which is useful for a busy business owner. We also deliver seminars – this business owner attended one on pensions, which he found to be *"excellent."*

Seminars play a vital role in our value-delivery. The feedback we've had to date has been exceptional. They provide trusted guidance for business owners to help them get more from their businesses. Seminars also show us where there's a demand for new services.

One service we have brought in-house is Private Wealth Management. After all, it's a natural addition to our core services as successful business owners will always develop a higher level of personal earning and we want to ensure they're making the most of their assets.
We have more seminars planned for the year ahead."

These examples are from Steven Carey and his team at Numbers UK Ltd in Plymouth, whose mission statement – 'Making Lives Better' – couldn't be clearer.

"We have many examples of how we're making a difference to our clients' lives, but here are just a few to give you a flavour of why we're enjoying our work so much at the moment.

A new client came to us in March. He was in a terrible state because he'd signed a two-year, fixed-price agreement with an online accountant who'd done nothing for him in three months. He was receiving VAT demands based on HMRC assessments because of the lack of VAT returns submitted by this accountant, tax demands based on late submitted accounts from the previous year, and a threat to collect two years' worth of fees from that accountant!

We were able to review his online agreement and find two or three ways in which the contract had been breached by the accountant concerned.
Carl now knows what information he needs to give us to do his VAT returns, and is now up to date. While the other accountant hasn't yet backed down, Carl knows he has someone "in his corner" and can go back to doing what he loves best: tending his allotment at the weekend without worrying what might greet him when he gets home.
What's most pleasing about this is that a lot of the client service has been delivered by one of our customer experience team rather than the accounts team, demonstrating that every team member knows what will achieve our goal of "Making Lives Better."

Another client whose company provides training in H&S and First Aid came to us two years ago, wondering why they "never seemed to make enough money." Using SSTW (Simple Stuff that Works)[†] as our agenda, we ran through their business and identified a lack of time for marketing and massive inefficiencies in their booking system which led to 90% of bookings falling through. By recruiting an admin assistant, and taking non-refundable deposits, we were able to free up their time, and ensure they got some compensation for their preparation time even if trainees then failed to show.

The result was a 243% increase in profits, and two very happy clients who could draw a living wage from their business for the first time in 10 years.

A third client lost a full year's profit in 2016 because he didn't hedge against the fall in Sterling after the vote to leave the EU. Purchasing in Euros left him vulnerable to the Sterling : Euro exchange rate, as all his sales are within the UK.

Using our forecasting software, we were able to show him the profit impact of various exchange rates for 2018 and 2019. Understanding this allowed him to allocate cash to fixing his exchange rate at a favourable level, meaning his biggest risk was eliminated. This freed him up to concentrate on driving sales and gave him the confidence to recruit a high-cost salesperson. The result is that this year's sales are up by 65% (against a target of 40%), profits are up by 330% and the purchase of a family holiday home in France is now an affordable reality rather than a pipe dream."

This example from Val Wishart and her team at Beyond The Numbers, Edinburgh

"Our vision is to help business owners achieve their dreams, goals and ambitions.

We do this in very small ways every day in everything that every team member does, but sometimes we really make a positive impact on our clients' lives in a big way too. Here are a couple of our stories.

---

† You can find out more about strategies around SSTW in *'What's Next For Accountants'*.

Making a Dream Come True

Claire was working as an insolvency practitioner with a large firm, but she was very unhappy with the way clients were treated, the way her team was treated, and the fact that her department seemed to be holding up the profitability of the firm.

She met with Val and explained her dream of leaving and setting up her own business, so that she could propel her services into a different offering to really help and support struggling businesses.
Currently, she was spending day after day coming up against brick walls at work and going home to her family at night exhausted and miserable, not even able to really enjoy her young children and the joy they should have been giving her.

Val suggested that they work up a plan together for Claire to leave and to set up her dream business. She worked with Claire on visualising the future, setting the goals and laying out the steps that would be needed to make it happen.

Once Claire had decided to take a leap of faith and go for it, we introduced her to an IT support company, a design agency for brand and website design, an insurance broker to take care of all her insurance needs, and an IFA to put pension planning in place. Of course she would also need the help of a good employment lawyer if she wanted to bring her team with her, so we connected her with one of our clients who happens to be the best employment lawyer in Scotland!

Val now works with Claire on coaching, planning, analysing performance and making sure that the numbers continue to work and to take her business in the direction she wants it to go. Claire's business has won national awards for the fresh approach to really helping clients and she's loving every minute of working in it.

She's also just bought a holiday home in Florida where she loves to spend time with her family. Her business has grown to a turnover of £1.8 million in just three years and is still growing fast.

Claire has given us a lovely video testimonial for our website and recently nominated us for a national accountancy award with the following words:

"I've worked with Val and her team at Beyond The Numbers since my firm was just a glimmer in my eye almost four years ago. She's been transformative both in my vision for my firm and in helping me to shape its future through her work with me. Val and her team have a tremendous can-do attitude and always wish to help in every situation. From working with accounts, through to tax returns, business advice and leadership coaching, Val and her team offer the whole package. Without her my firm literally would not be here. Her commitment to her clients is second to none, and she really does go beyond the numbers to provide a truly holistic approach to accountancy that's so sorely needed at this time."

We love Claire's story because our work with her has combined everything we love about what we do – we've really helped someone to achieve their dreams, we've connected our clients and strategic alliances together, and we're working with a client we really like and admire.

Hatching an Escape Plan
Bobby had a company operating in a high-demand market, specialising in providing bathrooms for people with mobility problems. He took pride in providing the best possible service to his customers and only hired the best teams to carry out the work. His showroom was full of thank-you cards from happy customers and almost all of his work came through word of mouth recommendations.

The company was incredibly profitable and really well run with happy customers and a happy team – the Christmas parties were legendary! So far this all sounds great, but underneath the success, Bobby was becoming more and more stressed. As a self-confessed control freak, he felt that he had to check every job, answer every query and phone call, and check the profitability of each job down to the spec of the light bulbs!

As the business was growing fast this type of control became overwhelming. He had two young children who never saw him and even when he was on holiday he'd spend the entire day on the phone instead of playing in the pool with them.

By sitting with Bobby and listening to his problems, Val helped him to realise that, as he was unable to change and let go of his tight control, it would be better if he sold the business and moved on to another project.

Once Bobby had accepted this and decided to look for a buyer, his relief was almost palpable – he was still working silly hours and controlling everything, but he had a new lease of life and was able to start seeing a future beyond the life he was currently living.

Val introduced Bobby to a couple of contacts who would look for the right kind of buyer and in the meantime set about helping him to restructure his role within the business to make it more attractive for sale. Once the right buyer was found, the due diligence process went very smoothly and quickly as we'd made sure that the books and records were in tiptop shape for easy handover.

It's taken two years but last month Bobby received a very large cheque for the sale of his business and headed off to Mexico for the first truly relaxing holiday he's had in years. He's now building his own house and taking the time to think through what comes next for him. Needless to say he has our number on speed dial to help him with that.

These are two of our big success stories, but we don't want to forget that even a kind word or a smiling *"no problem"* can make a big difference to someone's day!"

You may feel that you could easily deliver results like those above, and I have no doubt that you could, but are you actually doing so? In other words, are you regularly and consistently changing your clients' lives? I hope you are, but many of the accountants I talk to simply don't feel able to dedicate the amount of time it would take because their current model is based around producing as much compliance work as possible.

73

Making A Profound Difference
To Your Team Members

In Gearing we looked at the methods you can use to help develop a great team culture, and how investing in your team and helping them develop their skills to become the partners of the future will enhance their motivation. However, in addition to the many technical skills you can support them (including financially) to develop, don't forget to help them develop their softer skills, such as people and sales skills and business advisory too. After all, these are equally important, both to them and your practice.

I'm fairly confident that if you asked most accountants who are team members in a practice if they'd be willing to get more involved in business advisory or selling, they'd baulk at the idea. That doesn't necessarily mean they wouldn't and couldn't. It's fear. (Remember how earlier I described fear as simply a worry about the 'what ifs'?) With support, training and encouragement, though, you can help the people in your team to future-proof themselves. Yes, doing so may help them along the career ladder and mean they decide to move on from you, but surely that shows you've had a positive impact on someone's life and career and is something you should be proud of? Furthermore, the better the team culture you create the lower the risk of your best team members leaving to join larger more corporate firms. (If you're not convinced, I suggest you refer back to my suggestions in 'Gearing'!)

Growing your successors from the inside will mean that your legacy lives on.

74

Changing The World
One Impact At A Time

By helping clients achieve their business and personal goals, you'll also have an impact on the lives behind their businesses. In addition – as those businesses grow – you'll help to create jobs, which helps the economy, which in turn helps to make the country an even better place to live.

In other words, there's an even bigger game to play and I firmly believe that any business – your business, my business – can be developed for good.

Within this book I've often referred to the core values and beliefs of AVN. To remind you, here they are again:
- Success isn't really success if it comes at the expense of family, friends and health
- Most business owners need the help and support of an external business adviser
- Accountancy is a noble profession, one that can make a profound difference
- By helping accountants improve their practice and teaching them the skills to better help their clients we affect countless businesses
- Businesses can be developed for good.

I hope that throughout this book those beliefs have shone through. The final bullet point, of course – 'businesses can be developed for good' – is purposely ambiguous: long-lasting and able to do good in the world.

Most of us, when we're watching TV, listening to the radio or reading a news article and hear about some atrocity that's taking place around the world – from civil wars to starvation and poverty – recoil in disgust. Individually, of course, many of us try to do our bit. We run marathons, for example, or undertake other sponsored activities to raise money for charities such as research into cancer, strokes, or recovery from brain injury. (As I described in Chapter 7, the latter is a cause that's particularly close to my heart). When we come across stories about wars and poverty around the world, however, we realise there are global causes we can contribute to, too.

Although I'm sure I'm not alone in sometimes wondering why the governments of the countries concerned – or, indeed, our own – don't do more, the truth is that leaders from around the world have come together to recognise some of the problems. In fact, in 2015 the United Nations General Assembly agreed on 17 Sustainable Development Goals (also known as the Global Goals) which, if they're achieved by the target of 2030, will help to overcome many of the major injustices and challenges and make the world a better place in which to live.

These goals are represented in the image below and, underneath, I've explained them in more detail. I hope that some of what you read will resonate to the extent that you'd like to get behind them in some way.

THE GLOBAL GOALS
For Sustainable Development

The following descriptions of the UN Global Goals are not taken from their website as they have been worded in a more concise manner. The United Nations are aware of this and have given consent for me to use the United Nations Logo but have asked me to include the following text: "The content of this publication has not been approved by the United Nations and does not reflect the views of the United Nations or its officials or Member States"

The wording I have used against each goal is taken with permission from the GLOBALGOALS.ORG website. For detailed information about the United Nations Goals and the exact descriptions I recommend visiting https://www.un.org/sustainabledevelopment/sustainable-development-goals

1. **No Poverty: End poverty in all its forms everywhere.**

   Eradicating poverty is not a task of charity, it's an act of justice as well as the key to unlocking enormous human potential. Nearly half of the world's population still lives in poverty, and lack of food and clean water are killing thousands every single day of the year. Together, we can feed the hungry, wipe out disease and give everyone in the world the chance to prosper and live a productive and rich life.

2. **Zero Hunger: End hunger, achieve food security and improved nutrition, and promote sustainable agriculture.**

   Hunger is the leading cause of death in the world. Our planet has provided us with tremendous resources, but unequal access and inefficient handling leaves millions of people malnourished. If we promote sustainable agriculture with modern technologies and fair distribution systems, we can sustain the whole world's population and make sure that nobody will ever suffer from hunger again.

3. **Good Health and Well-Being: Ensure healthy lives and promote well-being for all at all ages.**

   Over the last 15 years, the number of childhood deaths has halved, which proves that it's possible to win the fight against almost every disease. However, we still spend an astonishing amount of money and resources on treating illnesses that are surprisingly easy to prevent. The new goal for worldwide good health promotes healthy lifestyles, preventive measures and modern, efficient healthcare for everyone.

4. **Quality Education: Ensure inclusive and equitable quality education and promote lifelong learning opportunities for all.**

   Education liberates the intellect, unlocks the imagination and is fundamental for self-respect. It's the key to prosperity and opens a world of opportunities, making it possible for each of us to contribute to a progressive, healthy society. Learning benefits every human being and should be available to all.

5. **Gender Equality: Achieve gender equality and empower all women and girls.**

Gender bias undermines our social fabric and devalues all of us. It's not just a human rights issue; it's a tremendous waste of the world's human potential. By denying women equal rights, we deny half the population a chance to live life at its fullest. Political, economic and social equality for women will benefit all the world's citizens. Together we can eradicate prejudice and work for equal rights and respect for all.

6. **Clean Water and Sanitation: Ensure availability and sustainable management of water and sanitation for all.**
    One in three people live without sanitation. This is causing unnecessary disease and death. Although huge strides have been made with access to clean drinking water, lack of sanitation is undermining these advances. If we provide affordable equipment and education in hygiene practices, we can stop this senseless suffering and loss of life.

7. **Affordable and Clean Energy: Ensure access to affordable, reliable, sustainable and modern energy for all.**
    Renewable energy solutions are becoming cheaper, more reliable and more efficient every day. Our current reliance on fossil fuels is unsustainable and harmful to the planet, which is why we have to change the way we produce and consume energy. Implementing these new energy solutions as fast as possible is essential to counter climate change, one of the biggest threats to our own survival.

8. **Decent Work and Economic Growth: Promote sustained, inclusive and sustainable economic growth, full and productive employment and decent work for all.**
    Economic growth should be a positive force for the whole planet. This is why we must make sure that financial progress creates decent and fulfilling jobs while not harming the environment. We must protect labour rights and once and for all put a stop to modern slavery and child labour. If we promote job creation with expanded access to banking and financial services, we can make sure that everybody gets the benefits of entrepreneurship and innovation.

9. **Industry, Innovation, and Infrastructure: Build resilient infrastructure, promote inclusive and sustainable industrialisation and foster innovation.**
    A functioning and resilient infrastructure is the foundation of every successful community. To meet future challenges, our industries and infrastructure must be upgraded. For this, we need to promote innovative

sustainable technologies and ensure equal and universal access to information and financial markets. This will bring prosperity, create jobs and make sure that we build stable and prosperous societies across the globe.

10. Reduced Inequalities: Reduce inequality within and among countries.
Too much of the world's wealth is held by a very small group of people. This often leads to financial and social discrimination. In order for nations to flourish, equality and prosperity must be available to everyone – regardless of gender, race, religious beliefs or economic status. When every individual is self-sufficient, the entire world prospers.

11. Sustainable Cities and Communities: Make cities and human settlements inclusive, safe, resilient and sustainable.
The world's population is constantly increasing. To accommodate everyone, we need to build modern, sustainable cities. For all of us to survive and prosper, we need new, intelligent urban planning that creates safe, affordable and resilient cities with green and culturally inspiring living conditions.

12. Responsible Consumption and Production: Ensure sustainable consumption and production patterns.
Our planet has provided us with an abundance of natural resources, but we haven't utilised them responsibly and currently consume far beyond what our planet can provide. We must learn how to use and produce in sustainable ways that will reverse the harm that we've inflicted on the planet.

13. Climate Action: Take urgent action to combat climate change and its impacts.
Climate change is a real and undeniable threat to our entire civilisation. The effects are already visible and will be catastrophic unless we act now. Through education, innovation and adherence to our climate commitments, we can make the necessary changes to protect the planet. These changes also provide huge opportunities to modernise our infrastructure which will create new jobs and promote greater prosperity across the globe.

14. Life below Water: Conserve and sustainably use the oceans, seas and marine resources for sustainable development.
Healthy oceans and seas are essential to our existence. They cover 70% of our planet and we rely on them for food, energy and water. Yet, we have

managed to do tremendous damage to these precious resources. We must protect them by eliminating pollution and overfishing and immediately start to responsibly manage and protect all marine life around the world.

15. **Life on Land: Protect, restore and promote sustainable use of terrestrial ecosystems, sustainably manage forests, combat desertification, and halt and reverse land degradation and halt biodiversity loss.**
A flourishing life on land is the foundation for our life on this planet. We are all part of the planet's ecosystem and we have caused severe damage to it through deforestation, loss of natural habitats and land degradation. Promoting a sustainable use of our ecosystems and preserving biodiversity is not a cause. It is the key to our own survival.

16. **Peace, Justice and Strong Institutions: Promote peaceful and inclusive societies for sustainable development, provide access to justice for all and build effective, accountable and inclusive institutions at all levels.**
Compassion and a strong moral compass are essential to every democratic society. Yet persecution, injustice and abuse still run rampant and are tearing at the very fabric of civilisation. We must ensure that we have strong institutions, global standards of justice, and a commitment to peace everywhere.

17. **Partnerships for the Goals: Strengthen the means of implementation and revitalise the global partnership for sustainable development.**
The Global Goals can only be met if we work together. International investments and support are needed to ensure innovative technological development, fair trade and market access, especially for developing countries. To build a better world, we need to be supportive, empathetic, inventive, passionate, and above all, co-operative.

Of course, the goals aren't listed in order of priority. They're all equally important if we want to make the world a better place for ourselves and for the generations that follow. However, the final one – Partnerships for the Goals – is the key to them all and one in which all our businesses can play a part.

Both ethically and morally, most of us want to give something back and to use our business for good by contributing a proportion of our profits to our chosen cause(s). (A side benefit is that research also shows that people are more likely to buy from businesses who take their social responsibilities seriously).

There are many ways you can get behind the Global Goals, from supporting local charities (their research will also help to improve lives around the world) to choosing to have a direct impact on global projects that are focused on combating the issues the goals address. Although there are many channels to help you achieve this, a particularly amazing one is B1G1 – Business for Good.

B1G1 supports projects that have been set up to resolve issues related to the Global Goals in some of the worst-affected parts of the world, with the overarching aim of creating self-sufficient communities that are better off. They also guarantee that 100% of what you give goes directly to the project you're supporting, as you pay a separate admin fee (either monthly or annually) to be part of B1G1. (Personally, I'm also pleased that rather than the heart-wrenching images we've come to expect, they choose to create smiles and positive impacts instead).

Giving just $0.01 can provide a village with access to clean water for a day, as their website describes: *"In the villages of Malawi, high infant and child mortality are caused by water and sanitation-related diseases. These problems are made even worse by a lack of knowledge about proper hygiene. Your contribution of a well and water pump is all that's needed to let people live the fullest of lives."* Meanwhile, giving $2,000 could build a science lab for a school in India: *"Spark the interest of children in the sciences by funding the construction of one science lab for a school. Currently, many schools in Bombay do not have the infrastructure or facilities for educating science studies. Your contribution to build a science lab will expose and encourage children to learn more about the sciences, benefiting their education in the long run."*

To make sure I do justice to the story behind B1G1.com, here it is in their own words, taken from their website:

"In 2007, a group of small-business owners had an idea. They asked, 'What would happen if we all gave back just by doing the things we do every day?' It was a question that deeply inspired them.

Three years and a great undertaking later, they were able to design the systems and processes necessary to make it work, and their dream is now a reality. The initiative was originally called Buy 1 Give 1, backed by the idea that companies would make a giving impact with each designated business transaction. Today, the B1G1 initiative has more than 2,600 businesses from around the world – each making significant impacts every day.

B1G1 is a social enterprise and non-profit organisation with a mission to create a world full of giving. Unlike conventional giving models, B1G1 helps small- and medium-sized businesses achieve more social impact by embedding giving activities into everyday business operations and creating unique giving stories. Every business transaction (and as a result, the business' day-to-day activity) can impact lives for as little as just one cent."

In 'Gearing' I described how most of us are actually motivated altruistically, and I'm pleased to report that this is borne out – at the time of writing – by the more than 180,000,000 impacts that have been created around the world by businesses just like yours becoming a member of and working with B1G1.

I'd also like to share the process that all of us at AVN (and many of the accountants we work with, too) go through on a quarterly basis as part of our commitment to make a difference, not only to the accountants we work with and their clients, but on a larger scale.

Although each member of AVN also contributes to charities and to the local and wider community in their own way and in their own time, the Global Goals are incredibly important to us as a business. The whole team is involved in deciding what we'll contribute to in the next quarter and in setting a giving-goal for us to strive towards. In addition, each team member chooses a Global Goal that's important to them personally and identifies a way of impacting on it every time something good happens (whenever we inspire an accountant, for example).

Below are some of the mechanisms we're currently using to give based around the goals:

- **Good Health and Well-Being** For every person that comes to one of our events, such as a workshop or Masterclass, a disabled child receives a music therapy session
- **Quality Education** For every person who attends one of our webinars, a child in Cambodia receives access to a schoolbook for a week. (For me, Goal 4 is particularly important because I strongly believe that better education puts people around the world in a better position to become self-sufficient and overcome at least some of the challenges they face).

- **Clean Water and Sanitation** For every Practice Growth Expert call one of our team has with a member of AVN, a family gets 30 days of clean water
- **Affordable and Clean Energy** Every time a new accountant becomes an AVN member, we light up a life with access to a solar kit for a year
- **Sustainable Cities and Communities** For every Practice Performance Assessment we complete we give 100 bricks towards building a house for a family in rural India (so far this has enabled three and a half houses to be built!).
- **Life below Water** For every invoice we raise, plastic and litter is removed from our oceans by funding clean-up operations
- **Life on Land** For every accountant that trials AVN, a tree is planted that will help save orangutans.

In addition:
- Our next team away day will be based around clearing litter and larger rubbish from a UK river, canal or beach
- In our Monday team meetings we use the B1G1 Giving app to make our impact there and then, which also allows us to celebrate each one with the app's 'cheer' function.

As we continue to introduce accountants to B1G1, we're able to appreciate more and more the collective impacts that all of us are having as a community. So, if you'd like to join us, then please think about joining B1G1 by going to: www.b1g1.com and entering the unique code: BM01352 – you'll get $11 worth of Giving Credits to kick-start some really smart giving.

Not only am I confident that you'll love it, but it's also a great way to show the world the profound difference our amazing community of accountants is making on a global scale.
Most importantly though, please do find time to identify a cause that's of particular importance to you and your team – whether it's close to home or further afield – so that everyone can get behind it.

To conclude the section, I'd like to end with this inspiring contribution from Peter Disney and Brendon Howlett's team at Wood and Disney Accountants in Colchester, which won them the AVN Changing Lives Award.

"I'd like to start by sharing a few examples of how we've been able to change the lives of some of our clients.

Case Study 1: Assistance with Start-Up Business

Although Ken had decided to establish his business with the perception of having a relatively quiet first year, it was clear following multiple meetings and discussions with our team that this was not going to be the case. In fact, we anticipated a potentially great business.

Our assistance became a major asset to his company and the trust he placed in us to discuss not only business matters, but also sensitive health-related issues, allowed us to agree plans for the company. Our knowledge and understanding have proved invaluable throughout Ken's inaugural period as the company continues to exceed expectations with provisional operating profit margins of over 40% in the first 10 months of trading.

Not only has Ken vastly exceeded his financial expectations, but as a direct result of the success of his company's first year, he's been able to find time to volunteer his services to those in genuine need over a difficult winter.. By doing so, he's showed he shares our philosophy of making small but positive impacts to people's lives through our giving and that he's exactly the type of client we want to work for.

We received an extensive testimonial from Ken, from which the following extract was most important to us: "It's not easy starting in business and a business is only as good as its team. I count Wood and Disney as part of my team. Well done!!"

Case Study 2: Gaining a Mortgage

Sophie was referred to us with the personal objective of gaining a mortgage after having received multiple rejections. In fact, following inadequate advice from her previous accountants relating to a company car and debt factoring, we were tasked with restoring her faith in the profession.

We're delighted to report that within one year of receiving advice and accounts from our team, she's just been approved for one.

Case Study 3: Overpayments towards Mortgage

Amanda and Paul had always wanted to own their own home and – as a result of the improved profitability of their business originating from engaging in business advisory services with us – they finally managed to gain a mortgage.

In fact, as a direct impact of our work and advice related to research and development claims the company has received a direct corporation tax saving of over £45K in the past four years. Amanda and Paul are now making regular overpayments towards their mortgage and have provided us with this awesome testimonial:

"After being with Wood & Disney for several years – and recently embracing Cloud computing and outsourcing payroll to them – I would like to say a big thank you to the whole team.
I'm constantly delighted with the comprehensive and tailored support we receive; they're a wonderful bunch of professionals. They provide us with prompt and friendly help and guidance whenever needed which is important when running a small company. They are forward-thinking and always take the opportunity to give advice on improving our profitability. I can't think of anyone I would trust more with our accounts."

Case Study 4: From Arrears and Penalties to Thriving Real-Time Business

Not all clients are perfect from the outset. Some are always late, don't keep up-to-date records, incur avoidable penalties and invariably pay in arrears. Andy, Graham, Richard and their team were guilty of all of these, until in 2016, they signed up to our highest service package which includes more regular meetings. Within two years the company turnover had increased by over 135% whilst maintaining an impressive profit margin of 25%.

As a result of the increase in turnover the company's VAT status required a change from cash accounting to invoice accounting. This caused further cashflow issues, as at the time, they were already owed a large amount by customers. As a result we took over the company bookkeeping and provided back-office solutions to improve the company's efficiency, reducing their debtor days from 82 days to 45 days which enabled them to pay their increased VAT bill without hardship.
As part of our continuous improvement our feedback forms suggested additional areas in which we could assist and we soon agreed numerous further projects with them in order to continue the upward trend in growth. Since then turnover has increased by a further 58%.

Now, not only do we look after the bookkeeping and the compliance services, but we also provide quarterly Zoom meetings. This has allowed us to progress into business advisory services and enabled a complete restructuring of the business with a positive impact on their personal lives. By adopting the systems and procedures we've introduced them to, they've switched from being a non-profitable 'D' client to a lucrative 'A' one and are delighted with the services provided to them.

Other Impacts

Our office entrance now proudly displays the UN Global Goals as well as both the B1G1 and Get and Give a Million logos. The latter is a programme initiated by Steve Pipe in which accountants commit to helping their clients generate one million pounds collectively in additional income ('Get a Million') and, as they do so, to give impacts through B1G1 ('Give a Million'). This is a powerful way to demonstrate to our clients the difference they're making by working with us.

We're proud of the impacts we've made through B1G1 and have set ourselves the target of making 10,000 impacts for the year. After five months we've already more than doubled this with 25,000 impacts in different countries! A few examples include:

- We've provided 100 days of dental hygiene to children in Morocco, thanks to a client in the dental industry
- We've donated a five-year supply of seeds to parents of malnourished children in Malawi to enable them to grow healthy crops, thanks to a client in the food and drink industry
- We're sponsoring and providing a training kit and equipment for a student to help find employment in Cambodia, thanks to a QuickBooks Online Training session with a client in the technology industry.

We're extremely grateful for the help and support we've received from AVN during this journey and have fully encouraged all the team to get involved where they can."

75

Tyres, Food And Excellence

To put this chapter into context, please bear with me while I tell you a seemingly unrelated story…

The year is 1900, the country is France. André and Édouard, two brothers who run a tyre manufacturing business, have put their heads together to come up with a strategy to increase sales. However, with fewer than 3,000 cars in the entire country, their challenge was two-fold: how to get car owners to need to renew their tyres more often, and how to encourage more people to want to buy a car – and therefore require more tyres – in the first place.

They discussed many ideas, but the one they settled on was to create a guide for motorists. As well as instructions around how to change a tyre and to check a car's oil and water, the guide would include maps of France, the location of fuel stations, and information about towns and cities around France that were worth a visit. (The additional mileage this encouraged, they reasoned, would put extra wear on tyres). Almost as an aside, they also recommended a few restaurants in each town and gave each of them a rating based on their experience:

 "A very good restaurant in its category"
("Une très bonne table sans sa catégorie")

 "Excellent cooking, worth a detour"
("Table excellent, mérite un détour")

 "Exceptional cuisine, worth a special journey"
("Une des meilleures table, vaut le voyage").

Despite the fact that there were less than 3,000 car owners in France at that time, they produced over 35,000 copies of their guide and made them available for free to anyone and everyone. They placed them in newsagents and hotel receptions – amongst other places – and encouraged people to take a copy.

The guide was called the Michelin Guide – free for motorists.

Given that well over a century later their tyre company – Michelin – is still going strong, we can infer that the guide did indeed encourage existing car owners to drive more and those who didn't yet own a car to buy one, both of which would have led to increased tyre sales. However, what the Michelin brothers hadn't expected was that soon after their guide was published, they would be approached by restaurateurs from all around the country enquiring why they weren't featured in it and how they could be,

as well as by the restaurants that did appear – but with a 1- or 2-star rating – asking what they needed to do to achieve a 3-star rating.

Of course, if the Michelin brothers had agreed to include every restaurant that asked, the Michelin Guide would have become very thick and, indeed, pretty much indistinguishable from the now defunct Yellow Pages (or other business telephone directories). Instead, they had the good judgement to retain a degree of exclusivity and, little by little, to put standards in place that establishments needed to meet in order to feature in the book. As more restaurants achieved these, the bar could be raised to retain exclusivity.

These standards, of course, included the quality and taste of the food but also, amongst other things, hygiene, customer service, presentation, overall experience and consistency. To avoid subjectivity and any ambiguity, the standards were also clearly defined and assessed by an objective professional assessor who would determine whether or not they were being met. That way, when an accreditation was given (or rejected) the decision would be highly respected and indisputable.

So successful were they that the Michelin Star has become synonymous with incredibly high-quality. In addition, the beauty of their initiative means that, should they choose to, restaurateurs have a set of standards they can strive towards implementing. Doing so will not only guarantee that the prestige of their restaurant is recognised, but that it will be sought out and visited by a higher standard of customer.

Although there must be many hundreds of thousands of restaurants around the UK, at the time of writing there are only:
- 155 with a 1-star rating
- 20 with a 2-star rating
- 5 with a 3-star rating.

Although I've never visited a 3-star-rated restaurant in person, I have looked one up on the Internet and what I found is instructive:
- Rather than a menu you're given a set meal – a food-tasting experience
- This menu costs a fixed-price per person of £255
- There's a six month waiting list.

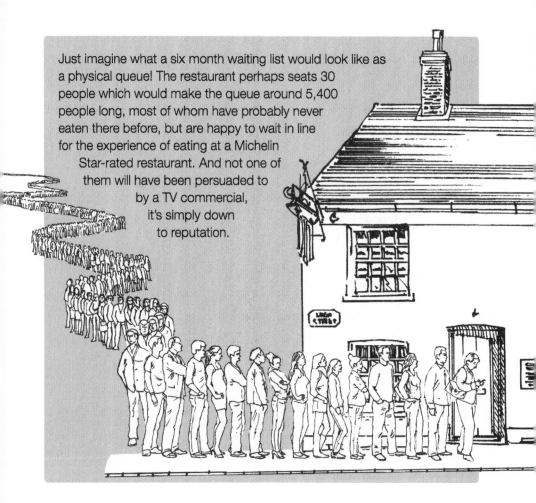

Just imagine what a six month waiting list would look like as a physical queue! The restaurant perhaps seats 30 people which would make the queue around 5,400 people long, most of whom have probably never eaten there before, but are happy to wait in line for the experience of eating at a Michelin Star-rated restaurant. And not one of them will have been persuaded to by a TV commercial, it's simply down to reputation.

Why have I told you this story? Because, when I heard it, it inspired me to want to create something very similar for the accountancy profession.

76

My Vision For The Accountancy Profession

There are many online sites on which Joe or Josie Public can review their experiences – whether these relate to a holiday, a hotel, a restaurant, a general trader or, of course, an accountant. Since potential customers are likely to check out these reviews, it's great to tap into these sites by asking customers to rate you on them. If the reviews are mostly positive, having at least some is better than having none at all as the odd negative one will generally be disregarded as long as:

- It's only one and the overwhelming majority are positive
- You've perhaps replied to it explaining what you've done to try to resolve the problem.

That being said, the challenge I find with these sites is that while they're great at identifying the consistently poor businesses, they're not so good at identifying the best. For example, if you check out a restaurant that has 38 reviews and only four of them are positive, you'll likely conclude that it isn't very good. In fact, it's probably averaged a 1-star rating.

But does a 5-star rating automatically mean a restaurant is outstanding? Personally, I know I've given five stars to my local pub (because the food and service were nice) and to a highly prestigious restaurant (because the food and service were amazing). In other words, a good business is just as likely to get a 5-star rating as an outstanding one, and only those that are consistently poor will stand out as such. Relying on these sites, then, won't guarantee that I'll find the best restaurant.

When I first learned about the story of the Michelin Guide (which I confess I hadn't previously connected to Michelin tyres!) Steve Pipe, founder of AVN, had just undertaken a considerable amount of research in order to write his book, *'The UK's Best Accountancy Practices'*.

At the time, Steve was still part of AVN, so we worked together to come up with what has since become AVNExcellence.

The firms Steve interviewed for his book – ranging from sole practitioners to firms with a small number of partners – were representative of those AVN typically work with. All the practices were profitable, successful, enjoyed what they were doing, and – above all – were making a profound difference to their clients. It was discovering the common threads amongst them that led to our creating (and continuing to develop, year after year) the standards that make up AVNExcellence.

The AVNExcellence standards – over 100 in all – fall under 11 categories and together form the blueprint for an excellent accountancy practice. The categories are outlined below.

1. **Excellence in Intent**

   The UK's most successful accountancy practices don't make excuses or moan about what the world is doing to them. Instead they take control of their own destiny. Their success is planned rather than accidental. They decide what they want, make whatever changes are necessary to ensure that they get it, and persevere when the going gets tough.

2. **Excellence in Measurement Systems and Decision-Making**

   The UK's most successful accountancy practices don't just rely on traditional accounting measures. Instead they work out what really matters – i.e. what drives their success – in both financial and non-financial terms. They find ways of measuring those drivers, set targets, use the results to make informed decisions and make people transparently accountable for performance and results.

3. **Excellence in Pricing and Cash Management**

   The UK's most successful accountancy practices recognise that the only sustainable way to provide a premium service is to charge a premium fee. They understand that clients hate surprise bills so rarely use timesheets for billing purposes. They also understand that, to clients, every bill is a value bill since they won't be happy unless it represents good value. Wherever possible, they use value pricing to make crystal clear that the value far exceeds the fee.

   Where value pricing isn't possible, they use pricing software to generate fixed prices that are acceptable to the client, and fixed-price agreements to formalise the arrangement. They also use Extra Work Orders to ensure that extra work is translated into extra fees, and collect most of their fees by direct debit – often by instalments and usually in advance of completing the work.

4. Excellence in Systems

The UK's most successful accountancy practices don't leave things to chance, and they don't rely on their people remembering what to do. Instead, they create systems to ensure that everything can be done to the same high standard, every single time.

5. Excellence in Service

The UK's most successful accountancy practices understand what excellent service means to the type of clients they want to attract and have focused their energy and designed their systems in order to deliver it. They focus on both the substance of service excellence (such as speed, accuracy and impact) and on the experiential aspect (such as showing genuine interest and using plain English and 'wow' factors).

6. Excellence in Proactivity

For the UK's most successful accountancy practices, 'proactivity' is not an empty promise on their websites and in their brochures. Instead, they've developed systems to ensure that genuine proactivity – of the kind clients really value – is part of their culture and habits. They've also discovered that the more proactive they are, the more additional services clients will want to buy from them.

7. Excellence in Measuring the Numbers that Matter to Clients

The UK's most successful accountancy practices recognise that profits are a consequence of doing the right things for the right people in the right way. They start by making sure that clients receive all the information they need about the numbers that really matter within their businesses, including success drivers and benchmarking comparisons.

8. Excellence in Improvement-Solutions for Clients

The UK's most successful accountancy practices know that as well as helping clients to measure the things that matter, they also need to help them create and implement improvement action plans in those areas. In particular, they help clients to create and to implement improvement action plans for their profit, cashflow, tax exposure, business value and personal wealth.

9. Excellence in Teamwork

The UK's most successful accountancy practices understand that the partners cannot and should not try to do everything. They recognise that leverageable success comes from involving their team fully at every stage, listening to them properly, and valuing their input. They share all the key numbers with them, trust them and delegate most of the work to them – but only after giving them the tools, training, systems and support they need to do the job properly. They also appreciate that their teams should be treated well and rewarded appropriately.

10. Excellence in Sales and Marketing

The UK's most successful accountancy practices don't leave referrals to chance. Instead, they use referral systems that leverage their time. They don't just look to clients and to bank managers for referrals, they actively cultivate a much wider network of referral sources. They understand that to get clients talking to other people about them, they have to give them a compelling story to tell. They also test a wide variety of marketing strategies to find the ones that work best for them. For example, many have found that holding the right kind of seminars is one of the best ways to win new clients.

11. Excellence in Doing Good

The UK's most successful accountancy practices don't just think of themselves, they also strongly believe in looking after other people and supporting future generations.

The AVN Roadmap is designed to help the accountants we work with integrate the standards outlined above within their accountancy practices in a logical, step-by-step way. And, in case you're concerned that this sounds a little too prescriptive, remember that just as no two Michelin Star-rated restaurants are the same, neither are two accountancy practices that have put the AVNExcellence standards in place. In other words the standards don't dictate how you should run your practice, but how to achieve a high standard in a way that suits your personality and the reputation you want your practice to have. We also – again just like Michelin – recognise the importance of objectivity and the assessors we use are unbiased and independent rather than employees of AVN.

When Michael Hemme from MDH, who I've featured in this book before, achieved AVNExcellence 6 Star – the highest standard possible – I asked him what AVNExcellence represents for him. Here's what he said:

"AVNExcellence is a lot of different things to a lot of different people, but from my perspective it's basically a blueprint. I had the bare bones of a business and good momentum with clients coming onboard, but to grow it successfully I needed to systemise. I needed to put so many things in place that it would have been impossible to do it all myself.

If you've got a blank bit of paper and you need to create something yourself, you can spend so long faffing around with it that you never actually get anything done.

When we first joined AVN, we looked at other firms that were successful and said, *"We'd like to be like them."* The way I could see us getting there was via the AVNExcellence model, because it incorporates really sound business practices.

Rather than having to create stuff, which always take longer from scratch, there's a blueprint. If you need to modify certain bits of it because it's really important to your business that's okay. I'd certainly recommend that every ambitious practice signs up to it."

As I pointed out earlier in this book, thousands of accountancy practices across the UK advertise their services almost identically by describing themselves as 'business advisers,' 'pro-active,' 'forward-thinking' and – somewhat ironically – 'different.' They probably have reviews from clients who state that they're great, but perhaps for the wrong reasons: they take calls late at night, work weekends, and produce tax returns before the deadline despite receiving the vital information at the eleventh hour.

My vision is that AVNExcellence accountants become sought after because of their reputation. Clients will be happy to wait for availability with them because they know their business will be looked after and that it'll grow and become more successful. AVNExcellence accountants understand who their ideal clients are and are rigid in sticking to this, which means they only work with the businesses they want to and let other accountants work with those they don't.

I regularly speak at SME business events about the benefits of working with AVNExcellence practices and distribute AVN's free book *'The Business Owner's Guide to the UK's Best Accountants'*. In addition, we also generate interest and leads by running ads and drip-feeding the benefits of working with AVNExcellence firms.

Would you like to achieve excellence within your accountancy practice? And to ensure that the business works for you rather than the other way around? If so, then you're welcome to a free copy of the full set of AVNExcellence standards – both so you can gauge where you are now and to use as a blueprint to develop your practice. (Remember, too, that if you'd like support, we'll always be here for you). To get a copy, get in touch with Shane in any of the following ways...

Linked in: **www.Linkedin.com/in/SLUKAS**

Tap in to additional learning and get access to world class training and resources via **www.improveyourpractice.co.uk**

Send an email and chat with Shane via **shane.lukas@avn.co.uk**

77

Closing Words

I hope I've demonstrated that it's possible to develop your accountancy practice into a thriving business and – despite the threats to the profession – prosper by letting technology produce meaningful data that you then interpret for clients. Just as importantly, I hope I've also shown how you can strengthen your practice's human-to-human relationships and, by helping clients identify ways they can make their businesses stronger, improve not only their and their families' lives but – if you choose to make your business a business for good – make a profound difference to countless lives and future generations around the world.

Your Next Steps To Improving Your Practice

You can score your accountancy practice in the seven key areas I've described to discover which you should focus on first here: **www.takethetest.today**

Or, if you'd like further help, I've created a free video training programme at: **www.improveyourpractice.co.uk**

You can also download a free digital copy of my book '*What's Next for Accountants*' at **www.avn.co.uk**

Finally, if you found this book as valuable as I hope, please do give it a great rating on Amazon and send me a screenshot. In return, I'll send you a physical copy of either '*What's Next for Accountants*' or '*Accountancy – It's Your Business*'.

Sincere Thanks

As well as the many inspiring accountants who've shared their stories in this book – for which I thank them again – there are other people I'd also like to acknowledge. During AVN's reinvention there were many members who – despite reaching the point of no longer requiring ongoing membership – continued to invest in us to support the changes I was carrying out. They did so because they trusted that the new iteration of AVN would continue to transform the lives of accountants and, through them, the lives of countless others.

Those people include:
- Gloria Murray of Murray Associates
- Nigel Bennett of Hallidays
- Paul Meades of Meades & Co
- Rob Walsh of Clear Vision Consultancy
- Shaz Nawaz of AA Accountants.

My thanks also go to Steve Pipe and Mark Wickersham for their continued friendship, support and passion for AVN's vision and purpose.

Finally, particular gratitude is due to Patrick McLoughlin of Accounting for Growth. Patrick is a huge advocate of AVN and – as well as providing regular external insight and strategic contribution – has become a good friend. His business specialises in generating appointments for accountants with high-quality new clients and, below, he explains why he loves working with AVN members:

"Firstly, they have the ability to help improve their clients' key numbers, not just present them. As we talk to hundreds of business owners every week I can say with certainty that business owners are screaming out for this level of support.

Secondly, the AVN members I've worked with typically generate twice the average fee of non-members. And because this extra revenue is from valued added, not compliance work, it's more profitable, too!

From the work we've done over many years with hundreds of UK accountants and thousands of UK businesses, the evidence is clear: accountants who've trained with AVN win better-quality clients and provide those clients with a better service. As a result, on average, they also earn twice as much per client and those fees are considerably more profitable."

Patrick and I have also collaborated on developing a podcast series in which we interview accountants from around the UK to glean insights about how they run their practices. I'm delighted to say that feedback has been wonderful, but don't take my word for it – you can check the series out for yourself and subscribe to: '*The Forward Thinking Accountant*' which you can find within the Podcasts app.